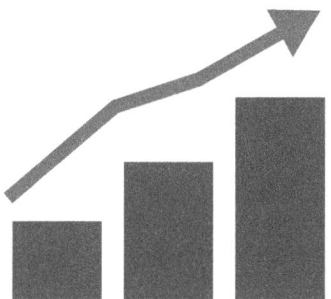

TSP Investing Strategies:

Building Wealth While Working for Uncle Sam, 2nd Edition

By W. Lee Radcliffe

Copyright ©2020 by Thrift Strategies LLC. All rights reserved. Printed in the United States of America. Except as permitted under the United States Copyright Act of 1976, no part of this publication may be reproduced or distributed in any form or by any means, or stored in a database or retrieval system, without the prior written permission of the author.

ISBN-13: 9798602600704

This publication is designed to provide accurate and authoritative information in regard to the subject matter covered and has been compiled in good faith by the author. However, readers should be aware that this information may be incomplete, may contain errors or may have become out of date. It is sold with the understanding that neither the author nor the publisher is engaged in rendering legal, accounting, financial, or other professional service. If legal advice or other expert assistance is required, the services of a professional person should be sought.

CONTENTS

Introduction to the Second Edition 5
   A Note About Piracy 11
Getting Started - The Background of the TSP 13
   A Brief History of Civil Service Pensions and the TSP 13
   The Funds 17
   How is the "stock market" different from an "index fund" and the TSP funds? 26
   The 'Blended Retirement System' - Now Military Members Receive a Match! 29
   The Risks of Saving and Investing - and of Not Saving and Investing... 34
   TSP Risks You Don't Have 39
   Pre-Investment Strategies 44
Strategy I - Assess Your Level of Interest and Risk Tolerance 47
   Rate Your Level of Interest in the Stock and Bond Markets 48
   Volatility and Dollar-Cost Averaging 50
   When The TSP Funds Decline, Have You Really "Lost" Anything? 54
   Consider Investing in an L Fund 55
   How Much Risk Should You Take? Gauging Your Reaction to a Severely Declining Market 58
   Scenario 1: The C Fund 60
   Scenario 2: The C Fund and the G Fund 68
   The Power of Reinvested Dividends 74
   Your Investor Type 78
Strategy II - Allocate Among TSP Funds Based on Your Tolerance for Risk 79
   The 'Thrift Van Winkle™' Approach to Investing 79
   Is 'Greed' Good? Not in Free Markets! 87
   For the Risk-Conscious Investor: Diversification Among Asset Classes 89
   What's an "Asset?" 90
   Strategic Portfolios for Risk-Conscious Investors 94
   Summary for Strategy II 102
Strategy III - Reallocate With the Help of Periodic Contributions 103
   Portfolio Drift and Periodic Rebalancing 105
   The Art of Rebalancing Over Time 111

Summary for Strategy III 112
Strategy IV - Use Volatility to Your Advantage..115
    The Art of Buying into Falling Stock Funds 119
    Caveats! 123
    Summary for Strategy IV 126
Strategy V - Build Further Wealth Outside Your TSP Investments 127
    Pay Off Consumer Debt 127
    Save For Major Purchases Using Appropriate Savings Accounts 139
    Investing in the 'Roth' TSP and Other Tax-Advantaged Vehicles 145
    Investing in Real Estate: Six Approaches..155
    Saving for College 162
    What About the Rest of Your Money? 167
    Summary for Strategy V..169
Strategy VI - Protect Yourself and Your Wealth 171
    Personal Insurance 172
    Property Insurance 183
    Wealth Insurance 188
    Digital Insurance 191
    Set up an "Active Duty Alert" When Deploying................................ 194
Parabolic Wealth 207
    Linear Growth, Exponential Growth, and Parabolic Growth 207
    Are You 'Crazy' Enough to Get Rich?...212
    Little Things Make the Big Things Happen 214
        The Impact of Fees on Investments 214
        Reinvestment of Dividends 217
        Increasing Contributions 219
        Time.. 220
    Parabolic Investing 226
Conclusion - Bringing it All Together 233
Endnote References.. 236

Introduction to the Second Edition

The 2011 publication of *TSP Investing Strategies* followed a decade in which markets declined dramatically not once, but twice. From 2000 to late 2002, the TSP's C Fund and the S&P 500 on which it is based fell by over a third, and small cap stock indexes (such as the S Fund) fell even further. This came on the heels of a major bubble era in U.S. markets in the late 1990s. After an uninspiring recovery that was marked by a major real estate bubble, investors experienced a near-depression fall in almost every major asset class in the 2008-2009 period, and the C, S, and I Funds dropped by over half. With these experiences as a backdrop, the first edition sought to answer the pressing question: *How might we best allocate our TSP investments in the wake of such market turmoil?*

Now, for the second edition published almost ten years later, I take a much broader look at markets in general and a deeper look at TSP investing behavior specifically. In doing the research for this book, I examined over 120 years of U.S. stock index and government bond behavior from the individual investor's perspective. I also conducted in-depth examinations into how the TSP funds have performed since their inception and how TSP investors reacted to different market conditions. In some cases, due to investor psychology that is both understandable and difficult to change, the data shows how investors have reacted contrary to their long-term interests. I hope that by examining market behavior and illustrating the solid returns of buy-and-hold investors over the very-long term, this second edition will provide TSP investors with greater confidence in maintaining balanced investing approaches through sometimes challenging market conditions.

To accomplish this much broader examination of market behavior, I threw out the spreadsheet. I instead took programmatic approaches to analyzing markets over extended periods of time. By conducting analyses using data analytic tools such as the "pandas" python data analysis library and graphing the results in data visualization libraries such as matplotlib and seaborn, I was able to test and view market behaviors in much more comprehensive ways that I was not able to do for the first edition. I still used spreadsheets, to be sure, but the combination of approaches and use of expanded datasets have enabled a much broader examination of markets over time.

And I did this in the context of asking, *how would these various market conditions impact regular investments made by regular TSP investors over their careers and beyond?* I was in some cases surprised by the results.[*]

Additionally, there have been a number of important changes in the TSP since the first edition of *TSP Investing Strategies* was published in 2011. The TSP now has a Roth option, which it did not offer when the first edition was published. Uniformed military personnel did not receive a match in 2011, nor were there any specific proposals to provide a match. Now, the Blended Retirement System (BRS), inaugurated in January 2018, provides contribution matches for uniformed TSP participants, much like their civilian counterparts receive. And as of the mid-2010s, new civilian federal employees have to pay more into their retirement system than their predecessors, which is a fundamental break from the near-parity established by design between the two retirement systems—FERS and the legacy CSRS—when the former was established along with the TSP to replace the latter in the mid-1980s.

While the increased contribution requirements for new FERS employees hired since 2013 do not impact the TSP directly (although it indirectly took away some investing power from newer TSP participants), the legislation that mandated the higher individual contributions points to the ever-present power of the U.S. Congress to alter government pension systems specifically—and Social Security and Medicare more broadly, as well as tax structures in general. This reality is a subtext of this book: *Congress can and will change government programs and tax law due to pressing fiscal constraints…* and the country certainly faces increasing fiscal constraints in the 2020s and

---

[*] I provide additional, up-to-date calculations and comprehensive visualizations on the book's companion site https://tspstrategies.com, and I describe the methodologies and data used in this book on github.com/TSPstrategies/2ndEdition.

beyond. The TSP is the one form of building individual wealth that federal employees and their uniformed service member counterparts have power over; they have no power over the future of pensions or social security. This is not meant as a value judgment but as a statement of fact, and one which younger generations especially have to take into account when planning for their futures.

Before moving on to the book itself, I'd like to highlight the choice of words in the subtitle of this book: *Building Wealth While Working for Uncle Sam*. I use the term "wealth" consciously and with positive connotations. Wealth is something that should be treated as separate from income: Income is the pay we receive biweekly or monthly, a portion of which we can use to save and invest and thereby build wealth. That wealth at a certain point will produce enough income—through interest, dividends, and growth—with which we can live independently and in conjunction with other sources of income. My premise in writing this book is that you can start from nothing, and through the power of hard work and diligent saving and investing in a basket of stocks and bonds (such as the funds offered in the tax-advantaged TSP), you can build wealth over time. There is no reason for uniformed military personnel and rank-and-file federal government workers (and anyone in any industry) not to participate in the wealth-building opportunities afforded by the TSP and similar tax-advantaged mechanisms over time. This is the foundation of America and another major subtext of this book: *Free markets are fundamentally the best producers of wealth in the world.*

Similarly, I did not include the word retirement in the title on purpose. In fact, I have gone to great lengths to avoid use of the word throughout this book. Yes, the TSP is technically part of a comprehensive system to provide retirement income after individuals leave the workforce. But it is so much more than that. It represents independence: of mind, of thought, of action, in the now and in the future.

I have several reasons for avoiding the word "retirement."

First, it's about vitality. The first definition of the word "retire" that appears in the Merriam-Webster dictionary is "to withdraw from action or danger: retreat."[1] Is that the mentality we want to have during our vital, working years? The term itself literally saps one's strength. As Yale professor John Bargh and his colleagues found in a classic 1996 study, thinking about the term "retirement" *slows you down*. In his study on the priming effects of using terms associated with old age such as "retirement," students who heard the terms actually walked more slowly later the same day compared to other groups who were primed with non-retirement terms.[2]

While there have been some questions about the replicability of the Bargh study two decades later,[3] I've personally seen examples of the general enervating effects associated with thinking overly much of "retirement," and I'm sure that many who are reading this book have as well. In one of several personal examples, within months of my arrival at a new civilian position two decades ago, one of my longer-serving coworkers consistently greeted me in the hallways by letting me know his "countdown"—that is, how many *days* until he was eligible to retire. Not months, not weeks, but *days*. What shocked me was that he was in his early 40s, and his countdown numbered in the multiple-thousand range. Guess how engaged he was at work, or how long he stayed employed in that position? He left government service less than a year after I met him (which was probably the right choice for him).

How many times throughout a given week do you encounter the same conversations? People who complain after the morning meeting of the *years* they have until they are eligible to retire, or those describing wistfully, or angrily, or wearily, what they plan to do on the *day* they can "retire"? It's all often said in good fun, or perhaps in a sudden fit of frustration with the regular stresses we all encounter in the office. More problematic are those who fit the term "Retired in Place" (RIP). This is a real phenomenon. How often have you gotten stuck with an extra task because management knows they can't count on certain others on your team who are "RIP"? There is quite literally a reason it is called re-*tire*-ment. Everybody who is obsessed with it is too 'tired' to work!

Second, this book directly links the building of wealth with the building of a sense of ownership and independence. Take, for example, the military pension system. Until the BRS was inaugurated in 2018, a uniformed service member had to serve 20 years before being eligible for a retirement pension. Serving less than that meant the soldier, sailor, airman, or marine received not a pension cent later in life, after service. What did that mean in practice? After completing a four-year (or so) initial service contract, you either got out or at a certain point you felt compelled to stay in, even if you didn't like the military as a career. Hitting your 10- or 12-year mark? Well, might as well stay in for *another eight or ten years*, just to be eligible to retire…or so went the mentality for many who served. That's a long time to spend doing something that you just might not like all that much. I both encountered and was caught up in that decision process when I served: I knew one mid-level non-commissioned officer in the mid-1990s who left after 12 years in the military, and most in our unit thought he was crazy for leaving "with just a few years left." (I admired him.) That's how rare and against-the-grain you had to be to leave at that point in a military career.

Even in retirement, a pension means *someone else*—in this case, taxpayers and current federal workers—is sending you a paycheck. You are dependent on others to provide for your retirement. That statement may sound a little extreme, because we all have paid and continue to pay into the traditional pension and social security systems. But let's be honest: With traditional pensions, we pay in less than we will take home in total "retirement" over many decades of our ever-lengthening lifespans. This means future generations—our kids and grandkids—end up paying for our retirements. Because of fiscal constraints, simple demographics and lengthening lifespans, pensions are increasingly at the mercy of Congress, either with lower COLA rates (lower "cost of living adjustments" to make up for inflation), changes in pension structures such as increased minimum retirement ages, increased required payments into the pension system for current workers, or perhaps new tax structures after retirement that could conceivably eat into a pension (and TSP wealth!) over time.

This brings us to the third reason for not using the term "retirement": Many readers of this book will not actually "retire" from government or military service. That is to say that most readers, particularly those in military service, will complete an initial term of service or two, and then leave to pursue other life opportunities. For example, initial reenlistment rates (reenlisting with between 18 months and six years of service) in the 2000s trended between the 30-40% range for the U.S. Army, 20-30% in the Navy, 20-35% in the Marines, and 40-50% in the U.S. Air Force.[4] Reenlistment rose to about 50-60% after a second enlisted term. Thus, two-thirds or more of enlisted personnel left the military after their first term of service, and half of those remaining left after a second term. This is increasingly true also for civilian government service. Just over 16% left federal government service in 2016 and again in 2017.[5]

Stay or go, no problem! You can use the TSP and other approaches to personal finance to set yourself up well to *continue building wealth* over a lifetime of earning, saving, and investing. The concepts presented in this book can be used for non-TSP index investments and other approaches as well.

Ultimately, in my opinion, if you want to live a vital, engaged, full life, a life that matters, don't become fixated on retirement. Instead, it is a matter of refocusing priorities. My motto is: *Don't plan for retirement, plan to build wealth!*™

This book is not for those about to retire, or for those who are obsessed about retirement. After reading this book, my hope is that you'll have so much confidence in your investing style that you'll want to check in on your TSP and other investments only occasionally. You'll be able to live a full and vital life, without thinking of "retirement," knowing that you're on the way to building *wealth*.

This book is for those just starting their wealth-building journeys and for those who are part-way there and who want to review where they are at and where they're heading. This book is for those who are interested in what the data says about actively building wealth over a lifetime of work and engagement. In this book, I try to reorient readers to focus on *what matters*: for their current situations, on growing their independence, on being fully engaged in the now and not in the three-decades-from-now idea of "re-*tire*-ment." This mindset allows us to focus consciously and conscientiously on the positive and possible, on service to our fellow (wo)man, to the country, and on hard and rewarding work. I fervently believe that with such an approach and with the right planning at the outset, positive results will follow.

Lastly, before starting this book, you should understand the disclaimers. I am a data analyst for the federal government and have 20+ years of service in both civilian and military positions. I am not an investment professional and except for my account I have no affiliation with the TSP, but I have studied the TSP and index investing behavior for more than a decade now. My driving motivation has been to answer the question, what does the data say about investing? I am providing my research in this book and on tspstrategies.com for informational purposes only, updated over time, in what is hopefully an accessible format for TSP participants about index investing and the history of the plan. Because much of the data is based on historical returns, both short-term and long-term future returns may differ from the findings presented in this book, and while I personally follow specific approaches covered in this book based on this research, I cannot accept responsibility for readers' investment decisions (or non-decisions and inaction). I provide a list for further reading on tspstrategies.com/long-term-investing/further-reading/ and citations in this book as places for readers to start for additional due diligence when researching prospective investments and approaches to investing. Seek the services of a fee-only financial planner for any questions about your personal financial situation and insurance needs or, for legal matters, a legal professional.

I wish you success in your wealth-building efforts!

A Note About Piracy

A large majority of readers have acquired this book through legal means by purchasing it, borrowing it from a friend, receiving it as a gift, or by checking it out from a local library. And I thank you for that!

But, as the author, I am aware that versions of this book as well as versions of the first edition have appeared in pirated formats on various platforms.

For those who have acquired a pirated copy, just know that this is illegal. This book is about ownership and empowerment, but by actively using pirated material, you are empowering crooks and thieves, not creators and authors who spend valuable time and money to produce their books and other intellectual property. And for those readers with security clearances or who need to get a security clearance, accessing or acquiring pirated material will impact your future background checks.

Also, who knows what was embedded in the file that you illegally downloaded, or that was hidden on the site you acquired it from? Is saving a couple of bucks worth the possibility of getting hacked?

Please, stop engaging in pirated activity, for your sake and for the sake of creators and authors everywhere.

NOTES

Getting Started – The Background of the TSP

The Thrift Savings Plan (TSP) is one of the greatest mechanisms through which to build wealth in the world. Established in April 1987, the TSP has grown to over $600 billion in assets more than 30 years later. By the end of 2019, almost six million participants were making net contributions of over $10 billion cumulatively each month.[6] Participants own their TSP accounts, so when they leave government service they can still access their personal accounts or transfer their money into an Individual Retirement Account (IRA) or another employer account and continue to contribute periodically each and every year thereafter to keep on building wealth over time.

A Brief History of Civil Service Pensions and the TSP

The TSP was created in the 1980s in an effort to modernize the Federal Government's retirement benefits system. The Federal Government's original retirement system, the Civil Service Retirement System (CSRS), had been created in 1920, and at the outset it paid a regular pension only after employees reached the mandatory retirement age of 70; employees only received a pension if they had worked 15 years or more with the civil service. CSRS also featured a disability retirement category, but again a pension was paid only if the disabled civil servant had 15 or more years of service.[7]

CSRS's initial retirement pension and approaches to pension calculations were quite limited in the beginning as well. Pensions initially ranged from $180 to a maximum of $720 a year, but in 1926 the calculation for pensions changed to a formula based on total number of years of service, up to 30, and the average of an employee's annual salary for the final ten years of service. The maximum annual pension was raised to $1,000 a year.

In 1930, the retirement age was lowered so that those with 30 years or more of service could retire at 68, two years earlier than the mandatory separation age of 70, with no reduction in their retirement pension. The pension formula was also modified that year to a five-year average instead of the ten-year average. The maximum pension a retiree could earn was increased to $1,200 a year.

Early retirements based on claims of disability had become an issue as well, given the possibility of leaving service with a pension much earlier than the minimum retirement age of 68. In 1942, the retirement ages were lowered to 60 with 30 years of service, or 62 with 15 years of service, in order to reduce the number of employees retiring on disability before they reached the ages of 68 or 70. Those with 30 years of service could retire even earlier with an immediate but slightly reduced pension between the ages of 55 and 60.

It's important to keep in mind the shorter lifespans of the era as well. A 40-year-old white male in 1931 could expect to live another 29 years on average (until about the age of 70), while a white female could expect to live another 31 years. An African-American male could expect to live another 23 years on average, and an African-American female could expect to live just over 24 years.[8] In 1940, just 53% of males and 60% of females who turned 65 that year had survived from the age of 21, and they could expect to live an additional 13 and 15 years on average respectively beyond that. In total, there were only 9 million people aged 65 and over in the United States that year, according to the Social Security Administration.[9] Thus, most civil servants who reached the age of 60 in that era had already outlived many of their compatriots.

In 1956, the minimum number of years required to retire at age 62 was reduced from 15 to 5. In 1967, the pension reduction for those leaving service between the ages of 55 and 60 was eliminated, and the service requirement was reduced from 30 to 20 years for retirement at age 60.

By the 1980s, however, the system was clearly unsustainable both fiscally and in terms of recruiting new talent. Moreover, workers in the CSRS had no access to flexible employer-sponsored, tax-deferred savings plans—sometimes called "thrift" plans then—that were growing in popularity in the private sector. CSRS participants also did not contribute to Social Security, so they were not eligible to receive Social Security for the time they worked with the government (and Social Security had millions fewer contributors because of the lack of government worker contributions). CSRS calculations of retirement benefits based on the number of years worked proved to be a challenge when switching jobs after a significant time in government because any future pension would be greatly reduced, and Social Security payments would be greatly reduced as well because former federal workers would only begin to contribute later in their careers. And with no access to tax-deferred savings or investment "thrift" plans, by mid-career, civil servants had little choice other than to serve out the rest of their career in government. After a lifetime of work, CSRS workers were entirely dependent on the government CSRS pension.

The opportunity to work multiple careers was therefore unrealistic since federal employees had to rely solely on a government pension, which in turn was based on the number of years of service as a percentage of the average of the last several years' salary.* Unsurprisingly, turnover in the Federal Government at the time was almost nonexistent. As Judith Havemann of *The Washington Post* noted weeks after the TSP and new FERS retirement system were introduced in 1987, while the federal government experienced a 40% turnover rate among those in their first five years of service, there was "very little mobility in government" once a worker chose to make government service a career. The old retirement system "tied some workers to hated or dead-end jobs with 'golden handcuffs'."[10]

The inflexible system, moreover, was not conducive to recruiting experienced workers to various levels of civil service, as pensions were based primarily on the number of years served. Thus, those who began a civil service career in their 40s or 50s would face a smaller pension than those who began federal government service in their early 20s, while giving up increases in Social Security and potential additional investments in a tax-deferred thrift or private 401(k) plan.

To help rectify these limitations while at the same time modernizing the federal government retirement system, on June 6, 1986, President Ronald Reagan signed legislation creating the new Federal Employee Retirement System (FERS), of which the TSP was a major new component.

---

* The CSRS pension formula was a complex one that averaged out to just under 2% per year of service over a career: CSRS workers with 30 years of service would receive 56.25% of the average of their highest three years' base salary as a pension, for example.

While FERS reduced the percentage used to calculate a worker's pension almost in half compared to the old CSRS, FERS employee mandatory contributions to the FERS retirement system were reduced, and they were also enrolled in and began to contribute to Social Security. They also became eligible to participate in the newly created TSP, which began collecting contributions in April 1987. At the outset, FERS participants could contribute up to 10% of their salaries to the TSP and enjoy tax-deferred growth, and they were eligible to withdraw the money after they turned 59½. In return for a reduced pension, they would receive up to a 5% government match on contributions to the TSP depending on how much they personally contributed. This same basic benefit continues to this day, although the overall contribution limits have risen significantly.

After President Reagan signed the legislation creating FERS and the TSP, all civil servants hired after January 1, 1984—around 588,000 by the time President Reagan signed the legislation—were automatically transferred to the new FERS system. The approximately two million remaining workers had until the end of 1987 to decide whether to switch from CSRS to FERS. Those who chose to remain in the CSRS could still take advantage of tax-deferred growth in the TSP by contributing up to 5% of their base pay to the TSP, although they did not receive matching contributions.

In its first year, the TSP had only one investment option: U.S. government bonds in the G Fund. The fund returned an annualized 8.75% in its first few months (a very high rate compared to the 2-4% annual returns in the G Fund in the 2000s!). In January of the following year, the TSP opened two new funds, the F Fund—a total bond index fund—and the C Fund that mirrored the S&P 500 index of stocks of large- and mid-sized companies based in the United States. By late 1988, total account holdings had grown to $2.5 billion, and the amount growing by an average of $5 million per day.[11]

(Uniformed military personnel would have to wait until 2001 to participate in the TSP. Military personnel would not start receiving a government match for their TSP contributions until 2018 as part of the new "Blended Retirement System," detailed later in this book.)

The TSP has expanded and improved greatly in the 30-plus years since it was established. The total value of TSP accounts surpassed $100 billion for the first time in mid-2000. On October 30, 2000, legislation was enacted that allowed over two million members of the U.S. uniformed services to open TSP accounts the following year. Two more fund options—the I Fund international equities index fund and the S Fund small-capitalization index fund—were inaugurated in May 2001. In 2005, a selection of "Lifecycle" L Funds was established that automatically adjusts investments based on the target-year of the L Fund. And contribution limits were gradually increased after 2002, with percentage limits eliminated in 2006 in favor of an upper contribution limit of $15,000, which is periodically adjusted upward based on inflation. From 2003, the TSP website began to provide daily closing values of each fund and to allow online interfund transfer requests. (The TSP until then allowed only one interfund transfer at the end of each month based on transfer requests received by the 15th of that month.) With these changes, the TSP has become more transparent and flexible, allowing TSP participants greater control over their investments.

The Funds[12]

According to fund information available on tsp.gov and associated websites of the underlying indices, as of the end of 2019 the six types of funds featured the following characteristics:

G Fund This fund invests in short-term, non-marketable U.S. Treasury securities specially issued to the TSP, and the U.S. Government guarantees payment of principal and interest. Thus, it is the safest of the funds as there is no "risk of loss of principal," according to the fund information. It has enjoyed a 2.30% compound annual return for the 10-year period from 2009 to 2018.* While this fund has never experienced a drop in share price, the fund has experienced the lowest return among the TSP funds over this 10-year time period.

F Fund The F Fund is invested to match the Bloomberg Barclays U.S. Aggregate Bond Index. This is an index of fixed-income securities (bonds) with maturities of over one year, comprising Treasury and Agency bonds, asset-backed securities, and corporate and non-corporate bonds. The fund became operational in January 1988, and it experienced a 3.73% compound yearly return from 2009 to 2018.*

C Fund The C Fund invests in the stocks of companies listed in the Standard & Poor's 500 (S&P 500) Index, which is made up of 500 large and medium-sized U.S. companies. The fund became operational in January

1988. At the end of 2019, major holdings in the C Fund included Microsoft, Apple, Amazon.com Inc, Berkshire Hathaway Inc, and Procter & Gamble. Between 2009 and 2018, the fund returned 13.17% on average annually, which was better than the 9.55% annual return it enjoyed from the January 1988 to December 2009 period.*

I Fund The only international fund in the TSP, the I Fund invests in all the companies listed in the "Europe, Australasia, Far East" or EAFE Index of publicly traded companies in developed countries outside the United States and Canada. The fund became operational in May 2001. The five largest companies in the I Fund at the end of 2019 were Nestle, Royal Dutch Shell plc, Samsung Electronics, Roche Holding AG, and Novartis AG. This fund experienced a 10-year 6.48% compound rate of return from 2009 to 2018.* (As of early 2020, TSP administrators planned to expand the holdings of the I Fund to include stocks of companies in developing countries and international small-capitalization stocks as well.)

S Fund The S Fund invests in domestic U.S. companies that are included in the Dow Jones U.S. Completion Total Stock Market (TSM) Index, which are not listed in the S&P 500 (C Fund) index. Like the I Fund, the S Fund became operational in May 2001, and it has returned 13.67% annually from 2009 to 2018.* Some of the major holdings of the S Fund at the end of 2019 were Tesla Inc, Blackstone Group Inc, Square Inc, and Lululemon Athletica Inc.

L Funds The L Funds or "Lifecycle Funds" opened on August 1, 2005. As of the end of 2019, there are five L Funds: L 2050, L 2040, L 2030, L 2020, and L Income funds. Each L Fund comprises a mix of the G, F, C, I, and S stock and bond funds listed above, and they slowly sell the more-volatile stock funds (the C, I, and S funds) as the funds' target dates near and invest more in the bond funds (the G and F funds) to protect investors from the ups and downs of the market and to provide more yield.*

Who actually manages the funds? Since 2011, the investment company BlackRock has managed the day-to-day transactions and investments of the actual funds except for the G Fund, which is invested directly in specially issued U.S. government bonds via the U.S. Treasury. The funds are invested in trust funds, not mutual funds or Exchange Traded

Funds. Because of the special nature of the trust funds, the TSP funds are not publicly traded and therefore do not have ticker symbols. They are also regulated by the Comptroller of the Currency, not the Securities and Exchange Commission (SEC).[12]

*Note: past performance does not mean this fund will grow the same in the future—the fund may enjoy a greater growth rate in the future, or it may go down in value as well.

The TSP generally enjoys high satisfaction among participants. According to a 2017 survey of TSP participants, 89% of respondents were satisfied with the plan compared to 85% in 2006 and a low of 81% in 2008, during the financial downturn. As a sign of TSP participants' engagement, 8 in 10 of those surveyed contributed at least 5% of their salary to their accounts, which was enough to receive a full government match (an automatic 100% return!). Just over half (51%) of FERS participants contributed over 5% of their salary, and 65% of uniformed service participants surveyed contributed over 5% of their salaries to their TSP accounts. The survey was taken before BRS was introduced, so military participants were not yet receiving matches (discussed further below).[13]

Most importantly, the TSP is among the cheapest investment vehicles in the world, especially compared to many 401(k) plans used by private employers. A 2014 study conducted by financial information company Brightscope found that 401(k) plan fees ranged from over 1% for smaller plans to around 0.4% for ultra-large plans of $1 billion or more. Moreover, the stock mutual fund investments that were offered in 401(k) plans had higher expense ratios that averaged 0.58% in 2013. While this was lower than the industry average (that is, mutual funds offered outside the sponsored plans) of 0.74%, the ratios were still quite high. Thus 401(k) participants in these plans end up paying as much as 1% to 1.5% of their assets in fees, which increases as one's investments increase. That 1.5% of a $100,000 investment is $1,500 each year. And as the total amount invested grows, so do the fees: 1.5% of $500,000 is $7,500 per year, for example.[14] It's obviously in the participant's interest to keep as much money as possible invested in one's own funds; we'll see the full impact of fees over the lifetime of investing in the final chapter, *Parabolic Wealth*.

These findings confirm an earlier study by Christian Weller and Shana Jenkins, who lamented the exceptionally large fees in many 401(k) plans in contrast to the TSP in the 2007 *Financial Planning*. Citing a 2004 Congressional Budget Office study, typical private-sector 401(k) fees were between 1% and 1.5% of assets, as found in the Brightscope study, which can result in a one-quarter to over one-third reduction in overall returns after a four-decade career. My research, presented later in this book, confirms the significant reductions in overall returns these seemingly small amounts can cause over a lifetime of investing.[15]

The TSP does not charge any up-front fees for investing in any of the funds, and all the funds charge very minimal administrative expense ratios, or fractional percentages of amounts invested each year to help pay for services such as support staff, the TSP website, and periodic correspondence with participants. The expense ratios are made up of "administrative expenses" and "other expenses," each having to do with running the TSP, such as operating the recordkeeping system, providing participant services, and the printing and mailing of notices, statements, and publications. Blackrock, which manages the buying and selling of shares on a daily basis, is also paid through these fees.

After falling considerably in the first 20 years of operation, net expenses have leveled to a weighted average of about .04% in 2018, or a mere $0.40 for each $1,000 invested in the stock and bond funds.

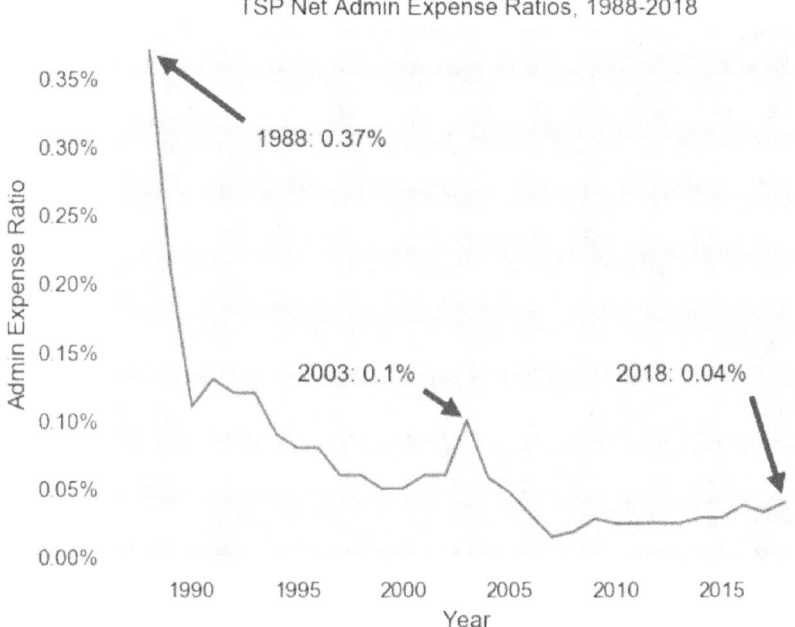

The TSP's expense ratios have dropped dramatically since it was first established in 1987, although there has been a slight uptick since the early 2010s (sources: TSP & FRTIB).

What many participants don't realize is that some of their fellow TSP participants actually subsidize some of the operating expenses by paying extra fees to take out TSP loans. Also, some FERS and BRS participants leave before their Agency/Service automatic 1% "vests," or legally becomes the property of the account holder. For BRS, for example, vesting happens after two years of service. If a worker or service member leaves before funds "vest," this money is forfeited to the TSP and helps to subsidize operations and lower fees for everyone else. Total expenses for 2018 were 0.052%, for example, but fees paid for taking out TSP loans reduced that amount by 0.002%, and forfeitures reduced it a further 0.01%, so the 2018 net expenses came to a mere 0.04%.

To be sure, private sector competition has driven expenses for similar index fund offerings to historic lows as well. Among the lowest expense ratios for a publicly traded index fund, Vanguard's "VOO" Exchange Traded Fund that tracks the S&P 500 index (and is exactly the same as the C Fund) is 0.03%, or $0.30 for each $1,000 invested as of late 2019. Its Total Bond Market ETF, which is exactly like the F Fund, features an expense ratio of 0.035%, or $0.35 per $1,000. Other companies offer similarly priced index funds as well.

Yet, a surprisingly large number of investment funds have expense ratios of half a percent (0.50%) or more. According to investment research firm Morningstar, the average for all funds in 2018 was 0.48%. This figure has declined from 0.93% in 2000, indicating that intensifying competition among asset managers has been driving down the price of investing (another sign of how competition in free markets improves our lives!). Expenses for index funds on average dropped to 0.15%, while those for managed funds dropped to 0.67%.[16] With the 0.48% average expense ratio, a similarly priced fund would collect $4.80 per year for every $1,000 invested, over *10 times* the amount charged in the TSP. And this is *in addition* to any other fees the fund may charge for the privilege of investing your hard-earned money in their mutual funds.

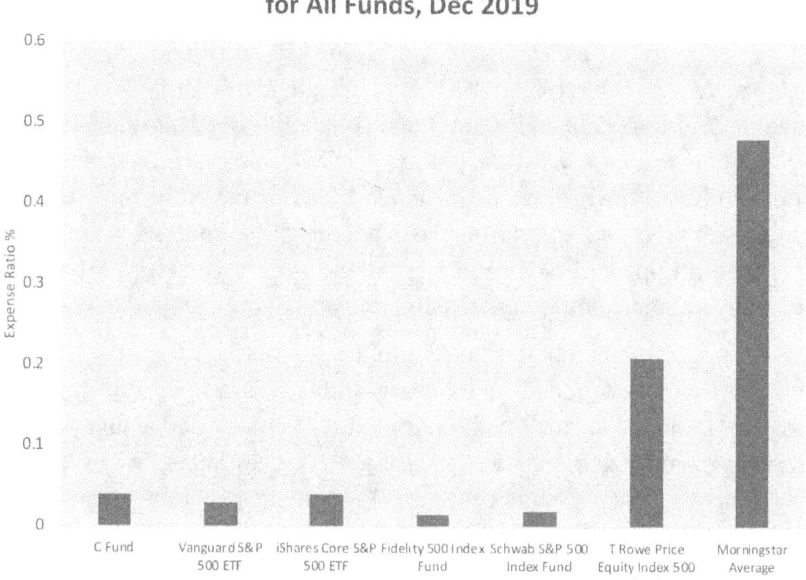

The TSP expense ratios are extremely low, but they face stiff competition in the private sector. Vanguard, Fidelity, and Schwab all offer competing S&P 500 index funds with net expense ratios that are less than the 0.04% net expense for the C Fund! (Sources: individual prospectuses of funds, December 2019)

Over time, these expenses can have a major impact on the growth of your funds. To illustrate this, let's say that after diligently saving and investing for many years you have a portfolio worth $500,000 in stock and bond funds. With the TSP's extremely low 0.04% expense ratio, the TSP would collect about $200 each year from your account to cover administrative expenses. If your $500,000 portfolio were instead invested in mutual funds charging a higher 0.48% expense ratio, you would instead pay *$2,400 each and every year*. That's a difference of $2,200 each year—meaning you would keep that extra $2,200 in your TSP fund, compared with mutual funds that charge greater expense ratios. And that difference grows as your account grows: A $1,000,000 portfolio would be charged $400 in the TSP but *$4,800* in the high-expense mutual fund. Thus, the less money the fund takes from you in expenses, the more you keep, and the more money that will continue to grow for you in your TSP account in the future.

Even one of the wealthiest individuals in the world, Berkshire Hathaway Chairman Warren Buffett, has repeatedly highlighted the detrimental effect of expenses over the years. In his 2004 annual letter to Berkshire shareholders, he wrote, "Investors should remember that…expenses are their enemies." Buffett attributed "investment management" fees as one of the three primary causes for investor underperformance over time. (The other two were investing "based on tips and fads" and a "start-and-stop approach to the market marked by untimely entries…and exits" into and out of the market.)[17]

In his 2006 shareholder letter, Buffett discussed more fully the relatively high fees that hedge funds charge private investors.* Private hedge funds are notorious for their high fee structure, as many hedge funds charge a 1.5% or 2% management fee each year and typically keep 20% of any *gain* in the funds, so that investors get only 80% of the gains of their investments (but investors of course fully suffer all the losses). Buffett illustrated how detrimental this high fee structure is to an investor. "[A] manager who achieves a gross return of 10% in a year will keep 3.6 percentage points—two points off the top, plus 20% of the residual 8 points—leaving only 6.4 percentage points for his investors…He will receive this bonanza even though an index fund might have returned 15% to investors in the same period and charged them only a token fee."[18]

In fact, Buffett was so sure that fees are a drag on a stock fund's performance that he declared at the May 2006 Berkshire Hathaway annual meeting that he would bet anyone $1 million that the S&P 500 index fund would beat a basket of any ten hedge funds over a ten-year period, with all fees included. A year later the owner of a high-fee private money management firm negotiated a bet with Buffett pitting a basket of five managed hedge funds against Buffett's choice of the Vanguard S&P 500 Admiral shares fund, with expense ratio at the time of just .07%. (The TSP's C Fund is exactly the same type of fund as the one chosen by Buffett.) They each invested

---

* Hedge funds are lightly regulated and privately-run funds that can make a wide variety of investments in addition to the buying and selling of stocks, to include buying and selling commodities, commercial real estate and debt, and foreign currencies. They can also "short" these investments—bet that they will go down—as a means to "hedge" or protect their other investments (hence the name for this type of investment fund).

$320,000 in a zero-coupon bond that would mature in ten years and be worth $1 million, and the bet officially began on January 1, 2008. The winner of the bet would give the money to the charity of his choice.[19]

Ten years later, Buffet won the bet handily. The index-tracking Vanguard fund returned 7.7% annualized over those ten years, despite experiencing one of the most significant declines in value since the depression in 2008-9. The basket of hedge funds picked by the asset manager returned a miniscule 2.2% annualized during that time.[20] The results beg the question: *Why would anyone want to pay the insane fees the hedge fund industry charges, to receive returns that underperform an index fund?*

There are many lessons we can take from this bet, the foremost being that one of the most successful investors in the world demonstrated significant confidence in investing in the S&P 500—the C Fund in the TSP—over the long run, so individual investors should be confident in putting at least a portion of their long-term savings in this index fund as well. (In case you're curious, Buffett gave his $1 million to Girls Inc. of Omaha, NE.)

In fact, the hedge fund fee model of "2 and 20" as it has been called is gradually crumbling. In the first half of 2019, hedge fund fees dropped to 1.2% on average, down from 1.6% in 2007, and performance-linked fees dropped to 14.5%. Yet, their 5.7% performance in the first half of 2019 still underperformed the S&P 500 and index funds that track it.[21]

Thus, if you invest in the TSP's C Fund, congratulations! You are, on average, consistently outperforming the big hedge funds of the world.

For any investment, your goal is to *keep* as much money as you can in your account so your investments continue to grow, and the lower the expenses and fees, the more money you can reinvest for long-term growth. To build wealth, you should pay close attention to minimizing expenses, and ultimately the TSP offers among the lowest expenses in the business.

So how are the TSP and other index-tracking funds able to keep expenses so low? One of the main reasons is because the funds invest passively in bonds and stocks according to broad indexes. The indexes list the company stocks and government and corporate bonds according to specific categories such as size, and fund managers purchase the stocks and bonds according to this list. The TSP funds thus go up and down as the broad stock and bond markets go up and down. Because there is no "research" involved as to which companies will do better than others—investors in these funds own them all according to broad metrics such as size—the index funds perform just as well as (or just as poorly as) the broad markets. These funds do not buy or sell stocks or bonds very often, and this saves TSP investors money since each trade requires the payment of a commission to buy or sell a stock or bond. And because the TSP manages over $600 billion in the five funds (with the L Fund holdings also invested in the original five funds), the TSP enjoys significant economies of scale.

How is the "stock market" different from an "index fund" and the TSP funds?

Broadly speaking, the **stock market** is the collection of all stocks traded in a specific country. In the United States, stocks are traded—bought and sold—on two major **stock exchanges**: the New York Stock Exchange (NYSE) and the Nasdaq (the acronym for the rather arcane "National Association of Securities Dealers Automated Quotation," which is no longer used). The NYSE is the older of the two, with origins dating to 1792.[22] The Nasdaq began as the first all-electronic stock exchange in 1971, and because of its tech-focused approach, it attracted more technology companies in its early years. One general way to know whether a company is listed on the NYSE or on the Nasdaq is to look at a company's ticker (or stock) symbol: If it has one, two, or three letters, it is most likely listed on the NYSE, but if it has four or five letters, it is probably listed on the Nasdaq.[23] Thus, "Ford" is listed on the NYSE as "F," and Microsoft is traded on the Nasdaq as "MSFT." Companies can switch exchanges, however, so you might see some four-letter symbols on the NYSE, and some with fewer than four on the Nasdaq. Both of these exchanges are located in New York.

The S&P 500 index—which is what the **C Fund** is based on—is a list of 500 or so of the largest U.S. companies. (The companies at the bottom of the list are not based strictly on capitalization, because company sizes can grow or contract quickly depending on how many investors are buying or selling their stock.) These companies are bought and sold on exchanges such as the NYSE or the Nasdaq, and BlackRock, the investment company that manages all the buying and selling for the C Fund as of 2019, buys shares of these companies on either exchange when

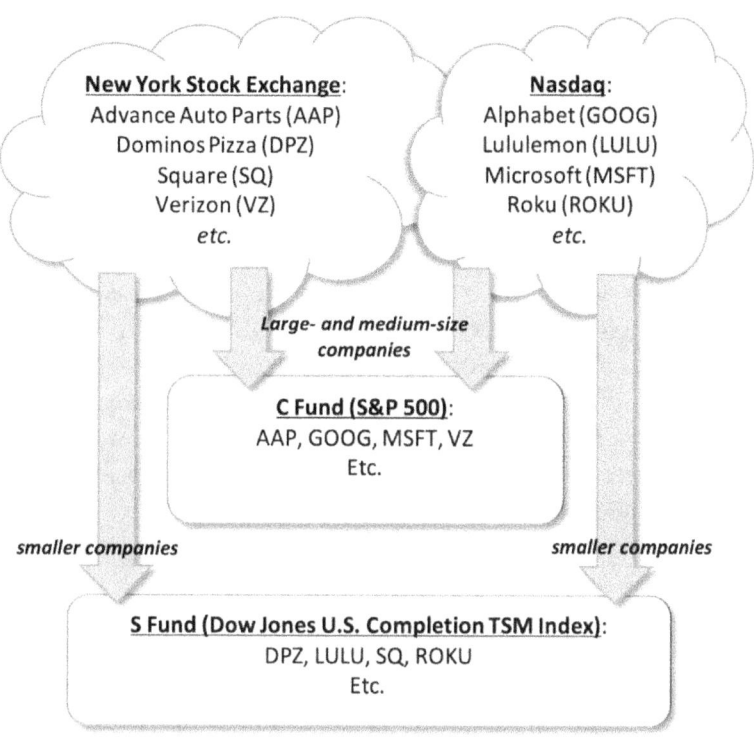

you invest money in the C Fund. It similarly sells shares of these companies via its respective exchange when investors take money out of the C Fund. The **S Fund** is made up of the smaller U.S. companies from the 501st or so to about the 3300th smallest company traded in the U.S. (Because new companies are often being created and "going public"—selling their shares to the public for the first time—or taken private or otherwise going out of business, the exact number of companies on the "Dow Jones U.S. Completion TSM" index changes often.) These smaller companies can also be bought and sold on the NYSE or Nasdaq. If you invest in both the C Fund and the S Fund, congratulations! You have invested in pretty much the entire U.S. stock market.

Outside of the United States, there are major stock exchanges in places like London, Frankfurt, Tokyo, and Seoul, and non-U.S. companies are bought and sold on these various exchanges. Since the **I Fund** invests in the major non-U.S. companies found on these foreign exchanges, if you invest in the I Fund in addition to the C and S funds, you are investing in companies that are listed on foreign stock exchanges as well.

Because there is no one person or team of people trying to calculate what company or companies will do better than others to improve investing results, the TSP does not have to pay what can be very high salaries for investment researchers and advisers, and this saves TSP investors lots of money. Active investment funds charge significantly for their research and staff, even though studies show that over the long term, a majority of active money managers actually perform worse than passive index funds such as those found in the TSP. According to Burton Malkiel, an economist at Princeton University who has written extensively on the topic, index funds have beaten active managers by almost 2% on average each year over long periods. The poorer returns of actively managed funds are due to investment fees to pay for staff and advertising, for example, and costs associated with increased buying and selling of stocks compared to index funds, according to Malkiel.[24] Even if a money manager can beat the market by one or two percentage points each year, the fees he or she charges investors for additional services, coupled with trading fees, can actually cause poorer performance on average for the individual investor over the long term.

According to Kenneth French, an academic at Dartmouth, many individual investors are simply "unaware that the average active investor would increase his return if he switched to a passive strategy"—that is, to index funds. French calculated the total cost of trying to beat the market at around .67% of a portfolio each year. Why don't more individual investors use index funds? "Financial firms certainly contribute to this confusion," according to French, and "[a]lthough a few occasionally promote index funds as a better alternative, the general message from Wall Street is that active investing is easy and profitable."[25] In other words, actively managing other peoples' money is a lucrative business because of the fees companies can collect.

It is true that over a one- or five-year period or even longer, some professional money managers do indeed beat the stock market, and they get a lot of media attention for their impressive performance over these relatively short periods of time. But almost none can do so over several decades or longer. Moreover, the odds of an investor choosing from one of the thousands of *underperforming* professional money managers are much, much greater than choosing the one or two who might actually be able to beat the market (or any index fund) over several decades. Decades of research shows that index funds beat a large majority of so-called investment experts over extended periods of time, so investing in the TSP's index funds is a winning strategy over time.

Additionally, most TSP participants receive a match from the government of up to 5% of their contributions, to make up for a lower pension. If you're eligible and contribute 5% of your $50,000 annual salary (only $96 every two weeks) into your TSP account, for example, the government will add an additional $96 per pay period. This *doubles* the money going into your account for the year from $2,500 to $5,000.

The 'Blended Retirement System' – Now Military Members Receive a Match!

The Blended Retirement System (BRS) was enacted by the National Defense Authorization Act of 2016. The BRS blends the traditional military retirement system (which features a "defined benefit" or pension) with a "defined contribution" portion that features a government match of participant investments of up to 5% of salary into the TSP, for up to 26 years of service. The default automatic enrollment is set at 3% of salary and is currently invested in the L 2050 Lifecycle Fund, and service members are highly encouraged to increase their contributions (and consider contributing to the Roth TSP as well!).

The plan also features the possibility of a lump sum distribution at retirement in return for a reduced military pension and a one-time, midcareer bonus in exchange for additional service (which is in addition to any career-specific incentives or retention bonuses you may be eligible for, too).[26] Uniformed personnel also get a perk that civilians do not get: They can contribute higher amounts while in a Combat Zone Tax Exclusion (CZTE) area, which for 2018 maxed out at $55,000 for your and the government's contributions.

The BRS became operational and began to sign up new members in January 2018. Membership has grown fast since then. As of September 2019, the last figures that were available as this book went to press, participation had grown to *618,000* members! Of those members, about 363,000 participated in the Roth TSP option, meaning that their after-tax contributions would continue to grow tax-free for decades, and can be used at retirement tax-free as well. Amazing! (See bit.ly/BRSgrowth for current figures.)

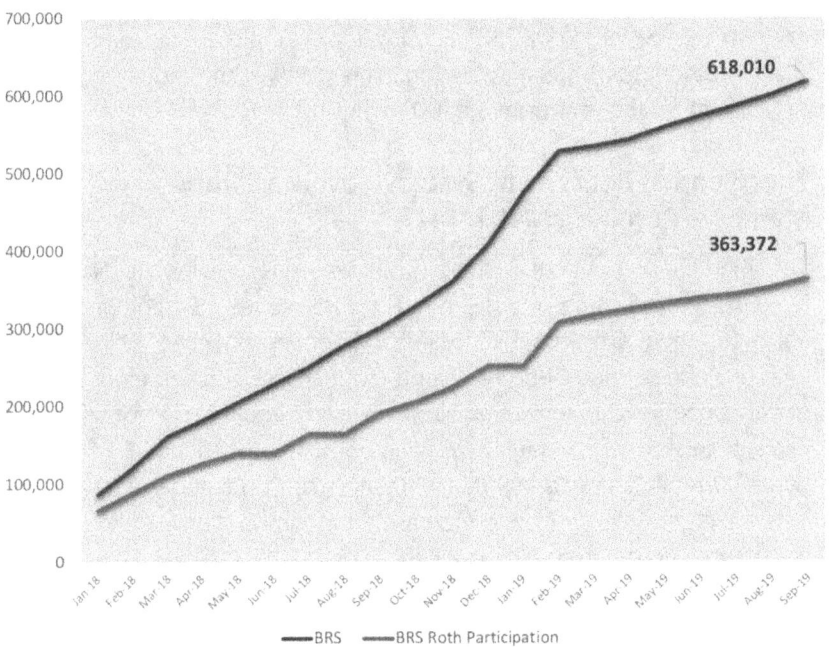

If, as a FERS employee or BRS participant, you *don't add* any money to your TSP account, the government will only add the equivalent of 1% of your pay into the low-return government bond fund. You lose the other 4% government match, because you are not contributing to your own account. When you do contribute, you receive a match based on how much you contribute up to 5% of your salary. If you contribute even 1% of your own pay to your TSP account, you get an additional 1% match from the government on top of the original 1% government contribution, for a total of 3% of your salary. Contribute 2% of your own money, and the government will throw in the original one percent plus 2% to match your contribution, for a total of 5%. (See chart below.)

If the TSP Participant contributes…	the government will add…	for a total contribution of…
nothing	1%	1%
1%	2%	3%
2%	3%	5%
3%	4%	7%
4%	4.5%	8.5%
5%	5%	10%
6%	5%	11%
7%	5%	12%
8%	5%	13%
9%	5%	14%
10%	5%	15%

And as the chart above illustrates, FERS and BRS participants are not limited to contributing 5% of their salaries. They can contribute 10% or more of their salaries and still receive the 5% match, as long as the contribution amount does not exceed $19,500 in the entire calendar year as of 2020. (This maximum amount increases periodically over time to match inflation.) Also, the TSP allows those aged 50 and over to make what are called "catch-up contributions" of up to $6,500 in 2020, for a total of $26,000. And since your contributions and the match are deposited directly to your TSP account, the entire amount for regular TSP accounts is exempt from all taxes until you withdraw it any time after you turn 59½.* (Roth TSP contributions are made

---

* You may withdraw TSP funds sooner, but under most circumstances the withdrawn amount will be subject to taxes and an additional 10% early withdrawal penalty—a big hit and something to avoid at all costs. You can also take out a "loan" and pay it back over time, but this means you miss out on any growth that your withdrawn investments might have enjoyed, and you generally have to pay back the entire loan immediately if you leave your job.

with after-tax dollars, and the original contributions as well as growth and government matching amounts can be withdrawn after you turn 59½.)

As you well know, taxes can take a significant amount out of your biweekly pay, leaving you with less to save. Depending on how much you make and whether you have deductions for a home mortgage, children, etc., federal and state taxes as well as deductions for Social Security and Medicare, healthcare, and mandatory retirement contributions, can take anywhere from one-fifth to one-third of your pay, meaning you might bring home no more than $0.67 to $0.80 for each $1 you earn after taxes are taken out. And you haven't even paid your bills yet, much less saved anything! If you save or invest some of that after-tax $0.67 to $0.80 in a taxable account, the interest and dividends on that money in most cases is also taxable each and every year, so you keep getting taxed again and again, year after year.

Participating in the TSP helps you to avoid this. Money you contribute to your regular TSP account is contributed *before* paying federal income and state taxes, so each $1 you earn and contribute to the TSP is a $1 you keep for long-term growth. And, with the match, that $1 becomes $2. Moreover, this $1—or $50 or $100 or $500 depending on how much you contribute each pay period—will grow without any taxes being taken out in any of those years that it is growing and collecting interest and dividends. Only many years later when you withdraw money from your regular TSP account is the money taxed (but not the remaining money in your TSP account), and money from your Roth TSP account can be withdrawn tax-free when eligible. Thus, you can choose to try to save and invest some of that $0.67 to $0.80 for every $1 you earn after taxes, or you can keep up to $2 by contributing to the TSP.

Your periodic contributions, any government match, the TSP's extremely low fees, and the tax-deferred nature of the TSP all mean that your TSP account can grow substantially over time. And your contributions themselves can grow over the years, as you are promoted from time to time.

Here's a basic illustration of natural contribution growth. Let's say you're just starting your first federal government job. You're in your mid-20s and start at GS-8, Step 1. Let's say you decide to contribute 5% of your salary to the TSP, which is enough to get a full match to double the amount that goes into your personal account. If you work hard during your government service and receive periodic promotions in addition to periodic step increases, your contributions will grow as a natural result of growth in your yearly pay.

Now, let's say you invest that amount into the large-cap C Fund, with holdings in large, well-known, and successful U.S. companies such as Apple, Google, Procter & Gamble, and Ford. If the fund continues to grow at the historic market average of just about 9% per year, give or take—its average from 1926 to 2018, according to Jeremy Siegel's *Stocks for the Long Run*[27] and Investopia[28]—your contributions would grow from $0 upon starting your first week of work to about $1,269,268 after a 30-year career, based on a 2019 starting salary in the Washington, D.C. metro area of $52,068. This assumes a 5% increase in your base pay each year that will automatically increase your TSP contributions and the government match by a similar amount.

This is a hypothetical exercise, of course, since indexes don't go straight up year after year by annual rates of 9% on a regular basis. But more on that later.

Depending on how you progress in your career, that 5% average yearly increase might actually be a conservative figure with additional promotions. Nevertheless, if the market performs as it has historically, and if you continue to contribute to the TSP throughout your career, you could end your career as a millionaire, and this is in addition to receiving a basic pension for federal government service.

What if you contributed 10% of your salary instead of 5% over this same 30-year period? Under the same scenario, your investment would grow to about $1,903,902 in 30 years—with a total out-of-pocket investment of only $346,000 (and $173,000 in matching contributions) over that time period.

But there are a couple of *big* caveats here. First, the above calculations were based on assumptions taken from very long periods of stock market performance over many decades. The market sometimes can perform quite badly over an extended period of time, even over several years or longer. There can be periods of significant and extended market declines, with some declines of 20%, 30%, even 40% or more. Sometimes, the markets recover quite rapidly, but at other times, they take many years to recover. The only TSP fund that has never declined in value is the G Fund; values of TSP accounts invested in the F, C, S, and I Funds *have* and *will* decline from time to time as part of market volatility. These can be times of great opportunity, as we will see in later chapters, but they can seem very painful for those who are not mentally and emotionally prepared for the declines.

Moreover, the returns noted above were not adjusted for inflation over time, so the actual purchasing power of that final amount—after taking into account the growth in prices over time of everything from food, fuel and clothes, rent and the price of a car—would be less than the final calculations suggest.

Despite these caveats, however, there is an important takeaway: *You don't have to continue working with the government or in the military* to continue to save and invest! You can (and should) continue to do so in any endeavor you choose to pursue, and you can continue to invest in an IRA or another company-sponsored defined contribution plan like a 401(k). Although the government does provide a 5% match of salary, you can probably get a similar match, maybe a little more or maybe a little less, in your next career too.

Market risks and the risk of inflation are therefore significant challenges in constructing a TSP portfolio that will provide meaningful returns over time. Let's look at these risks more fully before moving on to the various strategies in this book.

The Risks of Saving and Investing – and of Not Saving and Investing

Investing in anything is inherently risky. If you invest too conservatively, your investments might not keep up with inflation. If you invest in more volatile stock funds, you might experience sudden, prolonged declines in the stock markets. But in my opinion, the risk of not saving and not investing any of your hard-earned money in growth-oriented funds is greater than either of those risks because, if you don't save and invest, you cannot build wealth over time (nor can you get the TSP match!).

Inflation – One of the first major risks investors face over time is inflation. To illustrate the effects of inflation, imagine you're a new GS-8 employee contributing 5% salary, with the 5% match. Over a 30-year career, during which time you would have enjoyed the long-term average return of 9%, you'd end up with close to $1.3 million in your TSP account as noted previously. But over a 30-year time span, the prices of almost everything rise. Food and clothing become more expensive. Cars become more expensive, and rent becomes more costly, as well.

Annual inflation averaged over 3% in the 1900s. The adjusted average return of an S&P 500 index fund over 30 years, taking into consideration 3.5%+ yearly inflation, would drop from the 9-10% range to approximately 6% or 6.5%. Thus, the $1.3 million in your TSP would actually have the purchasing power equivalent to around $800,000 today. A dollar today will buy less tomorrow, because prices of common goods and services will continue to increase over time. And contributing 10% salary to the TSP, the amount 30 years from now would be about $1.2 million, adjusted for inflation, instead of about $1.9 million.

While these are still significant amounts, they are effectively reduced due to just 3.5% inflation per year. Moreover, inflation could be even worse in the future, and prices could grow by 4% or 5% or more a year. Indeed, by the end of the 1970s and into the early 1980s, inflation was growing by 10% or more in some years. With 10% inflation, prices of many things would *double* in just over seven years—a $20,000 car, for example, would cost close to $40,000 in seven years at 10% yearly inflation. While we will hopefully never experience inflation on this scale again, inflation of some sort is almost always present, and rapid inflation could wreak havoc on all of our investments inside and outside the TSP. Even the "safest" of the TSP funds, the G Fund, might not be able to keep up with rapid inflation, based on returns of around 2-3% over the past few years.

Higher inflation, moreover, can cause stock prices to drop in the short term. This is because the yield on bonds—that is, the interest rate that bonds pay to investors each year—goes up as inflation goes up to attract investors. The higher bond yields mean that investors can get a better interest rate in bonds in the short term than from stock dividends with some additional safety, and some investors will sell their stocks and invest that money in bonds to get better and safer yields. This happened in the inflationary 1970s as bond yields rose to over 10% by the end of the decade, so people invested in bonds that had higher yields and greater perceived safety than stocks that were languishing at the time.

Over the long term, however, stocks can better adjust to inflation because companies can improve productivity to lower costs, and they can raise prices of what they charge for their goods and services (not to mention develop new products and services to compensate), so that their earnings can recover and increase over time. And as inflation began to fall gradually from the mid-1980s, for example, investors enjoyed better returns in stocks over the next 18 years.

Ultimately, a well-diversified portfolio coupled with consistent additions to investments can help guard against the threat of inflation over the long term.

Declines in the Markets – TSP investors also face the risk of sometimes-sudden drops in the value of markets. While market declines can occur at any time—even during generally excellent economic conditions—some declines are more dramatic than others. They are sometimes followed by long periods of stagnation, when stock markets go for many years without increasing at all. In the United States, these periods include the Depression- and WWII-era period of 1929-1949, the extended period of "stagflation" (stagnation and inflation) of 1966-1982, and the post-Internet and post-real estate bubbles of 2000-2002 and 2008-2009.

Take the late 1960s and 1970s as an example. During this period, the U.S. faced a host of challenges, including major military operations in Southeast Asia, wars in the Middle East and South Asia, the resignation of a U.S. president, oil crises in 1973-74 and in 1979, rising inflation, rising unemployment, and multiple recessions. The S&P 500 began 1966 at 93.14 points, and, following many ups and downs, it closed on August 2, 1982, at 103.71—representing a rise of just 11% *over 16 years*, not including dividends. In fact, even after including dividends over those years, the stock market return was actually *-0.4* after adjusting for the high rate of inflation. Anyone who put money into the stock market in 1966 actually lost money by the end of 1981, after taking into consideration rising prices.[29] (These calculations do not take into account dollar-cost averaging, which can provide spectacular results and will be detailed later.)

In contrast, from 1982 through 1999, the S&P 500 enjoyed tremendous returns, growing from 103 in 1982 to a high of 1,527.46 on March 24, 2000—15 times its August 1982 value. Including dividends, between 1982 and the peak in March 2000, the S&P 500 returned an astounding 17.3% annually. Had you invested $10,000 in 1982, this would have turned into over $250,000 by the end of 1999, without adding anything to it. Indeed, between 1995 and 1999, the S&P 500 returned *over 20% each year*.

But even during this long-term "bull" market (when the general trend of the market was up), there were several sudden and dramatic declines, including a drop of over 22% *in one day* on October 19, 1987. After each decline, the markets recovered and often quickly went higher, adding to the excitement of the era. In the 1990s, many factors helped propel the markets upward, including falling inflation and commodities prices, the end of the Cold War, and new technologies that offered greater efficiencies for businesses around the world. Investors were excited as we approached the dawn of the 21st century and all the possibilities it offered. With markets peaking, however, some were becoming concerned that the stock market had increased too quickly despite the seemingly new and peaceful era.

In a speech in December 1996, Federal Reserve Chairman Alan Greenspan rhetorically asked about the potential impact of what he saw as "irrational exuberance" in the broader economy. "Clearly, sustained low inflation implies less uncertainty about the future, and lower risk premiums imply higher prices of stocks and other earning assets…But how do we know when irrational exuberance has unduly escalated asset values, which then become subject to unexpected and prolonged contractions as they have in Japan over the past decade?"[30]

Chairman Greenspan was referring to the Japanese stock and real-estate markets, which in the 1980s had enjoyed huge gains. The Nikkei 225, a major index of Japanese companies, had *quadrupled* in five years and peaked at 38,915.87 on December 29, 1989. Following several recessions in Japan in the 1990s, when Chairman Greenspan gave his speech in late 1996 the Nikkei was hovering around 19,000, half of its value seven years earlier. (And the Nikkei kept falling. In mid-November 2002, the index hit a new low of 8,197, a 79% drop in 14 years. At the end of 2009, on the 20-year anniversary of the popping of the Japanese bubble, the Nikkei closed at 10,546.)*

Always careful with his words, Chairman Greenspan highlighted the reasons for exceptionally strong U.S. stock market performance in the 1990s, while also warning that investors could become overly excited—exhibiting

---

* Despite the long decline of the Nikkei in Japan, the "Europe, Asia, and Far East" index fund—what the I Fund was based on and which held significant amount of Japanese stocks—had an annualized return of over 4% in that same 20-year period through 2009, with double-digit returns in the early 2000s. While this is not spectacular, it shows that even as stock markets in one country experience dramatic declines, growth in other areas can more than make up for the losses.

"irrational exuberance"—based on assumptions that the stock market would continue to go up in the foreseeable future, just because it had risen dramatically over the past 15 years. In pointing out that the Japanese stock market was experiencing a prolonged decline, Chairman Greenspan was implying that a future decline in U.S. stock markets was not impossible, either.

Perhaps the ultimate warning came in late 1999, when Warren Buffett predicted very low market returns into the early 2000s. Buffett wrote in his 1999 letter to Berkshire Hathaway shareholders that it was a "virtual certainty" that the S&P 500 "will do far less well in the next decade or two than it has done since 1982."[31] Buffett echoed this prediction in a November 22, 1999 *Fortune Magazine* interview that, after factoring in inflation, stocks might return a meager 4% annually over the next decade.[32]

Thus, in late 1999, Warren Buffett warned on multiple occasions that, instead of average returns in the double-digits (12%, 15%, even 18% as some were predicting into the foreseeable future), the best investors could hope for was an annual return of 4% into the 2010s, after inflation. Moreover, returns could be less than 4%, as he emphasized in the *Fortune* article.

Ten years after the predictions were published, it turned out that Buffett was correct in his forecast. With the bursting of the Internet bubble, the attacks of 9/11, subsequent allied military actions, and a relatively mild recession in the United States in 2001-2002, the S&P 500 suffered three years of significant declines in a row. The S&P 500 inched slowly upward from early 2003, but after barely making new highs in late 2007 the market then fell back again in 2008 and early 2009, and at the end of 2010 it still hadn't fully recovered from the losses in the early 2000s. (Following steep market declines in late 2008, however, Buffett declared in a *New York Times* op-ed that he was again buying stocks of American companies, issuing a new and more bullish forecast for the 2010s and 2020s.[33])

Thus, periods of stagnation and periodic downturns—like the extended stagflation during 1966-1982 or the downturns in the 2000s—are times when the stock markets return to their historical averages following years of "irrational exuberance." This is called "reversion to the mean"—that is, long periods of extraordinary growth that are followed by long periods of stagnation or by a sudden and steep decline, as the markets revert to their long-term average growth rate.

And, paradoxically, periods of long stagnation or sudden decline can be the best times to invest in the markets, because prices become increasingly cheaper over time. Just as we all like to buy things when they are "on sale," all things being equal, so it is with investing in the stock and bond markets. It is more advantageous in the long run to invest money when investments are cheaper, rather than when they are more expensive. We will explore "dollar-cost averaging" and ways to buy into declining markets a little later in this book.

TSP Risks You Don't Have

It is important to know that, by investing in the TSP index funds, one risk you *don't* face is company-specific risk, that is, the risk that you will lose *all* your money by investing it in one company's stock. Investing in one company is very risky because if the company goes bust, so does your investment! Even big companies can fail, and quite dramatically too. Enron, MCI, and Adelphia were some of the major companies that went bankrupt in the aftermath of the Internet bubble in the early 2000s, while Lehman Brothers and a host of regional banks went bankrupt during the financial crisis in 2008 and 2009. Thousands of investors lost all of their money invested in these companies.

The TSP stock funds, however, invest in hundreds or even thousands of companies, and it is impossible for them all to go bankrupt at the same time. Some companies might do poorly for some time, and the market might decline for fairly long periods as a result, but you will never risk losing *all* of your money by investing in and holding TSP stock funds. And over time, the TSP stock funds always recover and continue their upward trends (see *Parabolic Wealth* for a discussion of average recovery times).

Also, because these are *index* funds with transparent trading policies, and because no one individual controls them, there is no chance of losing money in a Bernie Madoff-type Ponzi scheme. Recall that investment funds controlled by Madoff had for decades provided relatively high returns, before Madoff admitted in December 2008 that his investment funds were really a scam and that he was taking money from new investors to pay returns to longer-term "investors"—and he was skimming millions for his own use! This type of fraud in any of the TSP funds would be impossible because of the stringent auditing and transparency requirements of the investments.

The Greatest Risk – Not Saving and Not Investing! For all the risks noted above, the greatest risk is to not save and to not invest *anything at all*. If you don't save and invest during your career, you will have few personal financial resources in your older years, aside from a very basic government pension—very little for yourself, and no financial legacy to pass on to your children or to your favorite charities.

According to the U.S. Federal Reserve's triennial study, "Changes in U.S. Family Finances," *saving* from income is an important wealth-building tool. The 2017 study declared: "saving out of current income is an important determinant of family net worth."[34]

The personal savings rates in the United States have recovered somewhat in the decade since the late-2000s "Great Recession," but even before then the number of households that indicated they save on a regular basis trended downward since 2001 for all age groups except the under-35 cohort. The rates for 2016, the last for which figures are available as of this writing,

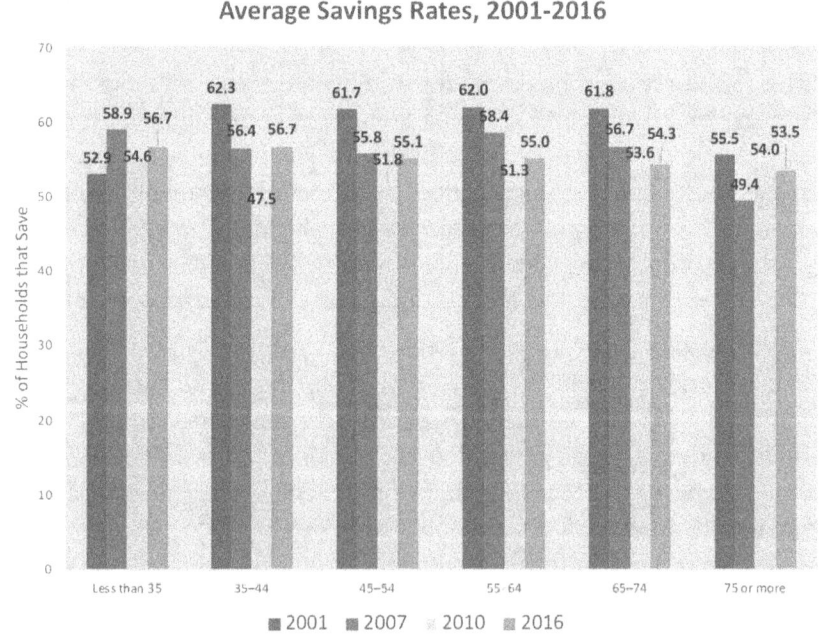

had improved since 2010, but in most age groups those savings rates were still below those in 2001.[35] Overall, the savings rate for households in the U.S. has grown from about 52% in 2010, to 53% in 2013, and to 55.4% in the most recent survey conducted in 2016. Also, the rates of saving increase as incomes increase. In 2016, for example, 42.9% in the bottom half of income saved, compared to about two-thirds of households in the 50-89.9% income bracket, to 80.2% of households in the top 10% income bracket.[36] (This again points to the difference between "income" and "wealth"—those who don't save and invest and otherwise spend all of their "income" might not have any wealth when their prime income-generating years end!)

In line with gradually improving savings rates since 2010, median and average household net worth (household wealth) have recovered as well since the "Great Recession." Except for a few dips in 2013, both the median and mean figures have increased since 2010. *

	2010		2013		2016	
	median	mean	median	mean	median	mean
< 35	$9,300	$65,100	$10,500	$75,400	$11,000	$76,200
35-44	$42,400	$216,600	$47,100	$347,500	$59,700	$288,200
45-54	$117,200	$570,100	$105,400	$526,000	$124,000	$724,100
55-64	$178,700	$878,900	$165,700	$795,400	$187,300	$1,164,400
65-74	$206,700	$842,500	$232,100	$1,047,300	$224,000	$1,058,900
Over 75	$216,900	$658,200	$195,000	$611,400	$264,800	$1,064,700

Median and mean (average) U.S. household wealth have improved since 2010, in nominal figures.[37]

The TSP is an excellent way to build wealth over time, as evidenced in the 2017 survey. It stated: "For many families, the amount of assets held within IRAs and Defined Contribution plans...are among the most important components of their balance sheets..." The TSP is technically a defined

---

* The word "mean" is the statistical term for "average"—a group of numbers added together and then divided by the count of items that were added together—while the term "median" represents the middle value of a series of numbers. The median helps when there are some outliers that skew an average too high or too low, such as if the savings rates of a few billionaires were included in the average savings of a group of regular workers—the average would look really big compared to actual savings rates for the regular workers!

contribution plan for federal government and uniformed service personnel. Moreover, stock holdings are a powerful driver of increased net worth, as "the mean value of stock holdings for families with holdings increased dramatically" by 2016.[38] Investing in and holding the stock index funds in the TSP (the C, S, and I Funds) is an easy way to take advantage of increasing values over time.

Even a small amount invested regularly each year can yield astounding results over long periods of time. As illustrated in a later chapter and at tspstrategies.com/1000-a-year/, a young worker investing just $1,000 at the beginning of 1980 (which is about $83 a month, less than $3 a day!) in the S&P 500, and who increased that same contribution by 5% in January each year over the following 40 years (from age 25 to 65, for example) would have over $905,000 at the end of 2019, despite the sometimes steep stock market declines over those 40 years. On a full-year basis, the index dropped seven times, including a *huge* 37% drop in 2008 and three consecutive declines in 2000-2002 for a total decline of almost 43%. That dropped what had been a $240,000 value at the end of 1998 to $155,000 at the end of 2002. Yet, with regular (and growing) investments, that amount was almost $1,000,000 17 years later. This is true, by the way, for any rolling 30- and 40-year period and when investing monthly, too, as detailed later in this book.

In terms of saving and investing, U.S. civil servants are doing a good job at contributing money to their TSP accounts. Participation rates, for example, are very high. In mid-2019, 91% of all FERS employees contributed money to their TSP accounts, with participation by new civil servants averaging around 98% due to automatic opt-in that was implemented in August 2010. (This means that around 2% of new feds opt out of participating in the TSP each month, however.) For CSRS employees, who are not eligible for a government match because of their larger pensions, approximately 77.5% contributed a portion of their income to the TSP. And about two-thirds of uniformed service personnel (63.7%) participate, a rate that is growing rapidly because of the Blended Retirement System.[39]

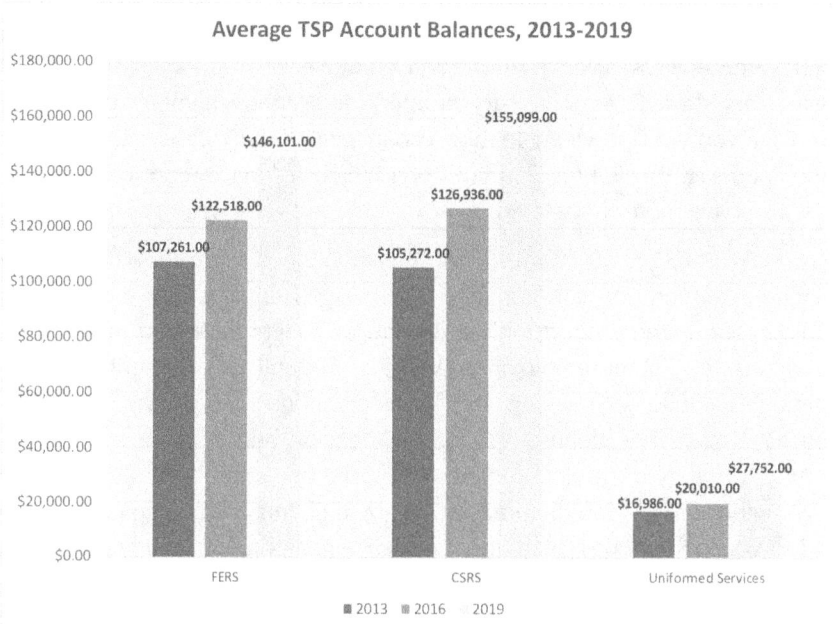

Average TSP accounts balances have grown steadily over the past decade. The above chart compares growth of FERS, CSRS, and Uniformed Services average TSP account balances from 2013 to August 2019.[40] Check tspstrategies.com for up-to-date figures.

Ultimately, saving and investing even a little at a time provides many benefits for you, for your family, and for the nation as a whole.

By saving and investing steadily over time, you can grow an increasingly substantial financial cushion for you and your family in your older years. This has a remarkable psychological benefit, because the more you have saved and invested, the more you feel in control of your own financial independence. You experience less financial distress. And the more you have control over your own finances, the more secure you feel in your personal life. By saving and investing, you are also setting a solid foundation for a more secure future for you and your family—you are building a *legacy*.

With the TSP, you can check your account any time. It is completely transparent: You know exactly what you have and how it has grown over the years. And the more you contribute, the more your TSP account grows. This is not the case with a pension benefit, as pensions are simple functions of calculating one percent or so per year of work multiplied by the average of your highest three years' salaries for civilian employees, or around 50% of your base salary after 20 or more years for uniformed service members depending on when you leave service. No more, no less. With the TSP, you choose how much you save and where you put it, and thus, you have more control over (but also have more risk related to) how you build your wealth over time.

Importantly, you can also take the money with you if you decide to change jobs, and you can continue to grow your investments even as you explore new career opportunities. You are no longer locked in the "golden handcuffs" of lifetime employment with the Federal Government. You can continue to build your savings and investments no matter how many jobs you have over your lifetime. While your pension benefit (after a minimum number of years of service) remains the same between the time you leave government service and the time you begin to collect it, you can continue to add to your TSP money even after you leave government service as long as you roll it over into an Individual Retirement Account (IRA), which is a relatively easy process to accomplish. Or you can keep it in the TSP and invest separately in an IRA.

Finally, by saving and investing in the TSP, you are buying U.S. Government bonds and the bonds and stocks of U.S. companies, depending on the funds you choose. This is very healthy for the U.S. economy, because these entities need our investments to continue to build and improve their products and services. And, if you invest in foreign companies through the I Fund, you are investing in the world economy, as well.

Ultimately, the TSP is an incredibly convenient and extremely cost-effective means for federal government employees and military personnel to build wealth in a fully transparent, portable, and ownership-focused way.

Pre-Investment Strategies

We have briefly reviewed the advantages of the TSP as a wealth-building mechanism, as well as the advantages and risks of any investing program. Through the strategies presented in the following chapters, I hope to further arm you, the TSP investor, with the knowledge to recognize various opportunities, while at the same time lessening the risks involved in investing over the long term.

Before getting started, I'd like to present two "Pre-Investment Strategies." These pre-investment strategies will help early TSP investors build a solid foundation for future growth, as we begin to explore the main strategies presented in this book.

Pre-Investment Strategy 1: If possible, contribute at least 5% of your salary to your TSP account.

- For FERS and uniformed personnel participants, the 5% contribution means you are eligible for the full government match, no matter what your salary may be.

- If you simply cannot contribute 5%—and I understand this situation well, since for the first six months of my government career I was unable to contribute 5%—try to contribute 1% or 2%, just to get in the habit of contributing even a very limited amount. Even a 1% contribution on your part actually works out to 3% of your salary when the matches are included. You will start to see some growth both in your salary and in your TSP account in the meantime, and you can increase your contributions slowly as you become more comfortable financially.

Pre-Investment Strategy 2: Build a basic emergency fund of at least six weeks' expenses untouched in an FDIC-insured bank account (or for credit unions, NCUA-insured).*

- Why six weeks? Because that was about the length of time many federal government workers were furloughed (or required to work without pay) during a major government shutdown in 2018-9, which lasted for 35 days. Similar furloughs lasted for 16 days in 2013 and for 21 days in 1995-6, and some personnel faced shortened work weeks (and smaller pay checks) for a time due to sequestration in the early 2010s. An emergency fund can be six weeks of expenses (what you have to budget and pay for that time) saved up, not six weeks of salary.

---

* FDIC stands for "Federal Deposit Insurance Corporation," and NCUA stands for "National Credit Union Administration," both of which insures bank accounts up to $250,000 in the unlikely event of a bank failure.

- Also, under normal circumstances, an emergency fund will help you pay for unexpected expenses without having to cut back on your TSP contributions suddenly. The emergency fund will also provide you with more peace of mind, as you establish yourself financially.

Now that we've taken a look at the TSP, as well as the importance of developing long-term savings and investing strategies to lessen the risks involved, let's now take a look at Strategy I to determine your level of interest in investing and your relative tolerance for risk.

STRATEGY I
Assess Your Level of Interest and Risk Tolerance

Now that we've reviewed the basics of the TSP, let's begin with the Strategy I for investing in the TSP. Before deciding on which TSP funds to invest in, the TSP investor should assess his or her level of interest in investing and identify tolerance for risk.

Identifying your tolerance for risk is particularly important, since success of the subsequent strategies in this book will be based on how much you can tolerate of the sometimes-wide swings in TSP fund values.

Upon determining your interest in actively following your TSP investments and your tolerance for risk, Strategy II will help you to decide how to allocate your investments among the TSP funds. Once you have allocated your TSP investments among the TSP funds, Strategies III and IV will help you to decide how to readjust your TSP investments periodically, since some funds do better than others over time and during different market conditions. Strategy V will provide a few more investment options to help you build even more wealth during your government service and beyond, and Strategy VI will discuss ways to insure yourself and family and protect your online account and identity.

The flow chart below illustrates how answering the questions in Strategy I will help to determine how to use strategies II-IV:

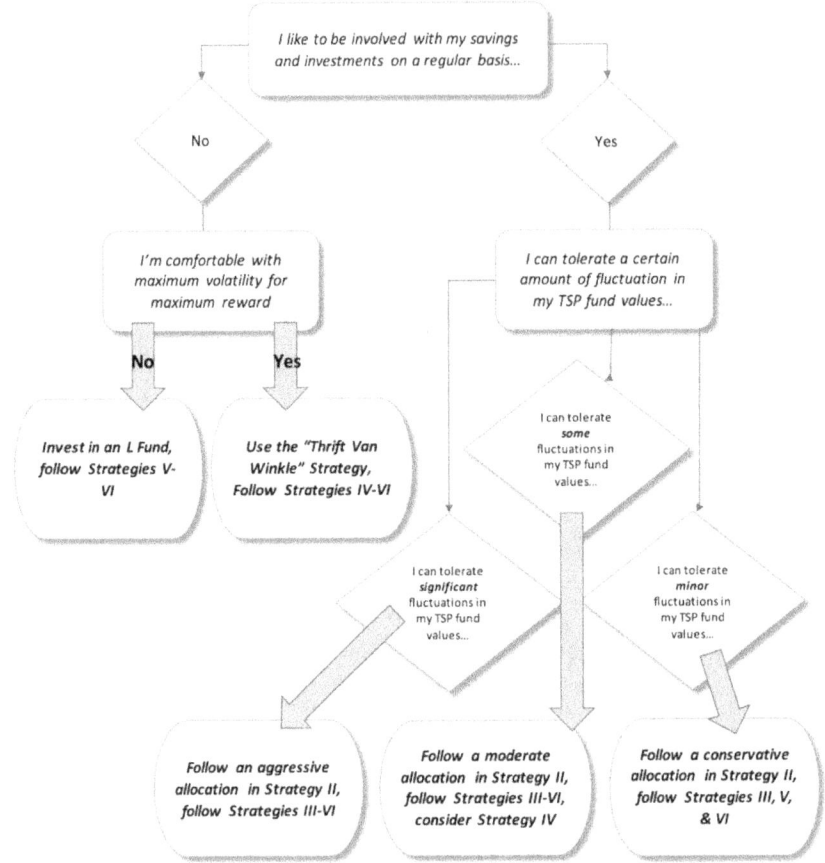

Rate Your Level of Interest in the Stock and Bond Markets

The first step in Strategy I is to determine your interest in investing. This is a fairly simple process. Ask yourself whether you like to check your TSP account periodically and whether you like to check on how the financial markets are doing from time to time.

This doesn't mean you have to be passionate about investing, because quite frankly, most of the time the money in your TSP account is not doing much of anything. It is often said that investing can be like watching paint dry, but watching your investments can be even more boring, because at least paint dries in less than a day! With your TSP, you'll add a couple hundred dollars every few weeks or every month, and maybe it goes up or down a percentage or two over a couple of weeks or a couple of months, but that's it. Being comfortable with the often-mundane task of following your TSP funds—and the financial markets—over time is important, however, as varying market conditions will require readjusting of TSP funds at times depending on the strategy you follow.

Here are a few questions to help you gauge your interest in investing:

	Yes	No
1) I like to check my TSP account every few weeks.	☐	☐
2) I like to check how the U.S. and international stock and bond markets are doing from time to time.	☐	☐
3) I like to read books on saving and investing.	☐	☐
4) When I hear the word "market," I think of buying fresh fruits and vegetables, not investing in stock and bond funds.	☐	☐
5) I know there'll be a lot of market ups and downs, but I don't care, just tell me what to set and forget for best overall returns in 30 or 40 years.	☐	☐

If you answered "Yes" to at least two of the first three questions, skim through the next section describing two set-and-forget strategies and proceed to the section after that. You are interested in investing.

If, however, you answered "Yes" to #4, and you know you're just not that interested in learning more beyond what is discussed in this book, perhaps one of the TSP's L Funds is right for you, described later in this chapter.

And if you answered "Yes" to #5, the *Thrift Van Winkle*™ approach detailed in Strategy II might be for you.

Before moving on to a couple of real-life market scenarios, it's important to discuss three important concepts: *volatility, dollar-cost averaging,* and *dividend reinvestment.* These concepts underpin both set-and-forget and more active investing approaches over the long-term. Let's review these now.

Volatility and Dollar-Cost Averaging

There is only one TSP fund that rises steadily over time, and that is the G Fund. As noted in the previous chapter, this fund is entirely invested in special U.S. government bonds that are issued solely to investors in the TSP. The daily interest rate is a weighted average of U.S. government bills and bonds, which averages to a return slightly below that of the U.S. 10-year government bond rate, or just under 2% annually in the late 2010s.

This means that each of the other funds experience *volatility* in their shares from day to day. Volatility is a measure of the dispersion or spread of returns for a given bond or stock—or for an entire market index such as the S&P 500 and C Fund.[41] The more a stock or index fund goes up or down in relation to its average price, the more volatile it is. *Volatility* therefore refers to the range of increases and decreases in a given index's share price over time.

In fact, there is even a measure for the volatility for the S&P 500 itself, called the "VIX". This gauge measures expected volatility for the index in the next 30 days, and it is sometimes called the "fear index" because the more the gauge goes up, the more volatile (and uncertain) the market is expected to be.

As for the TSP funds, the G Fund is the least "volatile" or movement-oriented of all the funds. But that doesn't mean it is necessarily the "safest" over the long-term, as we'll see below.

The F Fund, or bond index fund, is the second-least volatile of the funds. While it does sometimes experience negative trading sessions (when it drops a bit in value), the drops are fairly infrequent and not too steep. Thus, it is slightly more volatile than the G Fund. And the stock funds—the C, S, and I Funds—are much more volatile than the G and F Funds, because of the nature of the securities. The stocks of individual companies are priced partly based on how investors think their profitability will grow in the next year or two. For those companies that have high expected growth rates, their stocks will be more expensive (as measured by the "price-to-earnings" or PE ratio) than slow-and-steady growers. And those with limited growth prospects, or those whose businesses are contracting, will most likely experience declines in their stock prices, because they aren't expected to be profitable. Taken together, and especially with structural or external challenges impacting entire markets or economies (such as recessions), these can drive expectations in positive or negative directions, causing index prices to go higher or lower and driving volatility.

Sometimes changes in share prices are minuscule, but during times of great market upheaval, the changes in prices can be quite significant.*

The easiest way to visualize a given fund's volatility is to graph its regular returns on a *box plot*. A box plot shows the price trends over time in one graphic. The below box plots of the five main TSP funds are based on the monthly percentage-change data for each of the funds since May 2001 (when the S and I Funds started, in order to gauge the five funds' volatility from an equal starting point) and illustrate their volatility relative to each other.

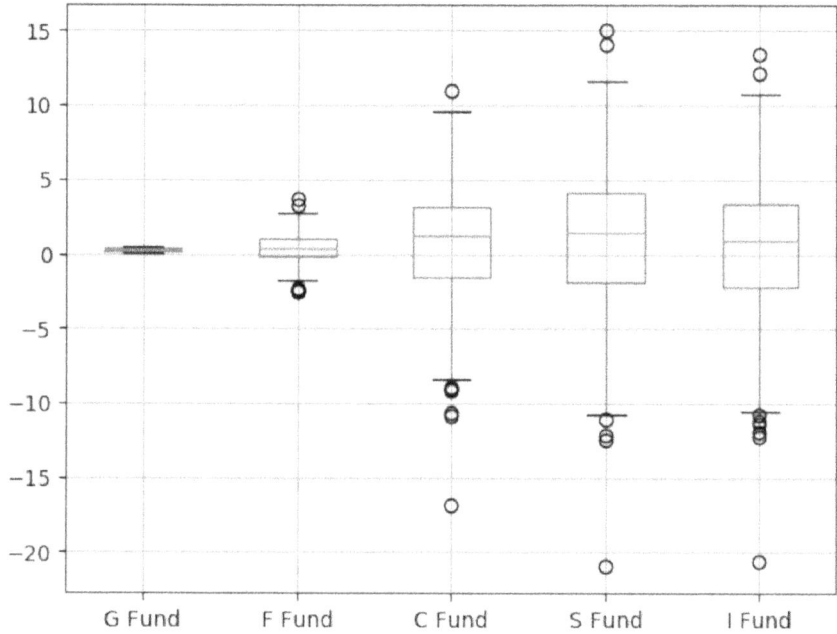

A box plot of the five individual TSP funds, representing monthly percentage change in the respective fund's value, from May 2001 to September 2019. Updated box plots can be found at tspstrategies.com/tspstats/.

The mid-line in each box shows the median percentage change, while the upper and lower portions of the box show the range of price changes

---

* Current share prices can be found at tspstrategies.com/current-prices/, and historical prices can be found at https://tspstrategies.com/fund-related-news/tsp-historical-fundprices/.

that are in first quartile (lower quadrant) and third quartile (upper quadrant) percentage changes for each of the funds. This area makes up the majority of price changes for that fund. The lower line or "whisker" represents the lowest monthly percentage change for the given fund, and the upper line or "whisker" represents the highest percentage change for the fund. The circles at the top and bottom are outliers. Ultimately, the funds with stretched datapoints are more volatile, while those with compact ones are less so.

As you can see, the G Fund is the least volatile. It neither gains much on a regular basis, nor does it ever go down. There are no outliers, which means that it is a steady fund over time. There is very little price movement.

The F Fund, another bond index fund, has some greater volatility, but for the most part it too has remained in positive territory except in a few instances. It hasn't declined more than about 3% over any given month even in rare instances, nor has it gained more than around 4%. It generally stays around the 2%-range on a monthly basis.

The stock funds, on the other hand, are quite volatile. The C Fund trends positive, but it has a number of negative monthly returns, including a decline of over 16% as indicated by the data in the box plot. In a few instances, it has increased by around 10%, too.

The S and I Funds are the most volatile of the five TSP funds, as evidenced by their respective plots. They both have returned about 15% in a couple of instances, but they both have fallen over 20% in just one month, too! As you can see by the lower whiskers, as well, there are a number of outliers that represent declines of over 10% each. These funds are technically called "high variance" because they can be very volatile.

The shares of the L Funds are more or less volatile based on their underlying mix of the stock and bond indexes. The L Income and L 2020 funds have more allocated to the bond funds (G and F Funds) than the stock funds (the C, S, and I Funds), so they are less volatile than the L 2040 and L 2050 funds, which have a significantly greater portion invested in the stock funds.

Dollar-cost averaging is a way to ameliorate or soften the volatility over time, and even use it to the investor's advantage. Dollar-cost averaging is the process of investing a little bit at a time, in regular intervals, so that over time, the average investment is better even as the markets fluctuate.

Here's an example, making investments of $100 over eight periods:

	Amt Invested	Share Price	Shares	Total Shares	Total Value
Investment #1:	$100	$40.00	2.5	2.5	$100
Investment #2:	$100	$42.02	2.38	4.88	$205.06
Investment #3:	$100	$47.62	2.1	6.98	$332.39
Investment #4:	$100	$40.00	2.5	9.48	$379.20
Investment #5:	$100	$37.74	2.64	12.12	$457.41
Investment #6:	$100	$35.71	2.8	14.92	$532.79
Investment #7:	$100	$33.33	3	17.92	$597.27
Investment #8:	$100	$40.00	2.5	20.42	$816.80
Total Invested: $800				**Total Value: $816.80**	

The above illustrates dollar-cost averaging in action. The first investment is made at $40 a share, so $100 invested means the investor gets 2.5 shares of the fund. The share price rises by almost 20% over the next two investment periods, and then it falls by a whopping 30% from its high. The share price lingers in the $30s, below the original share price of $40. But all the while, the investor buys more shares gradually through regular investments. Then the share price recovers and ends this period at $40, *exactly* where it began. It gained 0%. But because of dollar-cost averaging, your total investment has actually gained in value after eight periodic purchases of shares. Not too shabby, eh?

In essence, dollar-cost averaging uses volatility to your advantage by buying shares of good index funds as markets rise and fall and rise again. This is the underlying power of investing even small amounts at regular intervals in investment vehicles such as the TSP.

And a final note about the volatile stock funds before moving on: Over the very long term, those who take more risk in an intelligent and disciplined manner are rewarded more for their efforts. In fact, Thomas Stanley and William Danko, authors of *The Millionaire Next Door*, found that a large majority of the millionaires they surveyed—95%—invested in stock.[42] Stock markets have historically returned more than bond markets. (I provide details of my research into 120 years of investing in Strategy II and in later chapters that confirm this.) Thus, to truly build wealth it is important to embrace some risk by investing in at least one of the TSP's stock funds as part of a well-rounded portfolio. By accepting a certain level of risk, a person can be rewarded with greater returns over a 30- or 40-year work and investing career. There are ways to reduce risk while earning a higher rate of return by investing in multiple TSP funds, which we will examine in greater detail in Strategy II.

When The TSP Funds Decline, Have You Really "Lost" Anything?

It is important to remain aware that a decline in any given TSP fund is not the same thing as a *loss*. A *decline* in a fund becomes a *loss* when you sell it by transferring money out of the TSP fund and into another fund. If you do not transfer any money out of the declining fund but rather hold onto it until the fund recovers, you will not lose anything!

Instead of thinking of your TSP account as similar to a regular bank account, where a smaller amount of money means that you have less money to withdraw, think of your TSP investments like the house in which you live. Your house is a real asset: it has a value, and you can sell it when you want. The value of your house changes over time; sometimes the value falls, but it usually rises, over long periods of time. If you do not need or want to sell it, the value of your house is irrelevant to your day-to-day finances. You just keep paying the mortgage and sleep soundly, knowing that it is yours. You can, of course, refinance your mortgage to take money out for, say, a kitchen renovation or to build an addition to your home, but refinancing is, in effect, selling the rights to some of the value of your house to the bank in return for cash for other projects.

Thus, would you sell your house just because the housing market began to decline, or because the housing market had declined for several years in a row? Most likely, no. If you did not need to move, you would most likely keep your house until the market recovered, when your house could sell for a better price—and you could make more money on the sale.

Yet some people make this mistake when stock markets decline. They sell some or all of their funds after a decline in the mistaken idea that this action will protect the remaining portion of their money. But it is the *act of selling* that causes the losses. And then, once the market has "recovered," that is, once prices have moved back up to their original value, some will put money back into the funds that had already recovered. This would be the same as selling your house when the housing market had collapsed and then buying a new house after the price of houses have gone back up again. This action is simply not rational.

By not panicking and sticking to your investment strategies until the markets recover—and markets have in the past always recovered, given time—then you will be able to weather declining markets and even perhaps increase your investments with periodic additions in the process, knowing that a recovery will increase the value of your investments in the future.

Consider Investing in an L Fund

That's a lot to keep track of. Five funds—where to begin? How should you follow them, how do you know when to rebalance…should you rebalance at all, and when…?

If you don't like to follow your investments actively, or if you don't want the responsibility of making these decisions, that's ok! No need to force yourself to do what you don't enjoy doing or want to do. You've got other things with which to occupy your time, and you don't want to have to remember to check how this or that fund did over the past couple of days or weeks.

Luckily, the TSP offers a special type of fund for those who prefer to take a more passive approach to investing.

In 2005, the TSP introduced a group of funds called "life cycle funds," which automatically shift investments among the TSP funds over one's career from growth-oriented stock funds to more conservative bond funds.

When you are younger, your TSP money is invested in more growth-oriented stock funds, so that you might enjoy some growth of your investments in your early years of investing in the TSP. As you age, the money is gradually shifted to more stable, higher-yielding bond funds. This way, when you are ready to start withdrawing your money in your 60s or 70s, you will not have to be concerned that sudden and steep losses in the growth-oriented (and riskier) stock funds will impact your now more conservative and stable L Fund. This is all done automatically, and all you have to do once you've decided to invest in an L Fund is set your biweekly or monthly contribution amount and continue to put money into the fund on a regular basis.

As noted in the previous chapter, there are multiple L Funds with "target" dates that are set at ten-year increments, between 2020 and 2050. There is also an L Fund for those who are ready to withdraw their TSP money now—the L Income Fund. As an example of how the L Funds are designed to operate over long periods of time, let's briefly examine how the L 2040 shifts its investments from the time it was started to its target year of 2040.

When it was first set up in 2005, the L 2040 Fund was most heavily weighted toward the TSP stock funds. It had 85% invested in the three stock funds, with 42% in the C Fund, 25% in the I Fund, and 18% in the S Fund. The remaining 15% was invested in the G and F Funds. The amount allocated to the stock funds shifted gradually downward each year thereafter, so that as of fifteen years from its establishment—in 2020—the fund has about 72% of TSP investors' money allocated to the three stock funds and 28% allocated to the bond funds. This gradual shift will continue over the years, and by 2035—five years before the target date of 2040—the fund will have 60% in the stock funds and 40% in the bond funds, with one-third of the entire amount in the very stable G Fund. By 2040, the target date for this L Fund, it will have 70% of its holdings in the bond funds (with about 65% in the very stable G Fund) and 30% in the stock funds. The fund still allocates some money to the stock funds after 2040 to provide a little growth each year, even as the L Fund investor probably starts to withdraw money on a regular basis at that point.

The other L funds follow this same process but shift money from the stock funds to the bond funds earlier; the L 2020 Fund shifted a majority of its investments to the bond funds by early 2020 (after which it transitions to the L Income fund), while the L 2030 Fund will shift a majority of its investments to the bond funds by 2030.

Since the shift is pre-determined, the L Fund investor does not need to worry about how much to put in each of the TSP stock and bond funds. These decisions are already made for you, and they are done in such a way that you will most likely enjoy decent growth in your investments over time when you are young, while later your investments become more conservative as you are closer to an age when you might want to withdraw money from your TSP account in your post-career years. You just invest all of your biweekly or monthly contributions in one of the L Funds, and you are done.

Once that decision is made, you can just watch your money grow over the years of your government or military service and beyond.

After deciding to invest in one of the L Funds, the next step is to decide which L Fund to choose. Since the funds gradually shift from growth to income over several decades, L Fund investors generally try to match the year of the L Fund with their expected withdrawal date, sometime after they turn 59½ years old, when they can take it out as they choose. If the L Fund investor planned to begin to withdraw some of the money after turning 60 in 2038, the L 2040 fund might be the best fund in which to invest. If the investor turns 60 in 2033, perhaps the L 2030 fund is right, although the L 2040 might be better suited for those who expect to stay in the work force into their 60s and 70s. (As of this writing, TSP managers were planning to introduce L Funds for each 5-year period by 2022, which will provide greater flexibility in deciding on an L Fund specific to one's post-career plans.)

Indeed, much of your decision will depend on how long you plan to continue working. If you think you will likely continue to work in the years after you turn 60 and will leave your TSP account untouched, you should probably consider rounding up to the higher L Fund target year. If you think you'll want to begin to withdraw the money sooner after turning 60, you might want to consider rounding down.

This is not an exact science, as none of us can know when we will actually need to begin to withdraw money from the TSP. Our personal health, our family, our professional situation, and other factors in our late 50s, 60s, 70s and beyond will all play a role in our decision. If you are simply unsure about when you might want to begin withdrawing from your TSP account, and you are a cautious person by nature, perhaps it is better to choose an L Fund that is rounded down from the year when you turn 60.

Also, it is important to note that there will still be some volatility in your L Fund account, especially for those who invest in the L 2040 and L 2050 Funds. These funds allocate more to the stock funds within the TSP that tend to rise and fall in value more than the bond funds, and so your L Fund will also rise and fall more as a result. The L 2050 Fund, for example, declined over a three-month period in late 2018 and 2019, and in one month it dropped almost 7%. This is to be expected, but over the years the value of your L Fund will increase, despite the day-to-day gyrations of the markets, as you continue to add money to your TSP account through regular contributions.

The chart below shows the percentage gains or losses in each of the L Funds from 2012 to 2019. Notice that in 2018, all the L funds except the L Income experienced some losses in order of their higher stock versus bond holdings. These are full-year results—the individual funds have dropped on a weekly and monthly basis too.*

	L Income	L 2020	L 2030	L 2040	L 2050
2012	4.77	10.42	12.61	14.27	15.85
2013	6.97	16.03	20.16	23.23	26.20
2014	3.77	5.06	5.74	6.22	6.37
2015	1.85	1.35	1.04	0.73	0.45
2016	3.58	5.47	7.07	7.90	8.65
2017	6.19	9.86	14.54	16.77	18.81
2018	0.71	-0.36	-3.58	-4.89	-6.02
2019	7.60	9.38	17.60	20.69	23.33

If you have decided to invest in one of the Lifecycle Funds, still consider the lessons of volatility—the ups and downs—of the TSP stock funds especially, because the L Funds experience volatility as well. Or, if you feel like you have enough of an understanding about the L Funds and wish to move forward with your investing strategies, you can skim or skip the chapters for Strategies II-IV and continue to Strategy V for additional investing ideas.

Before moving on to additional allocation strategies, we should first determine what kind of investor you are by gauging your reaction to a significantly declining market, based on two scenarios detailed below.

How Much Risk Should You Take? Gauging Your Reaction to a Severely Declining Market

To remain successful in any long-term savings and investment program, you should be able to stick to your chosen investment and savings strategy through good times and bad. Sticking to a growth-oriented investment strat-

---

* Current share prices can be found at tspstrategies.com/current-prices/, and historical prices can be found at https://tspstrategies.com/fund-related-news/tsp-historical-fundprices/.

egy can be especially difficult during sharp market declines, because you will watch your TSP account drop 10%, 20%, or more in a fairly short period of time. And, as the months and perhaps years pass, it might seem like the market—and your TSP investments—will never go back up in value. But those who decide to change their TSP investment allocation during a severe market decline will suffer potentially serious losses in their TSP accounts.

In one dramatic example, what if you considered yourself very comfortable with market risk and invested 100% of your TSP savings in the C Fund in 1987? While the S&P 500 rose dramatically during the first half of the year, following a few months of significant declines in the fall you would have awakened one day to discover the value of your account had dropped by almost *one fourth in one day!* With $100,000 invested in the C Fund, a drop of this magnitude would mean that your account would now be worth around $77,000. Overnight. This happened on October 19, 1987, when the stock market fell almost 23% in one trading session. And this sudden decline was not limited to U.S. stock markets; international stock markets dropped by similar amounts. Investments in the C, S, and I funds all would have been affected. (Trading limits have been added to stock markets since then to prevent such drastic, single-day losses.)

Is this the kind of market risk that you are prepared to encounter? And what if the markets keep falling, even after such a spectacular one-day plunge? Would you sell all of your stock holdings in the hopes of keeping the remaining amount safe, or would you view the drop as an opportunity to add more to your investments for even greater potential future returns?

After the October 1987 crash, the S&P 500 fully recovered within a year and continued to increase thereafter. Had an investor put money into stock funds immediately after world stock markets plunged that day in October, he or she would have enjoyed a significant double-digit return on that investment in a very short period of time. But to do so, an investor would have to maintain faith in his or her investment strategy to survive the immediate aftermath of this type of market plunge.

As you undertake a long-term investment program such as the TSP, it is critical that you understand how you would react during periods of steep declines in your investment account. It is easy to remain invested in the stock funds when they might increase by 10% or 15% a year or more, but how will you react when they are *falling* by 10% or 15% or more? While some investors embrace risk and are comfortable with investing a majority of their savings in stock funds—and they believe they can weather significant drops in their investment accounts—others might prefer a more balanced investment strategy to smooth out the ups and downs of the stock and bond markets. However, it is difficult to know in advance how you might react to a significant downturn in the markets if you have not yet experienced one.

To determine your level of risk tolerance, let's take a look at how you might react in two scenarios during a period of significant market volatility.

In the first scenario below, you will experience a significant market decline while fully invested in the C Fund. In the more conservative second scenario, you will experience the same market decline with half of your portfolio in the C Fund and the other half in the G Fund. I won't reveal yet when this timeframe took place, but it is important to keep in mind that these market swings *really happened*. (And no, this is not a recounting of the 2008-2009 market decline.) As you read the scenarios, think to yourself how you might have reacted as your hypothetical TSP account balance fluctuated during this time.

Scenario 1: The C Fund*

At the beginning of the year, you have $100,000 invested in the C Fund. You've worked hard for a number of years to save and invest this money and have enjoyed watching your TSP account grow over the years. Indeed, the C Fund has enjoyed significant growth over the past number of years, although over the last couple of years there have been a few steep drops. But each time the market has recovered, and the previous year saw 20% gain before dropping slightly at the end of the year.

Despite the recent ups and downs of the market, you have decided to stay invested in this fund because of its long-term average growth of about 10% per year—you know at that rate your account will double every seven years or so, even without adding anything to it. It will grow even faster, since you contribute 5% of your salary of $65,000 a year to the TSP. That, coupled with the government match, means you are adding $250 to it each biweekly

---

* Returns for the C Fund over this period were calculated using the Friday closing price for the S&P 500, with the $250 biweekly contribution added to the recalculated TSP account total at the end of each pay period. This period does not include the re-investment of dividends, which will be discussed in a subsequent section.

pay period (only $125 of which is coming from your paycheck). You have several decades before you will retire, and at this rate, you expect to retire with over $1 million in your TSP account. Perhaps even more.

In fact, your $100,000 has *grown* over a subsequent year to about $121,000 by the end of the year. Pretty good after investing just $6,500 in total over that year!

But how well prepared are you mentally for a "bear" market, when the trend of the market is significantly down?

The stock market begins the new year with an upward pop to $125,000—more good news!—but then begins a minor drop of about 6% or so through February. This is not so bad—you understand that the stock funds can sometimes go down 10% or more every few years, so drops like this are to be expected. Besides, you are contributing $250 each pay period, so you are buying into the declining market as shares are progressively cheaper. Given the drop in the market, though, your TSP account has gradually decreased some through the end of March:

Pay Period 1, January	$124,987.26
Pay Period 2, January	$124,306.93
Pay Period 3, February	$121,781.29
Pay Period 4, February	$121,055.19
Pay Period 5, March	$117,708.24
Pay Period 6, March	$121,436.37

At the beginning of April, your TSP account recovers somewhat to around $119,500. Suddenly, however, at the beginning of May, the market plunges close to 5% in a matter of days, adding to the losses in March. Your account has been cushioned somewhat from greater declines because you've already added $2,250 since the beginning of the year, but as summer vacation approaches, you see that your TSP account is now only worth around $111,000. Even with the money you've added, your $125,000 account from the beginning of the year has dropped over 10% in six months. You continue to add $250 each pay period, so the actual loss would have been greater had you not been adding money each pay period. Here is how your account would look through the end of June:

Pay Period 7, April	$118,137.70
Pay Period 8, April	$119,509.59
Pay Period 9, April	$115,156.54
Pay Period 10, May	$117,638.67
Pay Period 11, May	$111,103.47
Pay Period 12, June	$111,609.68
Pay Period 13, June	$111,998.78

You experience a brief feeling of relief in August, as the market recovers by 6% and your account is back up to over $115,000. You take a final summer vacation thinking that a recovery is in store. But checking your account after you return, you find that the market has dropped even further, and your account is down to just over $111,000 in a month. The market recovers again somewhat in September, climbing to almost $113,000. Here is how your account has fared over the summer months through September:

Pay Period 14, July	$109,396.27
Pay Period 15, July	$114,558.24
Pay Period 16, August	$115,325.29
Pay Period 17, August	$111,451.52
Pay Period 18, September	$112,805.10
Pay Period 19, September	$112,003.28

In mid-October you notice a bit of a gain in your account, as it has increased to about $120,000. While this is not a full recovery back to your original $125,000 at the beginning of the year—even though you've added an additional $5,250 in total since January—it is a decent gain from six weeks ago.

Unfortunately, the gains do not stick, and the stock market plunges again. By December, the stock market is down for the year over 20%. Your C Fund falls to just over $101,000 before recovering somewhat to end the year at almost $105,000. You've added $6,500 in biweekly contributions from your paycheck over the year, but your TSP account is still down. Here is how your account performed through the last pay period:

Pay Period 20, October	$118,523.99
Pay Period 21, October	$119,198.73
Pay Period 22, October	$120,594.66
Pay Period 23, November	$115,956.13
Pay Period 24, November	$109,586.33
Pay Period 25, December	$101,487.74
Pay Period 26, December	$104,666.96

How do you feel?

At this point, ask yourself how you felt as your account continued to fall through the year. Your $125,000 is worth just about $105,000, even after adding $6,500 over the past year. What would your gut be telling you at this point, or at any point during the year?

1) Transfer the entire $105,000 now to the U.S. Government bond fund (the G Fund) to protect what money you have left from further declines; adjust your biweekly contributions to have everything go to the G Fund.

2) Transfer some of the C Fund now to the G or F bond fund to protect it; adjust your biweekly contributions to put half of the $250 in the bond fund every two weeks, as well.

3) Hold on to the $105,000 in the C Fund and hope that the market will go back up again soon; continue to add $250 to the C Fund each pay period, investing into the declining market for greater gains in the future.

4) Following the adage to "buy low and sell high," look for ways to increase biweekly contributions to invest even more in the C Fund as it continues to drop to improve long-term investment results when the stock market finally recovers (even if it takes years).

There is no "right" answer to the above questions. It is important that you answer these questions honestly, because this type of market might recur in the future. Again, this exercise is to determine how you would react to a severe market decline ahead of time, so as not to panic during a real downturn in the market when your hard-earned TSP savings are really at stake.

Keep these questions in mind as we continue the exercise into the second year, because *the declining market is just getting started.*

The next year begins with even more fluctuations in the stock market. You suffer more declines in your TSP in January, and in February, your account dips to $101,000 again. However, you continue to add $250 faithfully to your account each payday. By March, your account recovers a little and is back to almost $112,000 again. But there is little sign that this market will recover completely in the near future. Here is how your account looks through the end of March:

Pay Period 1, January	$108,073.96
Pay Period 2, January	$106,100.08
Pay Period 3, February	$107,891.62
Pay Period 4, February	$101,383.12
Pay Period 5, March	$107,672.87
Pay Period 6, March	$111,653.44

In May, the downturn begins anew, and your TSP account falls a stunning 10% to $99,000. Approaching summer, your account has fallen almost 20% below your original $125,000 account balance of 18 months ago to $98,682, even after adding $9,750 in new contributions since then. Here is how your TSP account performed through spring and into summer:

Pay Period 7, April	$108,377.18
Pay Period 8, April	$103,925.87
Pay Period 9, April	$101,813.92
Pay Period 10, May	$103,574.77
Pay Period 11, May	$98,682.20
Pay Period 12, June	$102,580.80
Pay Period 13, June	$101,161.07

Despite the steep declines over the past 18 months, the downturn still does not stop. In late July and early August, your account hovers in the $90,000-range. But then the markets plunge yet again as investors succumb to something close to panic. In late August and into September, your C Fund takes a real beating. At the end of September, your TSP account is now worth just over $78,000. Your account has fallen about 40% by this point, even after adding over $11,500 of new money over the past 18 months.

Here is how your account looks through September:

Pay Period 14, July	$96,184.49
Pay Period 15, July	$95,806.58
Pay Period 16, August	$91,031.60
Pay Period 17, August	$88,320.29
Pay Period 18, September	$81,698.51
Pay Period 19, September	$79,396.87
Pay Period 20, September	$78,511.80

What are you feeling now? Do you wish you had shifted everything from the C Fund to the G Fund at the beginning of the year…or even during the past summer? Your TSP account was worth over $108,000 at the beginning of the year. Now it's down almost 30% from even that reduced amount.

Or, on the other hand, are you wishing you had more money to invest in this severely declining market, feeling that the best time to invest new money is when the market is down significantly?

It is now October. The stock market does not stay down for long. Within days, your TSP account recovers to almost $88,000, although it begins to decline in value again in late November and early December. At the end of December, your account is now worth about $80,000. While this is a small recovery from late September, this is still down 36% from your impressive $125,000 account balance two years ago—and after you have added $13,000 of new money, $250 every pay period—since then.

Here is how your account looks through the end of this second bear-market year:

Pay Period 21, October	$79,052.28
Pay Period 22, October	$83,043.92
Pay Period 23, November	$87,643.12
Pay Period 24, November	$79,861.61
Pay Period 25, December	$79,535.29
Pay Period 26, December	$80,363.43

Will the stock market ever recover? Will your TSP account go back up in the next few months, or in a year or two, or will the declines continue?

No one can answer this, because no one knows. The experts say the markets always recover eventually, but what does that mean, really? Your $125,000—plus $13,000 in new contributions, or almost $140,000—is currently worth only about $80,000.

Now, how do you really feel?

Review the questions above again. How do you *really* feel about your account at the end of year two, after your TSP declined by 36% even after adding $13,000 in new money? Would you now, or at any time during the previous year, have done any of the following things?

1) Transfer everything now and put it in the G Fund to protect what money you have left; adjust your biweekly contributions to have everything go to the G Fund.

2) Transfer part of the C Fund into the G or F bond fund to protect that money; adjust your biweekly contributions to put half of the $250 in the bond fund, as well.

3) Keep everything in the C Fund, with the knowledge that the market will recover and go higher at some point in the future; continue to add $250 to the C Fund each pay period.

4) Following the adage to "buy low," look for ways to increase biweekly contributions to invest even more in the C Fund as it continues to decline to improve investment results over the very long-term when the stock market finally recovers (even if it takes years).

This scenario is taken from the last bull market of the late 1960s into the early 1970s when the S&P 500 *rose* by 19% in 1972, and then turned into the severe bear market of 1973-1974, when the S&P 500 fell over 14% in 1973 and over 26% in 1974. The S&P 500 experienced even steeper declines in August and September 1974 before recovering somewhat at the end of the year, as you witnessed. Again, this scenario is important because *it really happened*. Had you invested all your TSP money in the C Fund during years of similar declines, this is how your account would have behaved.

Here is how the S&P 500 looked from 1972 to 1974. Notice that in 1972, the year prior to the two-year example above, the market increased by almost 20% and many people were feeling pretty good about their returns in the stock market. By late 1974, however, some two years later, the market had fallen to almost half this level before recovering slightly.

Hypothetical Return of Investments in S&P 500, 1972-1974

This type of extended decline happens sometimes infrequently, sometimes twice in a decade. TSP investors experienced a similarly long, steep market decline in the 2000-2002 period, for example, and another sharp decline in 2008 and in early 2009. The chances are great that we will all experience another similarly steep decline again at least once in our investing lifetimes. Newer investors will almost certainly experience multiple such declines.

We'll take a look at how this all-stock TSP account would have performed in the 20+ years after the 1973-1974 bear market, but first let's first see how a TSP account would fare with only half of your money in stocks and the other half in bonds—$50,000 in the C Fund and $50,000 in the G Fund—under these same conditions.

Scenario 2: The C Fund and the G Fund

In this scenario, your $100,000 grows in the first year, but because you are investing $125 each in the C Fund and the G Fund, your year-end balance is about $117,000. It's helped by the G fund's interest rate that averages about 6.5% during the year due to increasing inflation.

Your TSP enjoys a nice little pop at the beginning of year 2, to over $119,000. The balance hovers in the upper-$110,000s through these months, even as you add money to it. Here is how your account looks during the first few months of the year:

	C Fund	G Fund	Account Total
Pay period 1, January	$62,493.63	$56,820.57	**$119,314.20**
Pay period 2, January	$62,153.47	$57,087.06	**$119,240.52**
Pay period 3, February	$60,890.64	$57,354.21	**$118,244.85**
Pay period 4, February	$60,527.59	$57,626.00	**$118,153.60**
Pay period 5, March	$58,854.12	$57,898.49	**$116,752.61**
Pay period 6, March	$60,718.19	$58,173.23	**$118,891.42**

While your C Fund experiences some further declines into May, falling about 10% in spring to under $56,000, your G Fund has increased somewhat, to $60,000. This is partly because of the G Fund's rise to around 7% due to increasing inflation. Prices for everyday items like food, clothes, and gas certainly are rising faster these days. Through late spring and into summer, your total account remains stagnant as it continues to hover in the upper $110,000s. By the end of June, because of a 10% decline in the C Fund your total TSP account is about $116,000.

Here is how your account looks through June:

	C Fund	G Fund	Account Total
Pay period 7, April	$59,068.85	$58,448.69	**$117,517.54**
Pay period 8, April	$59,754.80	$58,723.95	**$118,478.75**
Pay period 9, April	$57,578.27	$58,999.92	**$116,578.19**
Pay period 10, May	$58,819.34	$59,280.69	**$118,100.03**
Pay period 11, May	$55,551.73	$59,562.20	**$115,113.94**
Pay period 12, June	$55,804.84	$59,845.61	**$115,650.45**
Pay period 13, June	$55,999.39	$60,129.76	**$116,129.15**

As you make final plans for your summer vacation, your TSP account value continues to fluctuate only a few thousand dollars, between $115,000 and $118,000 over the summer months.

	C Fund	G Fund	Account Total
Pay period 14, July	$54,698.13	$60,420.00	**$115,118.13**
Pay period 15, July	$57,279.12	$60,711.03	**$117,990.15**
Pay period 16, August	$57,662.65	$61,009.18	**$118,671.82**
Pay period 17, August	$55,725.76	$61,308.17	**$117,033.93**
Pay period 18, September	$56,402.55	$61,608.02	**$118,010.57**
Pay period 19, September	$56,001.64	$61,901.36	**$117,903.00**

Your total TSP account value continues to increase through mid-October to just over $123,000, driven by a recovery in the C Fund. The balance begins to drop again, however, as Thanksgiving approaches, due especially to another sudden drop in your C Fund. Your G Fund, however, continues to exhibit steady gains. Through the final pay periods of the year, your account balance falls to around $116,000 again, but only off by a $1,000 or so from where your TSP account balance started the year. While your C Fund has declined by around 12%, even *after* adding $3,250 to it through the year, your G Fund is up by over 10%, with the increasing interest rates and the $3,250 you've added through the year making up the difference:

	C Fund	G Fund	Account Total
Pay period 20, October	$59,262.00	$62,195.50	**$121,457.50**
Pay period 21, October	$59,599.37	$62,483.26	**$122,082.62**
Pay period 22, October	$60,297.33	$62,771.76	**$123,069.09**
Pay period 23, November	$57,978.07	$63,059.57	**$121,037.63**
Pay period 24, November	$54,793.17	$63,348.12	**$118,141.28**
Pay period 25, December	$50,743.87	$63,637.66	**$114,381.53**
Pay period 26, December	$52,333.48	$63,927.95	**$116,261.43**

How do you feel?

At this point, ask yourself how you felt as your G Fund increased in value, while your C Fund decreased in value. Your $117,000 at the beginning of the year is now worth about $1,000 less and has an ending account balance of $116,261, even though one fund is up over 10% and one is down over 10%. What would your gut be telling you at this point, or at any point during the year?

1) Transfer the entire $52,000 from the C Fund—just under half of your total TSP account value—to the G Fund to protect what money you have left; adjust your biweekly contributions to have everything go to the G Fund.

2) Transfer a portion of the C Fund into the G Fund now to protect that money from possible further declines; adjust your biweekly contributions to put all of the $250 in the G Fund every two weeks as well.

3) Hold on to the $52,000 in the C Fund and hope that the market will go back up again soon; continue to split the $250 in the C Fund and G Fund each pay period.

4) Following the adage to "buy low and sell high," transfer some money from the G Fund ("sell high") to the C Fund ("buy low") now that it is down, to even the two funds out and possibly increase investment returns ten or 20 years from now. Increase biweekly contributions to invest each future $250 contribution into the C Fund as it continues to drop, to improve long-term investment results when the stock market finally recovers (even if it takes years).

As during Scenario 1 above, there is no "right" answer to these questions. It is important that you answer the questions honestly, because this type of market might recur in the future.

Entering year two, your TSP account recovers somewhat and by March it has again surpassed your original $117,000 account balance from a year ago, reaching $121,000. Here is how your account performs through March:

	C Fund	G Fund	Account Total
Pay period 1, January	$54,036.98	$64,225.16	**$118,262.14**
Pay period 2, January	$53,050.04	$64,523.16	**$117,573.20**
Pay period 3, February	$53,945.81	$64,821.96	**$118,767.77**

Pay period 4, February	$50,691.56	$65,120.82	**$115,812.38**
Pay period 5, March	$53,836.43	$65,420.48	**$119,256.91**
Pay period 6, March	$55,826.72	$65,727.24	**$121,553.96**

Your TSP account drops to $116,000 again in spring. The main cause of the drop in value is the falling C Fund, which, by the end of May, plummets to below $50,000. Your G Fund, meanwhile, has increased to above $67,000. By the end of June, you've added close to $10,000 of new money through biweekly contributions, but your TSP account total is just over $118,000, nearly the same as your $117,000 balance 18 months ago. Here is how your TSP account performed through the end of June:

	C Fund	G Fund	Account Total
Pay period 7, April	$54,188.59	$66,034.86	**$120,223.45**
Pay period 8, April	$51,962.93	$66,350.96	**$118,313.89**
Pay period 9, April	$50,906.96	$66,667.97	**$117,574.93**
Pay period 10, May	$51,787.39	$66,987.70	**$118,775.08**
Pay period 11, May	$49,341.10	$67,308.36	**$116,649.45**
Pay period 12, June	$51,290.40	$67,628.91	**$118,919.31**
Pay period 13, June	$50,580.53	$67,950.40	**$118,530.93**

Through the summer months your account total drops further, and in late August, the account suffers the largest decline in the past two years as it falls to $113,440. A month later, in late September, your account balance drops below $110,000 for the first time in several years, to $109,558. By this time, you've contributed a total of $11,500 over the past 21 months, and what would have been at least $130,000 has now settled at $109,000, due entirely to a significant decline in the C Fund, which has dropped by about 40%. Here is how your account balance looked through these months:

	C Fund	G Fund	Account Total
Pay period 14, July	$48,092.25	$68,279.89	**$116,372.13**
Pay period 15, July	$47,903.29	$68,610.36	**$116,513.65**
Pay period 16, August	$45,515.80	$68,941.83	**$114,457.63**
Pay period 17, August	$44,160.15	$69,280.41	**$113,440.56**

Pay period 18, September	$40,849.25	$69,620.03	**$110,469.29**
Pay period 19, September	$39,698.44	$69,960.71	**$109,659.14**
Pay period 20, September	$39,255.90	$70,302.43	**$109,558.33**

In October and November, your account balance recovers somewhat, however, as the C Fund increases by over 10% in value. Your TSP is now worth just over $112,000. While the C Fund fluctuates between $39,000 and $41,000—even *after* contributing $6,500 in the past two years—your G Fund continues its steady climb upward to over $72,000. This is partly due to inflation pushing rates up, which is good for your TSP bond funds but bad for your pocketbook because of rising prices generally. Here is how your TSP account performed over these last few months of the year:

	C Fund	G Fund	Account Total
Pay period 21, October	$39,526.14	$70,641.42	**$110,167.57**
Pay period 22, October	$41,521.96	$70,981.44	**$112,503.40**
Pay period 23, November	$43,821.56	$71,316.48	**$115,138.04**
Pay period 24, November	$39,930.80	$71,652.51	**$111,583.31**
Pay period 25, December	$39,767.65	$71,982.63	**$111,750.27**
Pay period 26, December	$40,181.71	$72,313.69	**$112,495.40**

At the end of these two years, you would have about $112,500 in your TSP account had you invested 50% of your regular contributions in the C Fund and 50% in the G Fund, or $125 to each fund. Total additional contributions amounted to $13,000 over the past two years, including the government match, and $19,500 since the exercise began with $100,000. A total of three years later, your TSP is still below its original value.

Now, ask yourself the same questions as you asked yourself after Scenario 1. Which of the following decisions do you think you would make, or would have made at any time throughout the past year, as you watched your account during this scenario?

1) Transfer the entire $40,000 remaining in the C Fund—now just one-third of your total TSP account value, down from half two years ago—to the G Fund to protect what money you have left; adjust your biweekly contributions to have everything go to the G Fund.

2) Transfer a portion of the $40,000 remaining in the C Fund into the G Fund to protect it; adjust your biweekly contributions to put all of the $250 in the G Fund every two weeks as well.

3) Hold on to the $40,000 in the C Fund and hope that the market will go back up again soon; continue to split the $250 in the C Fund and G Fund each pay period.

4) Adhering the maxim to "buy low and sell high," transfer some of your G Fund ("sell high") to the C Fund ("buy low"), following the considerable declines; change your biweekly contributions to put all of your new contributions into the C Fund.

Here's how the 50-50 allocation looked during the 1972-1974 time-period:

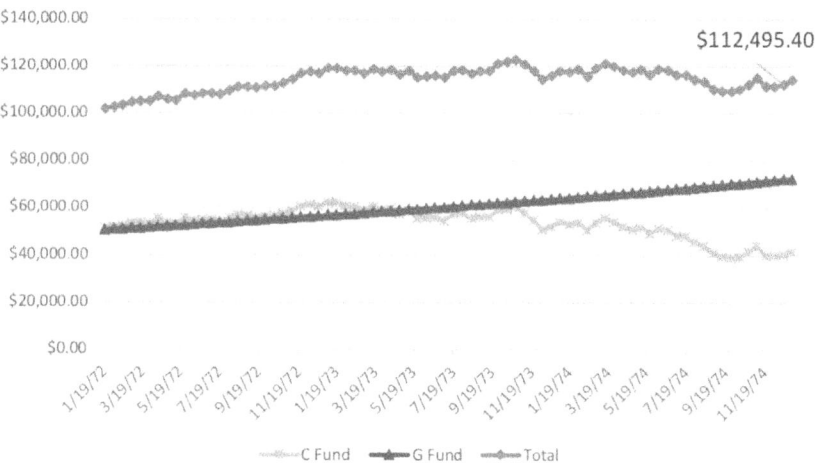

The exercises above were an attempt to demonstrate the concept of loss aversion. It is an important concept in behavioral economics, and we are all prone to it to certain degrees. Basically, psychologists and behavioral economists have found that for most people, losing hurts more than gaining feels good. We'll avoid making an optimal choice, if that choice has some identifiable potential loss or decline, even if the probable gain is significant. In investing behavior, this means that as declines continue to mount, we want to avoid even more declines in the near future and so we increasingly get nervous and feel the urge to sell.

It is important to understand the near-certainty of market declines—and the near-certainty of significant gains after the declines—in order to resist this all-too-human trait. We can combat this by (1) setting realistic investment choices based on an understanding of your tolerance for long-term declines so that you don't sell during the declines, and (2) seeing how markets have historically recovered after even the steepest declines.

Before discussing what type of investor you are based on how you answered the questions after scenarios 1 and 2 above, it is important to examine another concept that is central to dollar-cost averaging into index funds: the reinvestment of dividends. It provides a little extra ballast in the short term, but its power, coupled with periodic investments over the long-term, is truly evident over several decades as we will shortly see. It is instructive to see how the S&P 500 performed—and how the C Fund would have performed—in the 20 to 30 years after this major "bear" market.

The Power of Reinvested Dividends

The two scenarios in the previous section purposely left out one important element: the reinvestment of dividends.

The calculations for the S&P 500/C Fund above focused on changes in share prices and nothing else. These were indeed the results of investing during the *actual* movements in the markets at the time. But the results did not calculate *dividends* being reinvested back into one's funds.

Dividends are a stock's version of interest, paid from cash flow and profits. Most (but not all) companies pay back some of their profits to investors who took the risk to buy shares—provide capital—so that the company could continue to grow. Not every company gives their investors a share of the profit in the form of dividends. Some companies instead use funds to repurchase the shares of their own company's stock, which often has the effect of raising the stock price (because demand for the stock is higher and the number of remaining shares is smaller). Other companies, particularly fast-growing ones, prefer to reinvest in rapidly expanding the business. Still others simply can't afford to pay out a regular dividend, because of weak profits or losses.

In the case of index funds, a whole group of companies pay out some of their profits as dividends, and this is in turn paid to the investors of that index fund. The dividend rate for the S&P 500/C Fund has hovered around 2% in the past decade, give or take a few basis points. The dividend rate is higher for the I Fund and lower for the S Fund. Most investors take these dividends and "reinvest" them or use them to purchase more shares of the index fund. The TSP in fact does not list dividends separately from the index fund prices, since the dividends (and interest, in the case of the bond funds), is automatically reinvested in the funds.

Now, let's examine what happens when we recalculate Scenario #1 above to include the reinvested dividends. The short-term (1972-1974) results are still negative during this bear market, but they aren't *quite* so negative. The $80,000 without dividends becomes about $89,000 with dividends reinvested. And they really provide additional investing power years later, which can be seen in the chart below. By extending the calculations by just one year—a year of recovery in the markets—the dividend reinvesting approach grows to $131,210, while the no-dividend approach grows to a mere $113,867.

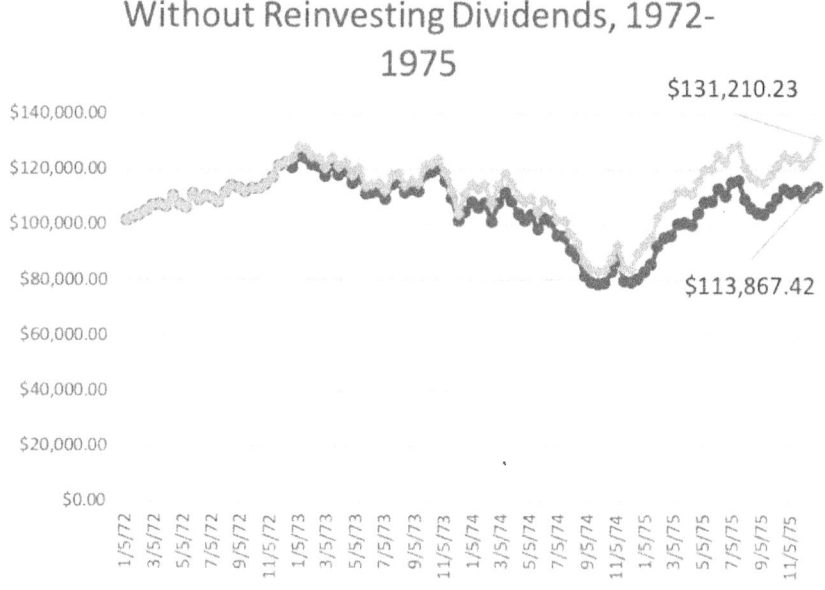

Performance of S&P 500 With and Without Reinvesting Dividends, 1972-1975

Dividend reinvesting, together with regular contributions, provide remarkable benefits even a year after the market begins to recover from a major downturn.

Without dividends, Scenario #1 dropped to around $78,500 at its bottom. With dividends, it dropped less, to around $83,100 at its bottom—more than $4,500 greater in value than without dividends reinvested during that time.

It also recovers more quickly. Scenario #1 ends at about $80,000 without dividends, but with dividends reinvested the adjusted figure would have been closer to $89,500 by the end of the year. This is because even more money, in the form of dividends, were reinvested in the final months of the year at its low point as well. This extra dividend rate is in turn due to dividends generally (but not always) rising even as index prices fall, so that a higher dividend (again, more money) can be reinvested into shares that are much less expensive than they previously were.

(In case you were curious, the 50-50 allocation increases by almost $5,000 to about $117,104 at the end of 1974, and to $147,676 at the end of 1975 with dividends reinvested in the C Fund portion of the investment.)

The dividend rate for the S&P 500 during this time actually rose in relation to the index itself. While it was about 2.7% at the beginning of the bear market in early 1973, it rose to over 5% by the end of 1974. The higher dividend, when reinvested, was buying even more shares on discount to the original price two years prior. Once the market started moving up again, the dividend payout also went up and added even more to the gains in the form of further dividend reinvestments in subsequent years.

(A note about dividend reinvestment in the TSP funds: According to tsp.gov, unlike most mutual funds and ETFs, which report dividend disbursements and capital gains/losses separately from the share price changes, the TSP funds do not receive or report dividends or interest separately from the funds themselves. This is because the tax treatment does not differ for the interest, dividends, capital gains, and tax-deferred contributions in the TSP under the Internal Revenue Code for defined contribution plans. Therefore, the F, C, S, and I Funds are credited with the interest and dividend income each business day as they are paid into the funds, so the daily change in TSP share prices reflects all investment income (interest, dividends, capital gains or losses, and securities lending income) net of TSP administrative expenses.[43])

And this shows itself over the longer term as well. In this scenario, had this worker left her position for another job outside the federal government and stopped contributions, but otherwise left the investments in the TSP to grow, her investments would have fared astoundingly well in the next few decades. By the end of 1996, her all-stock index fund would have been worth $2,461,225, and her 50-50 portfolio would have been worth $1,708,719.

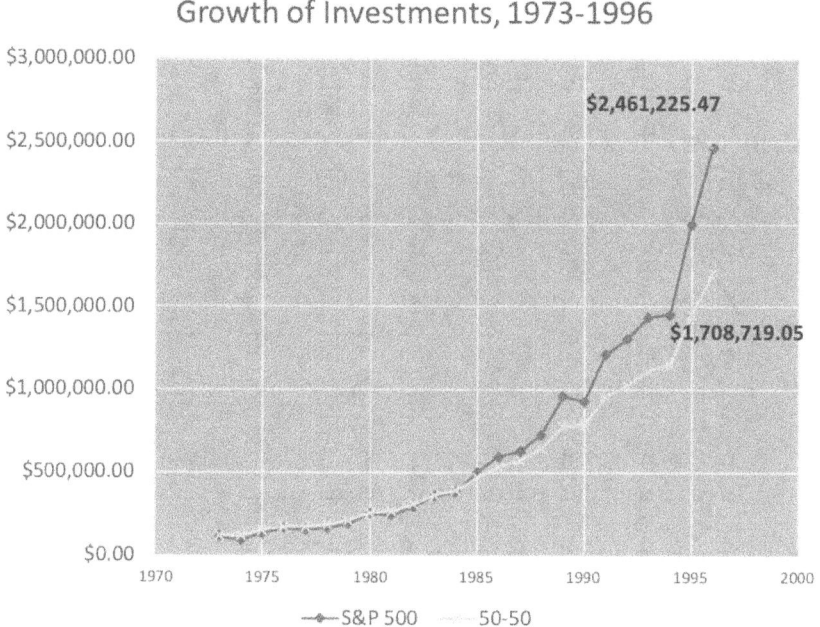

The 1973-1974 bear market looks like a tiny ripple when viewed over several decades from 1972-1996.

Looking at a chart of the S&P 500 over a 25 year period, from the early 1970s to the end of 1996, this early-1970s period looks like a mere blip in the market. Indeed, there appear to be even steeper and more sudden declines in the late 1980s and early 1990s. Recall that in October 1987, the market dropped over 22% in one day! Yet, on a percentage basis, declines in the 1980s and early 1990s were less than the decline in 1973-1974.

This is not to say that every 20+ year period will perform as well as 1975-1996. The stock market enjoyed a major bull run in the early 1980s through the 1990s, so these decades were particularly good for long-term stock market investors. And government bonds yielded an astounding 12% during some years in the early 1980s, due to rampant inflation. (In some ways, we are facing the opposite now given the historically low rates for government bonds.)

The next chapter will explore in a little more detail how investors would have fared investing in stock and bond markets over 30-year periods and longer. Some periods were better than others, but every 30-year period (with one slight exception), investing in the broad stock market out-performed investing in the government bond market.

Your Investor Type

Based on your reactions to the two scenarios above, you can now categorize your tolerance for risk among the following investor types:

- If you answered 1 in the first scenario and 2 in the second scenario, you are a conservative investor.

- If you answered 2 or 3 in the first scenario and 2 or 3 in the second scenario, you are a moderate investor.

- If you answered 3 or 4 in the first scenario and answered 4 in the second scenario, you are an aggressive investor.

- If you answered 1 following both scenarios, you are an extremely conservative investor. I would suggest reviewing the section on L Funds earlier in this strategy and considering an L Fund target year that matures no later than your early 50s.

But wait, what about the questions at the beginning of this chapter?

- If you answered "yes" to the question, "I don't care about market ups and downs, just tell me what to set and forget for best overall returns in 30 or 40 years" – and particularly if you also answered 3 or 4 in the above scenarios – see the Thrift Van Winkle™ section in Strategy II. Now that we've determined your interest in investing and your risk tolerance, Strategy II will provide sample TSP portfolio allocations based on your investor type.

STRATEGY II
Allocate Among TSP Funds Based on Your Tolerance for Risk

Perhaps one of the most difficult decisions to make when investing in the Thrift Savings Plan is how to allocate your investments among the TSP funds.

This is especially the case since the TSP funds can sometimes experience significant increases or decreases in value based on market conditions, as demonstrated in the previous chapter. When a given fund increases in value, the natural inclination is to add more money to the "winning" fund. At the same time, when a fund decreases in value, the natural inclination is to protect your remaining TSP investments by transferring money from the volatile to the less volatile funds.

But both of these inclinations would be detrimental to long-term financial gains. By having a buy-and-hold mentality and strategically allocating your TSP portfolio among the various funds based on pre-established parameters, you will be able to avoid selling when some TSP funds decline from time to time, and you will avoid overconfidence when some TSP funds increase significantly from time to time.

The *'Thrift Van Winkle™'* Approach to Investing

The simplest approach might be to invest in a single stock fund—the C Fund—during the span of your working life. This depends on your risk tolerance, which should be clearer now after reviewing Strategy I.

The *Thrift Van Winkle*™ approach to investing in the TSP is to invest all of your biweekly or monthly contributions in the C Fund, which matches the S&P 500 index.

Taking a narrow view, consider some market history comparing the C Fund's underlying stock index with the G Fund's government bond index over relatively short timeframes. The S&P 500's best five years was from 1995 to 1999, which saw annual returns of a whopping 28.55%. Its worst five years, from 1928 to 1932, saw a *loss* of 12.47%. In contrast, the best five years for intermediate government bonds was between 1982 and 1986, during which the index enjoyed 16.98% returns. The index's worst five-year annual return was +0.96% in 1955-1959. In other words, despite the generally better returns in the S&P 500, government bonds historically don't decline over these relatively shorter periods of time, but stock indexes can and do!

But lengthen the timeframes, and this is no longer the case. The best 20-year returns for the S&P 500 was between 1980 and 1999, which saw 17.87% annual returns, while the worst 20-year period, from 1929 to 1948, saw an annual return of 3.11% during that time, despite the depression and World War II. The best 20-year return for intermediate bonds was 9.97% between 1981 and 2000, while the worst 20-year period took place in 1940 to 1959, with an annual return of 1.58%.[44]

So longer-term, the U.S. large cap stock index does better than the bond index in both generally good and bad market conditions. But what does this mean for small investors, who dollar-cost average their contributions into stock and bond funds over 30 or 40 years?

To test this, I examined investing on a monthly basis over rolling 20-, 30-, and 40-year periods over 120 years, from 1900 to 2019. I started by testing a fixed amount ($250 a month) over a 30-year rolling period from 1900 to 1929, 1901 to 1930, and so on to the 1989-2018 time period. Then, I tested the same time periods but with amounts increasing yearly by 5%. I also tested returns without reinvesting dividends and returns when reinvesting dividends. I retested for 20- and 40-year rolling periods. (See this endnote[45] for further details about the methodology and data.)

Reinvesting dividends was the key. In *all* the 30- and 40-year periods examined save perhaps for one, whether with fixed-amount investments or increasing amounts, investing in a U.S. large stock index fund (similar to the

C Fund) outperformed investing in the intermediate-term U.S. government bond index fund (similar to the G Fund) when reinvesting dividends. This includes investing through major declines in the stock market, for example, in 1919-1921, 1929-1932, 1973-1974, 2001-2003, and in 2007-2009. Only in one 30-year period, from 1903 to 1932, were returns essentially tied.

When not reinvesting dividends, however, there were more instances of a stock index fund underperforming bonds over 30-year periods.

Before examining the results, it's important to highlight the difficulties experienced during many of these prolonged downturns. I fully understand the very real challenges and impact of severe declines in the market. Sustained downturns occur almost always in conjunction with major challenges in the regular economy and are often coupled with hugely impactful events such as war, recessions, and even depressions. These cause significant increases in unemployment and economic distress. As an academic exercise, it is interesting to see how investments over the very long-term fare despite the challenging economic conditions on the one hand, but on the other, it is important to always be aware of how the harsh economic realities detrimentally impact millions of American workers and families, and the sacrifices our military (and many civilian) men and women undertake to defend our country during these extremely challenging times as well.

Separately, as background, the S&P 500 has not always consisted of 500 companies. The daily price movements of stocks had been documented as grouped averages as far back as the 1880s, called the Dow Transportation Average (originally consisting of eleven companies) and the Dow Industrial Average (consisting of twelve companies). As these averages continued to operate (and became the "Dow Jones Industrial Average" consisting of 30 companies), the predecessor index for the S&P began keeping daily track of price trends for 90 companies in 1926. After a few additional increases in constituents, the current 500-company index became operational in March 1957.

Thus, general stock market indices and conditions in the first half of the 20th century differ somewhat from the post-1950s trends, both because the capital markets themselves were less developed in the first half of the 1900s (and were in particular marked by two world wars and a major depression) and because the make-up of the indices differed. Comparing rolling returns for the years prior to the 1950s with rolling returns after the 1950s is not quite an "apples to oranges" comparison, but more like "Fuji apples to Granny

Smiths" type of comparison. Apples, yes, just not the exact same apples. The important thing about including an expanded data set is that it includes a wider variety of market returns, and hypothetical returns during lengthy and extremely challenging conditions.

With that in mind, here are some of the highlights. The comparisons below are based on monthly investments over the course of 30 years, starting in January of the year indicated in the charts and ending in the 360th month of the investment (December). The contributions start at $250 per month in the first year and increase by 5% each year.* It should be noted that steady contributions of $250 per month for the entire 30-year period also saw stock returns better than bond returns in every 30-year period.

These figures are not adjusted for inflation, nor do they take into account average salaries during the given years (the average salary in 1950 was $3,300 for the entire year, for example[46]). This exercise was to gauge how any given 30-year period differed in terms of stock index returns versus bond index returns since 1900, using starting contributions that are realistic for young investors just starting their careers today.

The top-10 best 30-year periods of dollar-cost averaging into the U.S. stock market compared to investing in the U.S. 10-year government bond market is shown below. The absolute best 30-year period started in 1970 and ended in 1999, at the height of the tech-led bubble in U.S. equities. In fact, four of the top five best 30-year returns ended in the late 1990s. All the 30-year periods enjoyed returns of over $1.5 million, while bonds returned around $600,000 in the post-WWII years.

---

* The initial $250 monthly contribution equates to contributing about 5% of salary for an E-4 in his or her first year in the military, or a GS-4 on an unadjusted 2020 pay scale in his or her first year, and a government match. The amounts are invested into the S&P 500 index, with dividends adjusted and reinvested monthly. The investor's contributions total $99,658 ($199,316 with the government match) over the 30-year period. In order to provide a uniform comparison of investments over 30-year time frames during real-world investing situations since 1900, the figures are not adjusted for inflation.

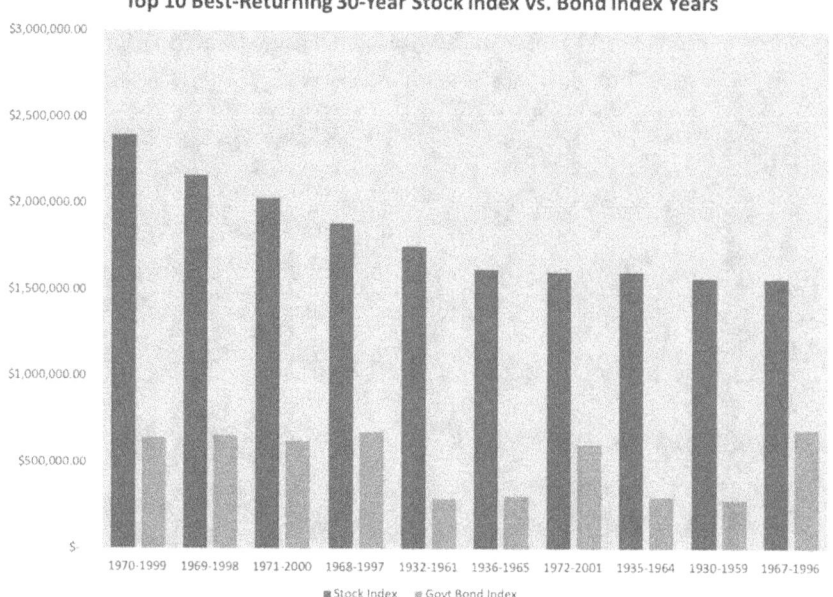

The top-10 best 30-year periods for dollar-cost averaging into the U.S. stock market by start year, compared to investing in U.S. government bonds during the same time.

Many of the worst-performing 30-year periods for the stock index took place prior to 1950. The three worst 30-year periods started in 1903, 1912, and 1902, and these periods ended in 1932, 1941, and 1931 respectively. Readers with even a cursory knowledge of history can understand why these were the worst-performing periods for the stock market as a whole for small investors, as the investing period ended during the Great Depression and as the United States entered into World War II.

Yet, only the absolute worst 30-year period for stocks underperformed those for bonds, but just barely. The period of 1903 to 1932 returned a paltry $326,593 for stocks, compared to $329,589 for bonds. The 30-year periods that began between 1903 and 1915 all featured returns ranging between the upper $300,000s to the low $500,000s. These returns were better than returns for bonds during that time, and investing during these challenging conditions will be discussed in greater detail later in the book.

For dollar-cost averaging during 30-year periods following World War II, even for those periods that featured low returns relative to other periods, investing in the U.S. stock market still did significantly better than investing in U.S. 10-year government bonds (see chart below).

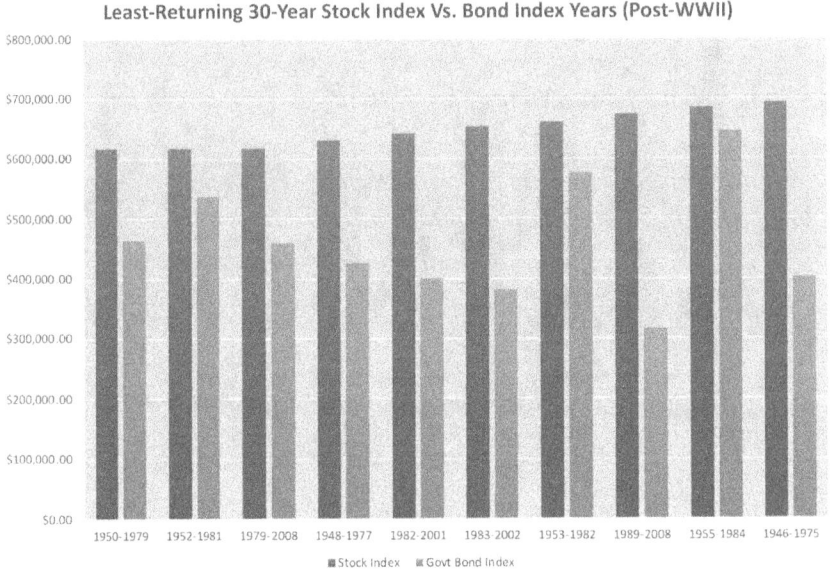

The least-returning 30-year periods for dollar-cost averaging into the U.S. stock market by start year (after World War II), compared to investing in U.S. government bonds during the same time. Calculations and data used in this research are available at bit.ly/TSP2ndEd.

The lowest-returning 30-year periods in the post-World War II era all returned between $600,000 and $700,000, compared to the government bond returns fluctuating between $300,000 and $500,000.

The difference in results varied widely for the 30-year periods examined, certainly, but there was no time when government bonds out-performed the U.S. stock index fund on an absolute basis.

This, then, is the *Thrift Van Winkle*™ strategy: Set all of your regular contributions to invest in the U.S. large cap stock fund (the C Fund) and forget about it. Go to sleep, in terms of investing. Don't pay attention to the financial headlines, they'll always deceive you.

The C Fund invests in large and medium-cap companies, many of which operate globally. Investors in this fund also enjoy some medium-cap growth in addition to the large company safety, and they also enjoy international exposure since the companies also derive some of their profits from overseas markets.

But if you want to get some further diversification in your stock funds, invest a portion also in the S and I Funds. The S Fund, as noted in a previous chapter, is the "completion" index and is thus composed of medium and small U.S. companies, while the I Fund is composed entirely of companies based outside the United States. Given the greater volatility of these funds, however, and in the case of the I Fund, weaker long-term returns, it is probably best to limit exposure to these funds to 20% or 25%.

This strategy doesn't mean you won't experience drops in the markets along the way. You *should expect* to experience drops, some small and some potentially quite significant.

In the previous chapter, you saw how one such historical decline impacted a significant investment. Can you stomach declines of as much as 50% over a year or two, while continuing to stay fully invested and continuing to buy into the fund as it declines?

You need to know this, because this is exactly what the *Thrift Van Winkle*™ approach to long-term investing requires. In the ten-year period between 2000 and 2009, for example, the stock index funds experienced not one but two significant declines, as illustrated earlier. The first took place over three consecutive years in 2000-2002, and a second decline of over 50% happened in 2008-9. In a 30-year period, you most likely will encounter multiple prolonged or steep declines.

During these times, you must know yourself and understand that you *cannot sell!* Selling during declines negatively impacts your investments in two ways: You get less for your investments than they will eventually be worth (you're "selling low"), and you are not taking advantage of buying into the stock market at a discount, when investments are cheaper relative to what they had been. Moreover, it will take considerable time to regain confidence to invest in stocks again, which usually only happens *after* the stock market has risen considerably, making it seem "safe" (less volatile to the downside) to invest again. By this point, though, the market and share prices have already risen, so you will have missed out on all of those gains. It's selling low and buying high, the opposite of good investing.

Thus, if you don't see these drops as opportunities, the *Thrift Van Winkle*™ is probably not for you.

But even for the most seasoned investor, steep declines can be nerve-wracking. There are a few ways to lessen your anxiety levels, if you are prone to them.

First, reduce the number of financial stressors in your life. This is accomplished first and foremost when you have a very low or no-debt lifestyle, and also when you have a bit of a financial cushion saved up and not too many revolving credit accounts open to keep track of. The more bills you have to pay, the more accounts you are paying down, the less wiggle room you have financially. This added tension will stress you, and behavioral psychology has shown that the stress can cause poor financial decision-making. This is discussed in Strategy V.

Second, if you are getting nervous about the declines in your funds, employ the technique discussed in Strategy III on using regular contributions to build up a cushion in a more stable bond fund to ease your concerns. Essentially, if you are unsure what to do during market turmoil and don't want to sell your stock fund(s) via an interfund transfer (as you know you shouldn't!), you can use your regular contributions to build up a bit of a cushion in a more stable bond fund for a little extra feeling of safety. See Strategy III for more details. (While this approach gets away from the *Thrift Van Winkle*™ investing strategy, that's ok! You need to feel comfortable with the long-term prospects of your investments, and this approach can be further leveraged in Strategy IV, too.)

Third, think 'crazy'. The concept of *loss aversion* discussed in the previous chapter is a real phenomenon that most of us are prone to feel, and this can drive us to make financial decisions in the near-term that seem safe but that can be objectively less optimum over the long-term. Certain types of individuals, however, are not as prone to these feelings, for a specific reason. We'll explore this concept more in the chapter titled *Parabolic Wealth*.

In about three or four decades, and a few years before you think you'll want to start drawing from the funds, start to plan to transition some of your holdings to the stable-value F or G Funds. This will depend on the markets at the time. The other lesson of this study is that fund investing that culminates in a market rally provides better returns than one as the market tanks—a bit of a truism, to be sure. This is in fact the primary downside of investing solely in the stock funds. As you near the time you want to use some of those funds, you don't want to experience a major drop in your stock index fund(s). By starting to prepare up to five years away from when you'll start tapping your wealth, you will be able to secure funds to use in the near-term to weather the downturns and save your stock-oriented funds for more years of potential growth. In this way, unlike with the L Funds, you have control over when, how, and how much to transition your funds from growth-oriented stock funds to more stable bond funds.

While this book is focused on investing strategies at the beginning of one's investing lifetime, *Parabolic Wealth* will address the challenges of falling markets in later years. There are many books and articles focused on preparing you for using your funds as you near needing them, and an excellent one to start with is "Investment Portfolio Torture Chamber," which details findings related to an asset mix in retirement (and coincidentally resembles the "moderate investor" allocation below).[47]

Is 'Greed' Good? Not in Free Markets!

"Greed, for lack of a better word, is good. Greed is right. Greed is good..." So states the villainous and rapacious Wall Street tycoon Gordon Gecko in the 1987 Hollywood movie, "Wall Street," as he talks about the need to restructure the failing (and fictional) Teldar Paper.

But is "greed" really what drives the entrepreneurial spirit, is it really the essence of free markets and capitalism? After all, "greed" is one of the seven deadly sins. It implies taking advantage of others to sate one's personal desire for material gain, which by definition can never be sated. The "greedy" person will always want more and will stop at nothing to get it.

If this is capitalism, no thanks! Who wants to participate in a system that takes advantage of others for the mere material gain of an oligarchic few?

But "greed" is *not* what underpins free markets and capitalism. "Greed" is *not* what drives the entrepreneurial spirit. Quite the opposite, in fact. "Greed" is *not* good.

The founder of modern economics, Adam Smith, rather referred to the "profit motive" as the driving force of free, modern economies. He discussed this motivation in what became the first academic treatment of modern economics, *An Inquiry into the Nature and Causes of the Wealth of Nations*—published in 1776, the same year as American independence. (What a year!)

Enterprises of all sizes, from individual proprietorships to large corporations, seek to "profit" from their efforts. They are motivated by profit because without it, they can't keep the lights on, they can't pay their workers, they can't invest in researching and developing new and innovative products. The opposite of "profit," after all, is "loss." And no private enterprise can survive long on losses.

In a free market, "greedy" profiteers can't survive for long either, because many other competing enterprises will see the profits being made in a particular industry, and *they'll* soon offer similar products and services at lower prices to get some of that profit and attract more customers. Still more competitors will enter the market, and they'll figure out how to make still better products, produce them more efficiently, and offer better service to attract customers, driving prices down even further. If companies don't compete with better products and services, they'll lose money and go out of business. This entire process creates jobs, so that workers have more choices in a given industry. Companies have to offer better pay or benefits to attract and keep skilled workers. It is a virtuous cycle.

Thus, in free-market capitalism, "greed" leads to the downfall of a company, not to its success! This is the reason for the saying, "innovate or die": If we don't innovate, our competitors will put us out of business with their own innovations.

Note how Nobel Prize-winning economist Milton Friedman described the win-win of the "proposition that both sides to an economic transaction can benefit from it." Friedman explained in a 1955 essay titled "Liberalism, Old Style":

"A gain to a purchaser need not be at the expense of a loss to the seller. If the transaction is voluntary and informed, both sides benefit; the buyer gets something he values more than whatever he gives up,

and so does the seller. In consequence, voluntary exchange is a way to get cooperation among individuals without coercion. The reliance on voluntary exchange, which means on a free market mechanism, is thus central to the liberal creed."

This is how we as a democratic and open society benefit from capitalism based on free markets and individual freedoms. Is there a need for some regulation? Of course. No system is free from "greedy" and law-breaking businesses and executives, just like no political system is free from corrupt political leaders or self-dealing government bureaucrats. Free markets naturally balance and temper human endeavors, even as government—made of and by the people themselves—lightly regulates them, polices them, and defends them.

For the Risk-Conscious Investor: Diversification Among Asset Classes

In Strategy I, you saw how two different model portfolios performed during a severely declining market. In the first scenario, your $100,000 was fully invested in the C Fund, while in the second scenario you invested half your money in the C Fund and the other half in the G Fund. Over the three-year period in the exercise, the two-fund TSP portfolio performed much better than the one-fund portfolio. The two-fund portfolio suffered only minor declines, ending the period with close to $117,000, while the one-fund portfolio, despite rising to $125,000, suffered significant declines and had approximately $89,000 by the end of the two-year period (with dividends reinvested).

Why the more-even performance in the two-fund portfolio? Because you diversified your account with funds from different asset classes. The C Fund, a growth-stock fund, did better during the go-go days of the 1960s, the 1980s, and the 1990s, while the G Fund, a safe bond fund, did relatively better as a refuge for investors during uncertain economic times in the 1970s, the early 1980s, and in the early 2000s. They performed differently under different market conditions.

The funds performed differently because they represent two different asset classes: The C Fund is a domestic U.S. large-capitalization stock asset class, while the G Fund is a U.S. Government bond asset class. Additionally, like the C Fund, the S and I Funds are both stock asset classes, but the S Fund is a domestic U.S. small-capitalization stock asset class, and the I Fund is an international, large-capitalization stock asset class. While their performance will sometimes mimic the C Fund because they are both "stock" asset classes, some will perform better than others over time because of the different types of investments within this general stock asset class. The F Fund, in turn, is a U.S. total-bond asset class that includes U.S. Government debt, corporate debt, and asset-backed securities such as mortgage securities, which is a slightly different asset mix compared to the G Fund, which only invests in U.S. Treasury securities.

What's an "asset?"

An "asset" is anything that retains value. Any asset that generally increases in value over time is considered an *appreciating asset*, while any asset that decreases in value over time is a *depreciating asset*. Your house is considered an appreciating asset because, in general, its value increases over time. Your car is a depreciating asset, because its value decreases over time (in fact, a car's value decreases as soon as you drive it off the dealer's lot, which is why cars should not be considered long-term investments).

Stocks, bonds, and real estate are generally appreciating assets, because they can increase in value for investors over time. Taken separately, they each can be considered an "asset class." Commodities—such as oil, natural gas, gold, silver, wheat, timber, etc.—make up a separate "asset class." Each of these asset classes tend to perform better at different times and under different market conditions, so when commodities or bonds are increasing in value as a group, stocks might fall, and when stocks as an asset class are increasing in value, bonds might decrease in value relative to stocks.

The TSP features two broad "asset classes": two bond funds (the G and F Funds) and three stock funds (the C, S, and I Funds). There has been some discussion in past decades about adding new funds with different asset classes, such as a special real estate or a commodities fund, although these discussions never progressed beyond the very early stages. Whether such investments are ever added or not (real estate will be discussed a little later in this book), it is important to remember that each of the stock funds includes companies that focus on real estate and commodities, so by investing in the TSP stock funds, you are investing a little in the real estate and the commodities sectors too, albeit indirectly. This—and the potential added cost and increased complexity of any new types of funds—are two reasons why new funds are yet to be added.

Finally, keep in mind that you are an asset as well. You are an asset to the government because of the value you bring each day in fulfilling your office's mission. Be sure to invest from time to time in your greatest assets of all by continuing your education and staying fit and healthy.

We looked at the five funds' general volatility as illustrated in the box plots in Strategy I. The box plots demonstrated that some funds have significantly more volatility (S and I Funds) than other funds (G and F Funds). We also looked at dollar-cost averaging as a basic strategy that takes advantage of differences in volatility.

This brings us to the key element of diversification. To diversify, you want funds that are not correlated or that are negatively correlated.

Correlation is measured on a continuous scale from -1 to 1. A negative correlation means that when one fund goes up, the other goes down, and a positive correlation means that when one goes up, the other is going up too. A "1" correlation means the two funds are perfectly and positively correlated, while a 0 means there is no correlation. And a "-1" means the two are negatively correlated.

You don't want funds that all go up at the same time, and you don't want funds that all go down at the same time. If this were the case, you can't take advantage of relative changes in different asset classes during market turbulence.

Looking at the monthly return of the funds again, we actually find a very significant correlation between the stock funds. The C and S Funds from 2001 to autumn of 2019 have a 0.9276 correlation coefficient, which means that most of the time, when one goes up, the other is going up too, and vice versa. Similarly, the C and I Funds have a 0.8729 correlation coefficient.

Conversely, the stock-bond funds have very limited correlation. The correlation coefficient for the G and C Funds is -0.1736, so that the movements are not at all correlated. Their movements do not happen in tandem, either positively or negatively. And the correlation coefficient for the F and C Fund is similarly -0.117. While these coefficients change over time—the G and C Fund monthly returns have a 0.0151 correlation coefficient since 1988—they generally hover around the same correlations (see chart below).

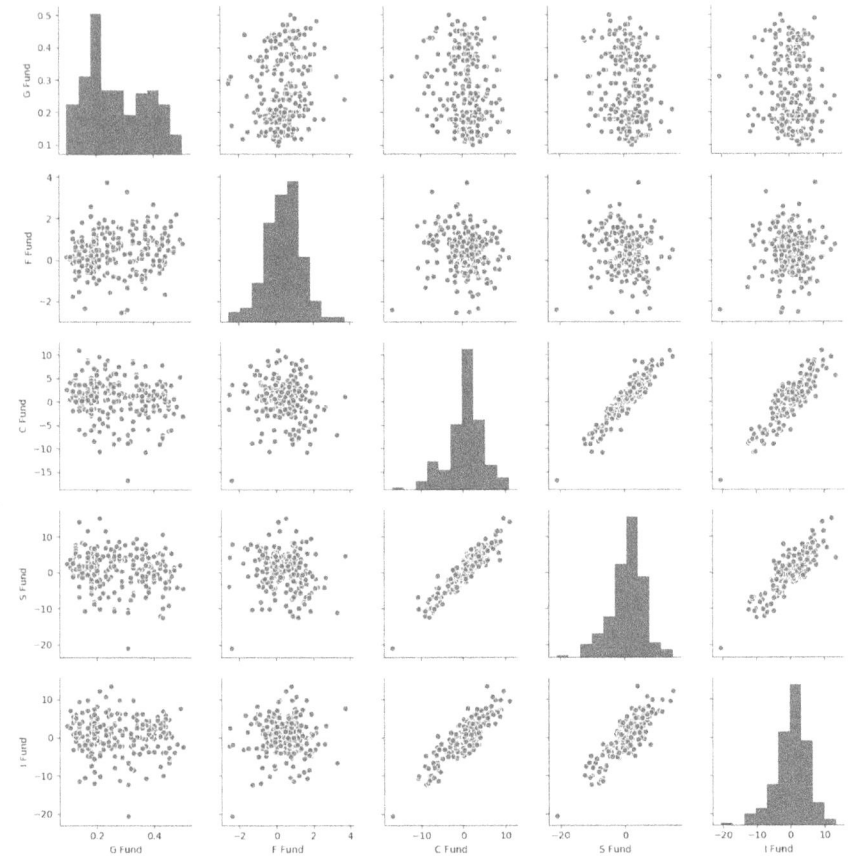

The above scatter matrix compares monthly returns between the funds since January 2001. The stock funds are highly correlated, as you can see in the relatively uniform scatter plots in the bottom-right quadrant. The bond funds, particularly the G Fund, are uncorrelated with the stock funds, as you can see in the scattershot patterns in the top two rows. Interestingly, the G and F Funds are relatively uncorrelated as well, with a coefficient of 0.17.

Thus, if one is to have a diversified portfolio—made up of investments that are uncorrelated or negatively correlated—one should invest portions in both the stock and bond funds. And given the lower levels of volatility, relatively speaking, in both the G and C Funds—and especially given their almost total lack of correlation—these two funds can serve as the core holdings for the risk-conscious investor. This is discussed further below.

Relatedly, I ranked the funds from best to least return for each trading day from the summer of 2003, when the current daily pricing structure became operational, to the summer of 2019. The rankings counts total how many trading sessions a particular fund closed in relation to the other funds: "1st" indicates that that fund closed with the best relative return for that day, "2nd" indicates that fund had the second-best return for that day, and so on to "5th", which indicates the fund had the least return for the trading day. "Least return" could mean an actual decline, or just a very low positive (or 0) return. Note how few times the G Fund was last in the rankings, when all the other funds would have outperformed that fund for those days.

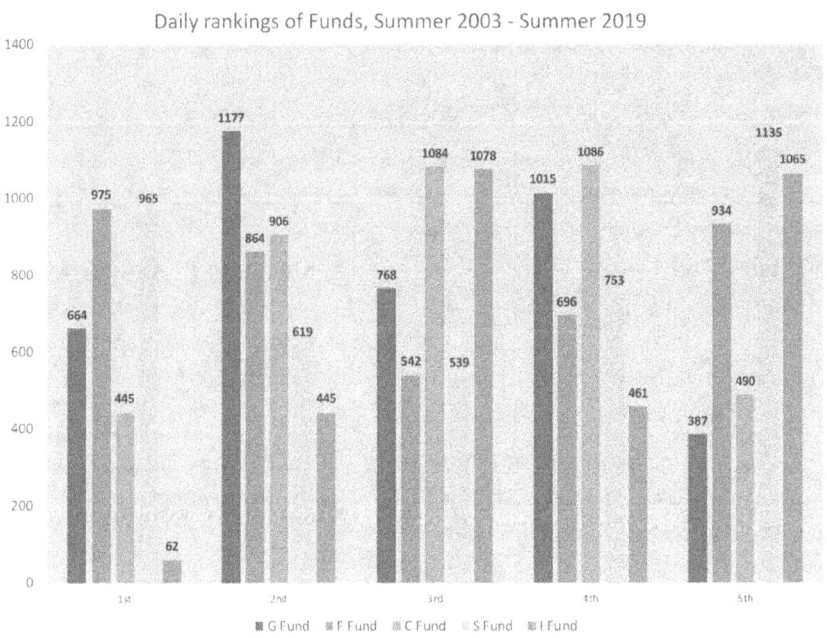

Daily relative performance of each fund from summer 2003 to summer 2019. The S Fund in particular ranks highly in both 1st and 5th place, which reflects its high volatility, while the I Fund ranks highly in the 3rd and 5th rank. The C Fund consistently ranks in the 2nd-4th range.

I undertook this calculation to further illustrate the general randomness among the funds. There are many outside marketers that claim they can improve your results by telling you when to buy and sell, sometimes on a daily basis. This was in fact the reason the TSP instituted a two-transfer limit on interfund transfers per month, to prevent over-trading that raises costs for all TSP investors. The data hopefully illustrates for you that these are bogus claims. There is just too much volatility and uncertainty over any given timeframe to be able to predict with any consistent accuracy how funds will behave. Over the very long term, the rankings (and therefore the relative returns) are random. Yes, they all trend upward, but some outperform others for a while, then the performance switches. You can't time this in any consistent way over the long term. Avoid these sales pitches.

Strategic Portfolios for Risk-Conscious Investors

In Strategy I, we identified what type of investor you are based on your reaction to two scenarios featuring two different TSP portfolios—a *conservative investor*, a *moderate investor,* or an *aggressive investor.*

The conservative investor using the model portfolio below will experience less volatility during difficult markets. In return for the greater degree of safety, he or she will also probably experience a lower return over the very long term. The aggressive investor, on the other hand, might experience significant volatility, but as a result, will most likely experience a higher return compared to the conservative and moderate investors. The moderate investor will experience some volatility at times but also more growth over the very long term than the conservative investor.

By understanding these trade-offs in advance, you will be more likely to stick with your chosen investment strategy over the long term and will avoid selling your declining funds during down markets.

Portfolio for the Conservative Investor

For the conservative investor, a basic 50% allocation to stocks and a 50% allocation to bonds (similar to Scenario 2 in the previous chapter) will provide some growth while also protecting the total TSP account value during significant declines in stock markets.

The simplest way to divide this 50-50 allocation in the TSP is with 50% to the C Fund and 50% to the G Fund. For those who adhere to the "KISS" principal (*Keep It Simple, Stupid!*), this is one of the simplest allocations to have in the TSP.

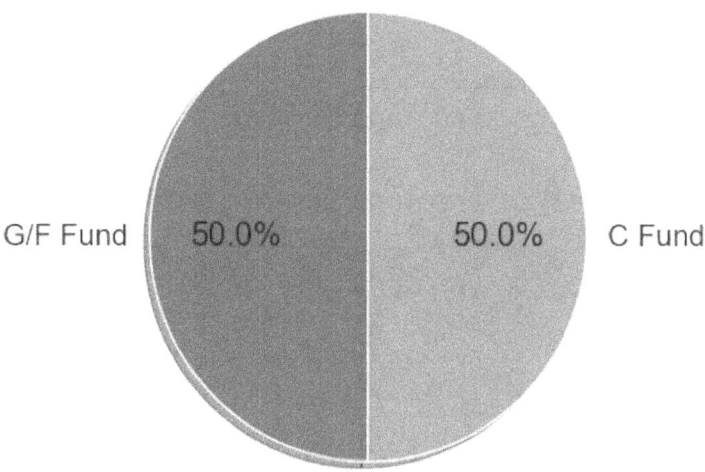

A conservative 50-50 stock-bond allocation.

A chart illustrating approximate returns of a 50-50 allocation strategy compared to all-stock and all-bond allocations for the 1957-1986 time period is shown below. The 30-year period is about the median return for all the 30-year post-WWII periods examined and detailed in the previous section, with the 50-50 allocation returning just over $800,000. This particular timeframe also includes the 1970s period used for demonstration purposes in Strategy I. The example is based on a monthly investment of $250 the first year that increases by 5% each year, starting at the beginning of January 1957 and ending in December 1986. Further examination of these allocations by year can be found at bit.ly/TSP2ndEd.

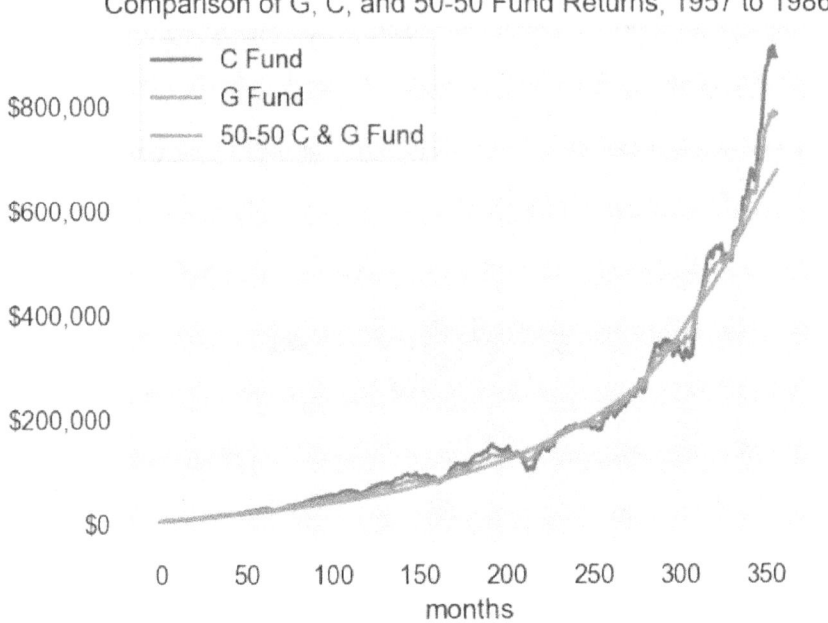

Comparison of G, C, and 50-50 Fund Returns, 1957 to 1986

A sample return of the conservative asset allocation of 50% stocks to 50% government bonds over 30 years, from 1957 to 1986 (the median return of 30-year periods for the stock index fund in the post-WWII era). The all-stock portfolio ended the 30 years at $937,265, the all-bond portfolio ended the period at $681,551, and the 50-50 portfolio ended at $809,408.

The chart illustrates how the all-stock portfolio can underperform the all-bond portfolio multiple and extended times in one's investing lifetime. The 50-50 portfolio helped to ease the declines. The all-stock portfolio dropped from a high of over $146,000 in the 193rd month to a low of just over $97,000 in the 213th month, for example, for a total decline in value of over $48,000 in the 20-month period. The 50-50 portfolio, on the other hand, dropped from a high of $127,000 to about $115,000, or a drop of just $12,000. (The third line, representing an all-government-bond fund investment, rose from $108,000 to $134,000 during this time, because of rising interest rates.) The all-stock and 50-50 portfolios recovered fairly quickly and stayed about even with the government bond fund, but they experienced some downturns again at around the 300th month. The two funds then grew significantly in the last 18 months of investing, which is a theme that will be explored in greater detail in the chapter *Parabolic Wealth*.

While this basic allocation does not feature complete diversification among all the stock and bond asset classes, the C Fund contains at least some of the attributes of the S and I Funds indirectly, providing more diversification in stocks than many realize. The C Fund includes a large majority of companies in the U.S. stock market (about 80% of all publicly traded companies), so you are getting some exposure to medium- and smaller-sized companies in addition to the largest U.S. companies that make up a significant portion of the C Fund. And many of these U.S.-based companies held in the C Fund have large global operations (think Microsoft, Disney, and Caterpillar) earning significant profits from their overseas sales, which provides good international exposure as well.

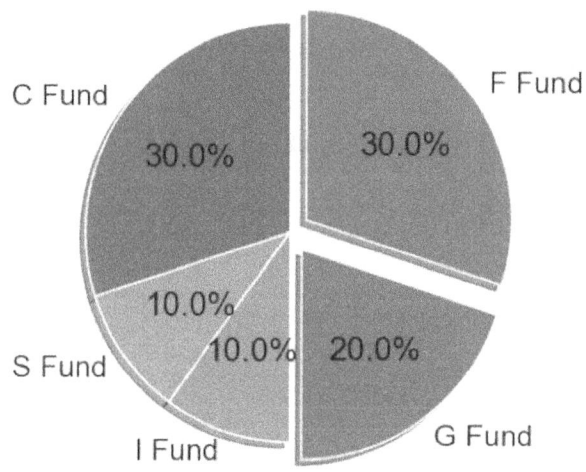

A diversified, conservative TSP portfolio

But for those conservative investors who would still like a slightly riskier allocation among the TSP funds, an example 50-50 stock-to-bond ratio with the following model allocations provides some exposure to all the funds: 30% in the C Fund, 10% each in the S Fund and I Fund, and 20-30% in the F Fund with the remainder in the G Fund. The addition of the small-cap and international funds provides a little more potential growth—and a little more risk—while maintaining an overall less-risky, 50-50 stock-to-bond allocation.

The F Fund, in turn, includes a significant amount of corporate and other asset-backed bonds in addition to U.S. Government bonds, thus expanding beyond the basic G Fund government bond holdings.

Portfolio for the Moderate Investor

For the moderate investor, a 65% total allocation to stocks and a 35% total allocation to bonds provides some extra opportunity for growth while still protecting the total TSP value from significant swings in the market. This might be the preferred portfolio for a majority of risk-conscious investors, as the 65% in stocks allows for a little extra growth over time, while the 35% allocation to bonds protects investors from most kinds of downturns investors can expect to experience in U.S. and international equities markets. Moreover, this leaves a significant cushion to use to invest during periodic downturns in the stock funds, as will be discussed in Strategies III and IV.

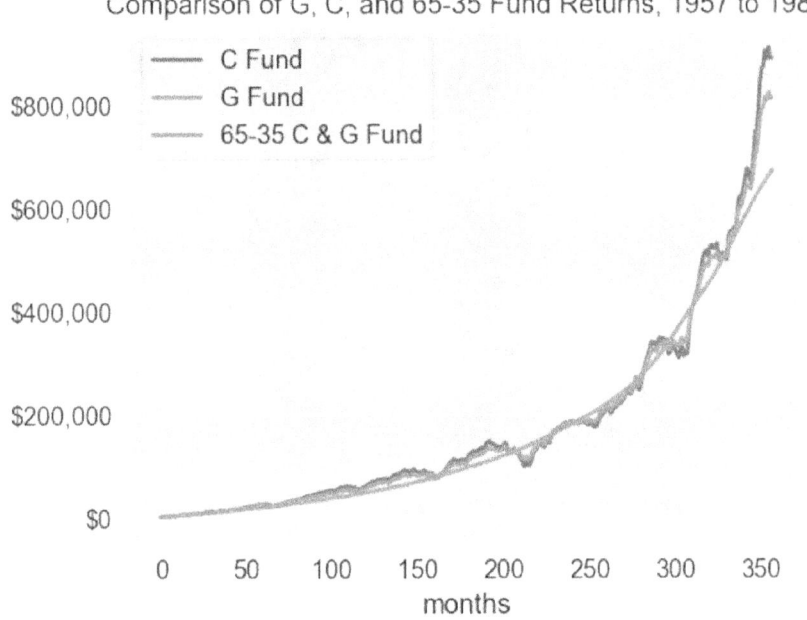

Comparison of G, C, and 65-35 Fund Returns, 1957 to 1986

A sample return of the moderate asset allocation of 65% stocks to 35% government bonds over 30 years, from 1957 to 1986 (the median return of 30-year periods for the stock index fund in the post-WWII era). The all-stock portfolio ended the 30 years at $937,265, the all-bond portfolio *ended the period at $681,551, and the 65-35 portfolio ended slightly lower than the all-stock portfolio at $847,765.*

As with the 50-50 allocation, the 65-35 dips along with the all-stock portfolio in the 1970s (from the 193rd month investment to the 213th one) from a high of $133,000 to a low of $110,000, a decline of about $23,000. This compares to a decline of $48,000 in the all-stock portfolio, and a gradual increase in the government bond portfolio.

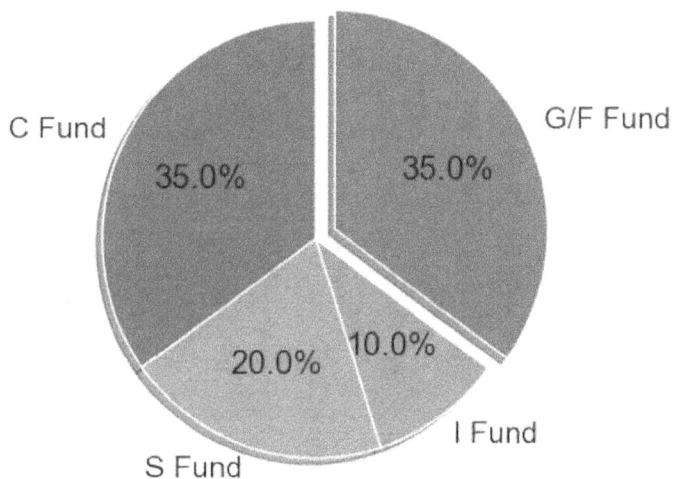

An alternate, diversified moderate portfolio.

The simplest way to diversify a moderate portfolio is to invest 65% in the C Fund and 35% in the G Fund, similar to the "KISS" allocation strategy above. For those who wish to further diversify their 65% stock allocation, 30-35% of the total portfolio could be invested the C Fund, 10-20% in the I Fund, and 10-20% in the S Fund, based on preference. For the bond allocation, 15-20% could be invested each in the F and G Funds, give or take 5-10% among the funds.

Portfolio for the Aggressive Investor

For the aggressive investor who is seeking greater potential long-term growth and is comfortable with sometimes significant volatility (and declines!) from time to time in their portfolios, an allocation of 80% to stocks and the remainder in bonds provides growth potential while also leaving a significant cushion for investing during declining markets, as discussed in Strategy IV. An 80% allocation to the C Fund and 20% to the G Fund is the easiest allocation.

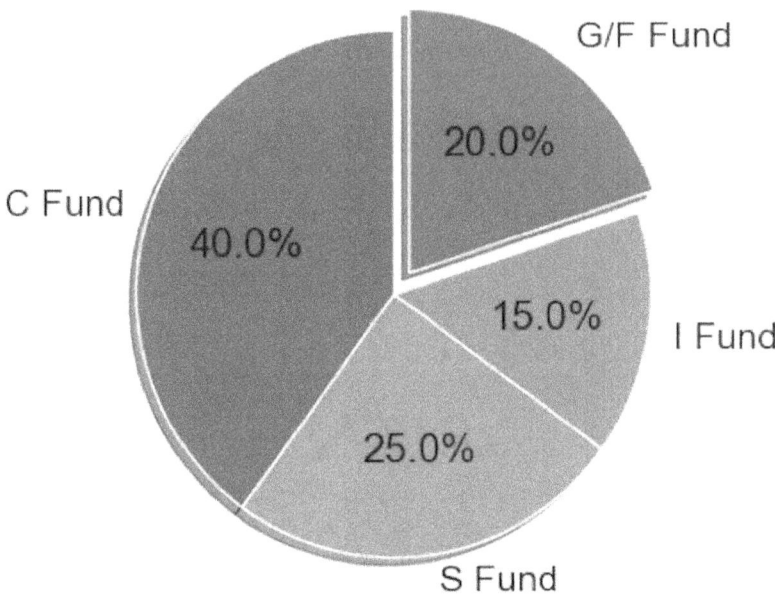

An alternate, diversified aggressive 80-20 portfolio.

A more diversified allocation could include 40% invested in the C Fund, 15-25% in the I Fund, and 15-25% in the S Fund, with 10% each in the G and F Funds, with 5-10% difference in allocations among the funds based on personal preference.

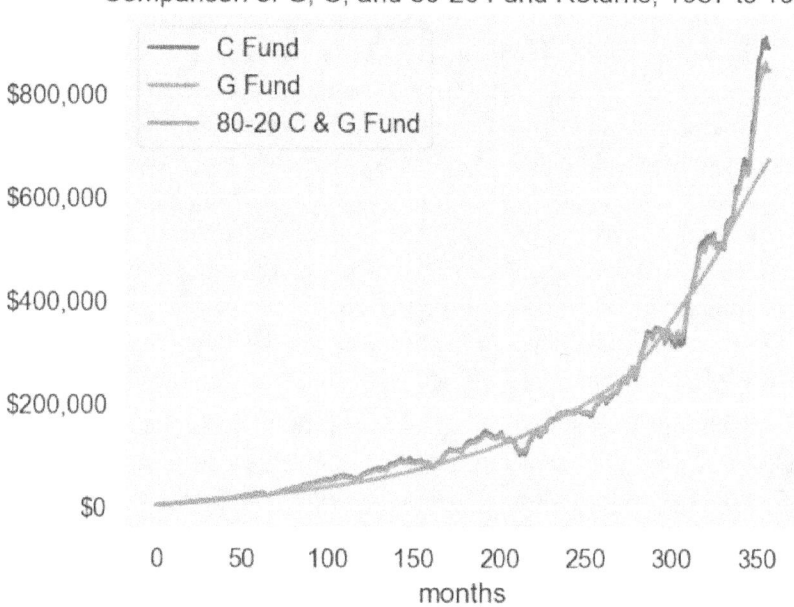

Comparison of G, C, and 80-20 Fund Returns, 1957 to 1986

A sample return of the aggressive asset allocation of 80% stocks to 20% government bonds over 30 years, from 1957 to 1986 (the median return of 30-year periods for the stock index fund in the post-WWII era). The all-stock portfolio ended the 30 years at $937,757, the all-bond portfolio ended the period at $681,551, and the 80-20 portfolio ended at $886,122.

As with the previous allocations, the 80-20 allocation dips along with the all-stock portfolio in the 1970s, as seen in the graph (from the 193rd month investment to the 213th one) from a high of over $138,000 to a low of $104,500, or a decline of about $34,000. This compares to a decline of $48,000 in the all-stock portfolio, and a gradual increase in the government bond portfolio. It also declines again around the 300th month of investing but recovers more quickly than in the 1970s timeframe.

Some readers will have noted that even this "aggressive investor" TSP allocation puts relatively less in the TSP stock funds than some of the longer-term L Funds. The aggressive allocation in early 2020 has about 2% less invested in stocks than the L 2050 Fund, with an 82-18 stock-bond allocation.

Later L Funds (L 2055 and after) will have even more invested in the stock funds as they open for investors.

The lower stock-to-bond allocations in the conservative and moderate investor strategies are designed to protect against major fluctuations in one's TSP total account value during times of significant market swings, as noted previously. The lower allocations also provide flexibility for more active investors to re-allocate during significant market swings. The L Funds in contrast are monolithic and reallocate daily, which reduces the opportunities to invest after steep market declines. Their stock-to-bond ratios also steadily decrease, limiting the upside potential growth especially in later years, as the stock portion of a portfolio can really start to grow compared to the bond portion. This will be explored further in the upcoming *Parabolic Wealth* chapter.

The bond allocation in the aggressive portfolio is also intended to leave significant resources to buy into declining markets, as occurred in 1973-74, 1987, 2000-02, and in 2008-09. These strategies are detailed more fully in the next two chapters.

Summary for Strategy II

The TSP investor should allocate his or her investments among the stock and bond funds based on risk tolerance identified in Strategy I.

- If you are a conservative investor, allocate 50% of your portfolio to the stock funds (C, S, and I) and 50% to the bond funds (G and F). Rebalance your TSP account over time according to Strategy III and consider the recommendations in Strategy V.

- If you are a moderate investor, allocate 65% of your portfolio among the stock funds and 35% among the bond funds. Rebalance your TSP account over time according to Strategy III and consider the recommendations in Strategy V. (The more adventurous moderate investor might also want to consider Strategy IV, with the understanding that this strategy entails greater fluctuations in one's total TSP allocation strategy.)

- If you are an aggressive investor, allocate 80% of your portfolio among the stock funds and 20% among the bond funds. This investor will also be the most active when employing Strategies III and IV. Also consider the recommendations in Strategy V.

STRATEGY III
Reallocate With the Help of Periodic Contributions

Once you have established a target allocation among the TSP funds based on your investor type, it is useful to know how to rebalance your holdings among the funds, since your individual fund totals will fluctuate due to changing market behaviors over time.

When investing in several TSP funds with different average growth rates, some of the funds will increase in value faster than others. This is called *portfolio drift*, or the slow change over time from a target allocation to one reflecting recent market conditions.

Under historically average market conditions, the stock funds should grow at their long-term average of about 9-10% per year, and the bond funds should grow at their historical rate of about 2-3% per year. Even within the first year under these average market conditions, the stock funds will represent a slightly greater proportion of your TSP account, because the total investment in the stock funds will grow more than the investment in the bond funds.

And if the stock funds enjoy a few years of outsized growth—such as in the late 1990s, when the C Fund grew by over 20% each year for five years—they will increase in value disproportionately compared to the bond funds. Conversely, during significant declines in the U.S. and world stock markets, the stock funds will contract more quickly relative to the bond funds. And in the 2010s, the bond fund interest rates fell to average returns of 2% or less a year, so that the mean-reverting stock fund returns outpaced the bond funds by an even greater margin.

Thus, when U.S. and world stock markets are performing well, your TSP holdings might change from a 65-35 or 50-50 allocation between stock and bond funds to 72-28 or 56-44 allocation or greater within a few years. While the increase in value of the stock funds over the bond funds might make you feel wealthier—and no shame in that!—this also means that an unexpected stock market correction or significant decline in U.S. and world stock markets will cause a greater proportion of your portfolio to decrease quickly in value as a result. Several years of portfolio drift will create a disproportionate allocation between your stock and bond funds, and as a result, more of your TSP would be impacted by any market declines.

Portfolio drift is illustrated below, based on the 50-50 conservative allocation from 1957 to 1986, as discussed in the previous chapter. The 0.5 trend line is the ideal allocation for this investor, and the fluctuation above the line indicates that the stock fund allocation has grown to a greater percentage of holdings compared to the bond fund holdings, while the line's movement below the 0.5 trend line means the stock fund holdings have fallen below the 50-50 allocation.

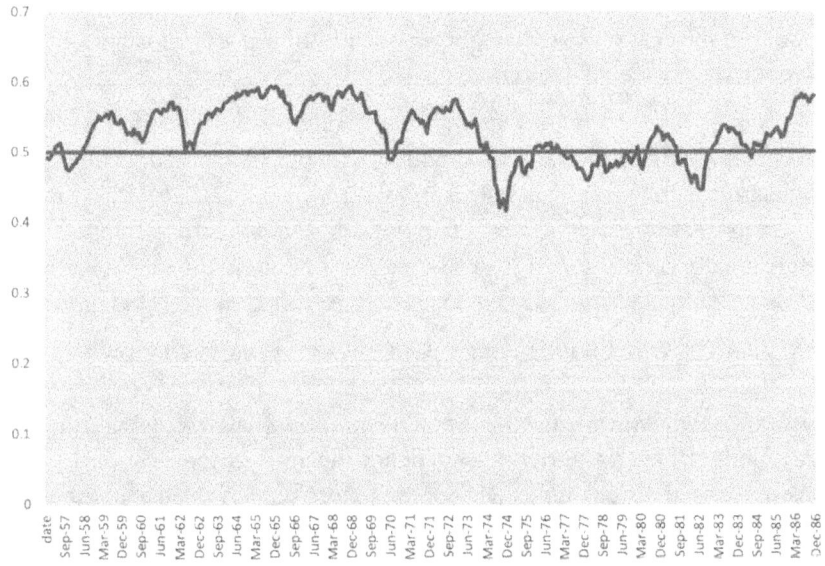

The actual holdings of the 50-50 strategy between the stock fund and bond fund drifted higher and lower due to market conditions, with stock fund holdings doing better relative to the bond fund holdings in the 1960s, then falling in value relative to the bond fund holdings in the 1970s, rising slightly and then falling again in the early 1980s.

Therefore, from time to time the TSP investor will want to readjust or rebalance his or her fund holdings back to the original allocation to remain aligned with one's investor type. Rebalancing from a fund or funds that have enjoyed significant increases also forces the TSP investor to focus on investing more in the relatively cheaper funds, as they potentially represent better values in relation to the higher-returning funds.

Portfolio Drift and Periodic Rebalancing

As an example of how an investor's portfolio can naturally change or "drift" from a target allocation, the following example portfolio shows an early-career moderate investor with $100,000 in her TSP account that experiences significant growth in the stock funds relative to the bond funds.

Mia Williams, an 8-year employee of the Department of Energy, has $100,000 in her TSP. As a moderate investor, she has allocated her portfolio among all the funds as described in Strategy II—$35,000 in her large-cap C fund, $20,000 and $10,000 respectively in the S and I Funds, $15,000 in the G fund, and another $20,000 in her F fund. In total, Mia has 65% of her portfolio in the stock funds and 35% in the bond funds. Her last promotion was to GS-11, and she makes about $70,000 a year. She contributes 14% of her pay to the TSP, and with the government match, she invests about $500 every two weeks to her TSP.

Mia enjoys a year of significant growth in her stock funds, with the C fund growing approximately 15% and the S fund growing close to 20%, while the I Fund steadily decreases by 7% in one year. Her bond funds enjoy steady returns, with the G and F funds growing at 2% and 3%, respectively. This growth, in addition to her $13,000 worth of contributions, brings her total TSP holdings to just under $124,000. This also means, however, that Mia's 65-35 stock-bond allocation has drifted to over 67-33 in a year, reflecting the greater growth in two of her three stock funds, and a decline in the other (see below).

	Beginning balance	TSP Fund Allocation	Drifted balance	TSP Fund % Holdings
G Fund	$15,000.00	15%	$17,273.27	13.934%
F Fund	$20,000.00	20%	$23,249.60	18.754%
C Fund	$35,000.00	35%	$45,568.43	36.759%
S Fund	$20,000.00	20%	$27,297.30	22.020%
I Fund	$10,000.00	10%	$10,576.67	8.531%
Total	$100,000.00		$123,965.27	

If Mia's stock funds continue to enjoy increased growth over several years, her allocation would drift even further away from her chosen 65-35 allocation.

Now, Mia has the option to rebalance her funds back to her desired TSP allocation, at any time, using the interfund transfer on the TSP website. On the "interfund transfer" page, Mia would see the dollar amount in each of her funds and the total percentage this represents in her TSP portfolio—as the "% Holdings" figures appear above. Next to each of these percentages, Mia would fill in her original target allocation percentages for each fund for a moderate investor, or 15-20-35-20-10, respectively. After providing her email address to receive final confirmation of the interfund transfer and re-confirming her interfund transfer request, the whole process is done. One or two business days later, Mia receives an e-mail from TSP confirming that the transaction took place.

TSP investors can use this reallocation method to rebalance among the funds at predetermined times during the year—every three months, for example, or at the end of each year. Alternatively, investors can rebalance once their accounts have drifted beyond a certain percentage in fund holdings—for example, if any of the funds have drifted 5% above or below their desired values. Rebalancing via an interfund transfer doesn't have to be undertaken too often; there is no need to keep funds at *exactly* the set percentages, especially since some drift naturally occurs in both directions on any given trading day. Also, the TSP administrators limit interfund transfers to no more than two in any given month, so more active TSP investors will have to keep these limits in mind too.

Let's take another look at the 50-50 allocation strategy in the 30-year period from 1957 to 1986. Setting 5% drift from the 50-50 balance as our trigger to rebalance, this era would have required 14 rebalances, eight because the stock fund grew beyond its 5% upper range, and six when the bond fund was 5% overbalanced. By rebalancing to 50-50 when each fund hit its upper threshold, the total final amount grew to approximately $833,464 at the end of 30 years. This compares to the $809,000 return of the non-rebalanced 30-year investment (and the $937,000 total return of monthly investments in the C Fund).

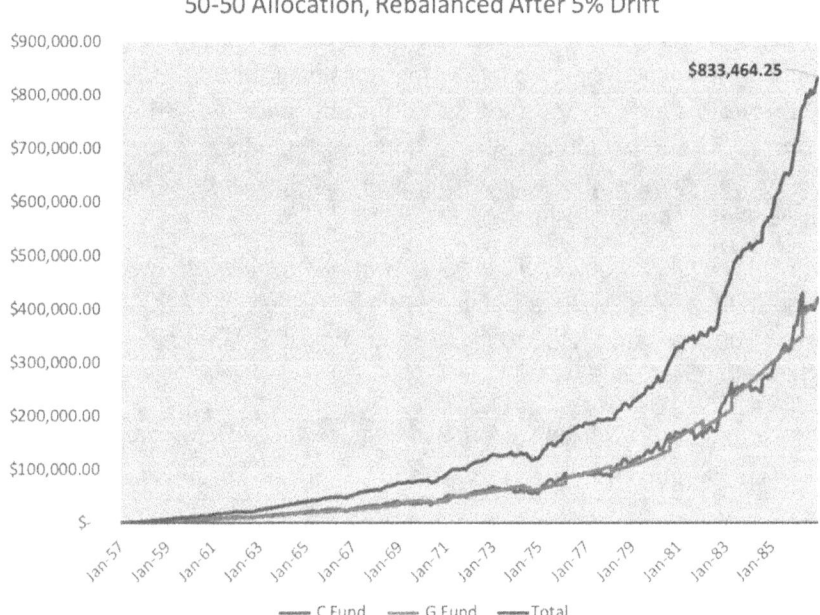

Return of the 50-50 allocation between the C Fund-like S&P 500 and the G Fund-like government bonds from 1957 to 1986, with monthly contributions that increased by 5% each year. The lines representing the C Fund and G Fund are more closely associated than in the non-rebalanced fund illustrated in the previous chapter, and the total return line features a smoother rise as well.

One thing should be noted in this example, however. The rate on the government bond rose to an astounding 12% per year or so in the early 1980s, and the rate was otherwise elevated throughout the last half of the 1970s and 1980s. Inflation was in general quite high in the late 1970s and early 1980s. This thus increased government bond returns by an historic extent, and the rates have since dropped to around 2% as of late 2019.

As a general illustration of the concept, however, this example shows how rebalancing can both soften the gyrations of market activity and potentially improve returns over the long run.

Rebalancing via Biweekly Contributions

For buy-and-hold investors, interfund transfers are an unsatisfying exercise. As noted above, by using an interfund transfer to reallocate your investments all at once, you are immediately selling shares from some TSP funds to rebalance the amounts in the remaining funds. But because most TSP investors are also investing in those same funds via periodic contributions, an investor would invest new money again in those same funds in the weeks and months after rebalancing, assuming the investor's contributions mirrors his or her total allocation.

Let's take a look again at Mia's portfolio to illustrate the reallocation process more closely. By rebalancing, Mia had to sell over $2,000 from her C and S Funds to add $1,300 to the G Fund, almost $1,500 to the F Fund, and $1,800 to the I Fund.

	Before Rebalancing	After Rebalancing
G Fund	$17,273.27	$18,594.79
F Fund	$23,249.60	$24,793.05
C Fund	$45,568.43	$43,387.85
S Fund	$27,297.30	$24,793.05
I Fund	$10,576.67	$12,396.53
Total	$123,965.27	$123,965.27

If Mia's biweekly contribution allocation is the same as her TSP account's total contribution, she would be investing around $175 into the C Fund, $75 into the S Fund, $50 into the I Fund, and $75 and $100 into the G and F Funds every two weeks. Within 14 pay periods—half a year or so—Mia would have thus re-invested the same amount into the C and S Funds as she had sold during her interfund transfer. The biweekly contributions in effect negated some of the rebalancing activity.

Why sell something just to turn around and buy it back again?

Under normal market conditions, there is another method to rebalance one's TSP holdings that does not require TSP investors to shift any money from the growing funds to rebalance the remaining funds. Instead of rebalancing via an interfund transfer, you can invest in the underweighted funds via biweekly contributions.

Rebalancing via biweekly contributions takes more time and patience to complete (hence the question on your level of interest in investing in Strategy I), but it has the advantage of avoiding the sale of any investments in any of the funds, at least for a time. You can remain a "buy and hold," long-term investor using this method. You are simply investing new money via biweekly or monthly contributions in the underweighted funds, instead of selling shares from the funds that have enjoyed significant growth.

Let's take a look again at Mia's situation to see how this would work. Mia, a buy-and-hold TSP investor, does not want to shift money out of any of her stock funds—they've gained so much already, after all—and she instead wants to let her stock-fund holdings continue to grow. Therefore, she will simply add money to her unbalanced bond funds using her biweekly $500+ investments, until she has reached her desired allocation of 65-35 once again.

To do this, Mia changes her $500 biweekly contributions to go entirely to the bond funds and I Fund—33% each (or about $165 per fund). To accomplish this, Mia would access the "biweekly contribution" page in her TSP account (instead of the "interfund transfer" page) and would enter 33% each in the G, F, and I Funds. Once she enters her e-mail address and confirms the transaction, the TSP administrators send her a message within several days confirming the change. Mia would not add any new money to the two stock funds until her other funds have re-attained their target allocations.

Or, she could elect to allocate contributions to one fund by putting 100% ($500 in her case) into the fund of her choice.

Because she continues to invest a significant amount in her TSP account via biweekly contributions, in just six pay periods—just three months—Mia would have added a total of $3,000 to the G, F and I Funds (or that amount to one fund), thus increasing their values in a relatively short amount of time.

Because her TSP total value has increased due to the additional $3,000 in contributions, Mia would want to contribute a few more pay periods to the bond funds to reach the 65-35 balance, assuming no major increases in the stock funds. And, if her stock funds continued to enjoy significant returns—which is great, of course!—Mia can continue to add to the funds to fully re-balance her TSP account even as her stock funds continue to grow.

Once Mia was satisfied with her total allocation, she could change her biweekly contribution again to reflect her original allocation preference, with 65% of her biweekly contributions going into her stock funds and 35% going into her bond funds. Alternatively, in anticipation of further long-term growth in her stock funds, Mia could set her biweekly contributions to add a little more to her bond funds, relative to her stock funds—say, 25% or even 30% of her $500 biweekly contributions each to the G and F funds, with the remainder going to the stock funds.

Importantly, this process can be reversed during significant declines in the stock markets, too. Let's say Mia's stock portfolio suddenly declined 10% or 15%, thus slightly over-weighting her bond funds relative to her stock funds. She could then increase her biweekly contributions to invest more into her stock funds, thus investing into these funds as the stock market declines and as stocks become progressively cheaper.

Moreover, this technique does not violate the TSP's policy against frequent trading, so aggressive investors will retain their two interfund transfers per month to use during significant down markets, as will be discussed in Strategy IV.

Lastly, if you are concerned that the market might drop, and you feel like you should "do something" to prepare for it but don't know what to do, as an interim measure you can switch your biweekly/monthly contributions to invest in the G and/or F Funds, for a little extra peace of mind. You can keep the rest of your portfolio invested in the asset mix you have previously decided on, without needing to sell any of your growth-oriented funds. Then you can use these extra funds in the G and/or F Funds to invest in the stock funds in case of a decline, as detailed in the next Strategy. Just remember to switch back to your chosen asset contribution mix in time for more long-term gains!

The Art of Rebalancing Over Time

For this method to be effective, the TSP investor must first be contributing a healthy percentage of pay via biweekly contributions. A contribution of just a few percent of pay every two weeks is probably not enough to rebalance one's TSP holdings by using contributions alone. If Mia were contributing 4% of her pay instead of 14%, her biweekly contributions would drop to under $250, effectively doubling the time it would take to rebalance the stock and bond funds in her TSP account. Biweekly contributions of 10% or even 15% substantially improve the success of this strategy (and add more quickly to one's TSP account too).

Also, as one's TSP account grows over time, rebalancing via biweekly contributions will naturally take longer to accomplish. If, instead of $100,000, Mia had $300,000 in her account, it would take her much longer to rebalance her funds with her $500 biweekly contributions. Her $300,000 would have grown to over $344,500 at the end of the year, with about $112,000 in the two bond funds and over $232,000 in the stock funds (see below). To regain her 65-35 allocation, Mia would have to increase her bond fund holdings to $120,000, and the I Fund to $34,450. With a $500 biweekly contribution, it would take about a year to add the additional $13,000 or so to those funds, assuming marginal growth in her stock funds. But if the I Fund were to recover or grow more in value than the other stock funds,* it would take less time.

	Beginning balance	TSP Fund Allocation	Ending balance	TSP Fund Allocation
G Fund	$45,000	15%	$47,879.05	13.896%
F Fund	$60,000	20%	$64,467.02	18.711%
C Fund	$105,000	35%	$126,861.30	36.819%
S Fund	$60,000	20%	$76,115.64	22.092%

* Note that Mia's biweekly contributions slowly increase the total amount in her TSP account and, as a result, increase the target amount to achieve the 35% allocation for the bond funds. With close to $345,000 in her TSP in this example, Mia would have to increase her bond allocation from $112,500 to $120,000 to achieve the 35% allocation. But by adding $8,500, her TSP total increases to $353,000, which means Mia's 35% bond allocation target is now $123,550, requiring a few more contributions to the bond funds to fully rebalance. In reality, all the funds will fluctuate every day, making exact target allocations unrealistic.

I Fund	$30,000	10%	$29,222.45	8.481%
Total	**$300,000**		**$344,545.46**	

Moreover, one's TSP account could fluctuate greatly during times of significant market volatility, causing significant portfolio drift in a short period of time. If Mia's stock funds experienced a drop of 30% during the year, her $232,000 would have declined in value to $162,400, and now her TSP account would be close to 59-41 stock-bonds, thus overweighting her bond funds relative to the stock funds for the moderate investor allocation. Mia here would allocate all of her biweekly contributions to the stock funds to invest into the rapidly declining stock markets. Given the severity and rapid nature of the declines, Mia could additionally request an interfund transfer to shift a few percentage points from her bond funds to her stock funds, to bring it back to a 60-40 or 62-38 stock-bond allocation, even as she continues to invest her biweekly contributions into the stock funds to gradually regain her 65-35 target allocation.

Thus, rebalancing via biweekly or monthly contributions becomes more of an art than a science, as your TSP account total value grows and as you encounter significant volatility in the markets from time to time. If your preferred target allocation has drifted 5-10% in one direction even after allocating biweekly contributions into the underweight funds, an interfund transfer of a few percentage points might be necessary to regain a more optimal allocation.

In the next chapter, Strategy IV will further discuss how to invest into significantly declining markets and is primarily intended for aggressive investors due to the potentially significant shifts in fund values. Conservative and moderate investors who are comfortable with their investment allocation and rebalancing strategies can skip to Strategy V.

Summary for Strategy III

- Review your TSP account periodically—quarterly or twice yearly—to ensure your TSP funds are allocated according to your investor type.

- Under normal market conditions, if your TSP funds are more than a few percentage points different than their target allocations, rebalance by either an interfund transfer or by using periodic contributions to increase the underweight funds slowly over time. To ensure greater success with this method, contribute an adequate percentage of your base pay—10% to 15%—via your biweekly or monthly contributions.

- During times of significant market volatility, when the allocation of one or more of your funds has drifted by more than five percentage points from your target allocation, reallocate a few percent via the interfund transfer, in addition to biweekly contributions to the underweight funds.

NOTES

STRATEGY IV
Use Volatility to Your Advantage

To achieve truly significant growth in wealth over time, TSP stock fund investors should be prepared to invest into significant market declines at predetermined intervals, when stock funds become increasingly cheaper.

However, as illustrated in Scenarios 1 and 2 in Strategy I, having a significant portion of one's portfolio invested in the TSP stock funds when stock markets decline will cause commensurate declines in one's total TSP account value as well. This is why Strategy IV is recommended only for those with an appetite for risk. Only those who can withstand significant declines in their TSP account over potentially long periods of time (from several months to several years or longer) should consider using this strategy.

Yet, the rewards of investing into stock funds as they decline can be quite significant over several decades. The former fund manager Peter Lynch illustrated the long-term benefits of buying into major market declines in his 1993 classic *Beating the Street*. Lynch commissioned research that found that $1,000 invested in the S&P 500 index on January 31 each year from 1940 to the beginning of 1992 would have grown to over $3.5 million after 52 years and a total investment of $52,000. This equates to a 12% average yearly return, which is very good. But by adding $1,000 each time the market dropped 10% or more—which according to Lynch happened 31 times over those 52 years (on average about once every 20 months)—the investor's $83,000 total investment would have been worth over $6.2 million by the end of 1992.[48] The extra $31,000 invested during market downturns ultimately grew to *$2.7 million* in this scenario!

I similarly recalculated returns based on investing at the start of January instead of January 31 each year from 1940, and doing so produced a total return of $3,649,336 by the end of 1991. However, for full-year returns, there were only five years that dropped by over 10%. Other years came close, such as 1940's 9.78% drop and 1962's 8.73% drop. As we have seen in previous chapters, however, several years had *multiple* 10% declines, such as the 1973-1974 bear market. But even factoring in these fewer down years on a full-year basis, adding an additional $1,000 to the investment in the January after that 10% decline, the extra $5,000 in total additional investments brought the returns to $4,145,719 at the end of 1991—an extra $500,000!

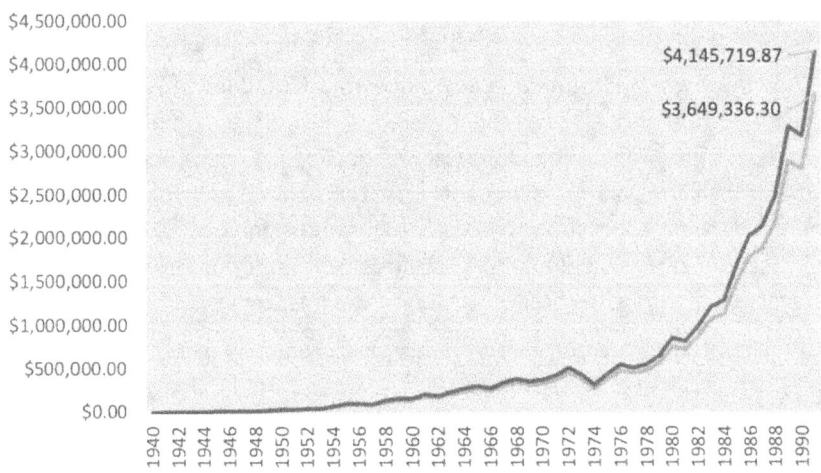

Return of $1,000 a Year in the S&P 500, 1940-1991, and Extra $1,000 Invested After Each Drop of 10%

This was an extremely unique period, of course. Stock prices were extremely low in the 1940s, after the Great Depression and during World War II, so that any investment in the stock market then would have enjoyed significant gains over 50 years later. However, while returns will differ depending on when one starts investing, this same general approach can be applied at any time. By investing a little extra when the stock market declines at predetermined percentage intervals, an investor will see greater gains over the long term than if he or she just continued to invest the same amount among the funds each year.

Let's recalculate this same $1,000 yearly investment over a more current time period, from 1980 to 2019. Forty years is a more realistic timeframe to consider since a 20- or 25-year-old might invest in stocks until she is 60 or 65 and then choose to enjoy her wealth fully thereafter. It should be noted that 1980-2019 also includes steep market declines in 2000-2002, and 2008-2009, so that any investment would have experienced significant fluctuations.

But let's add a little twist. Instead of investing $1,000 in a lump-sum at the beginning of the year, let's invest $100 a month, every month, for the entire 40 years. That would amount to a total investment of $48,000 as of the end of 2019. Doing that and just that every month would have yielded $711,887 from January 1980 through to early December 2019. Not bad, eh?

Now let's undertake the same exercise where we contribute an additional $1,000 to our investment every time the market declines by 10%. That happened 22 times over that 40-year period, on a month-to-month basis. There were a few other instances of 10%+ declines on a non-monthly basis, but we get most of the declines at least.

By investing an additional $1,000 after each decline of about 10%, our intrepid investor would have turned a $70,000 investment (the original $48,000 plus a total of $22,000 for the $1,000-per-downturn investments) over 40 years into $1,114,240! Notably, the addition of the extra $22,000 following significant market declines, in addition to investing during thick and thin, added over *$400,000* to her account.

And this was with a flat contribution rate for the entire time. A majority of TSP investors likely can—and will—contribute more than $1,000 per year or $100 a month into TSP stock funds and other investments. Imagine what the result might be if, instead of investing $1,000 per year, your investments including the government match was $5,000, $10,000, or even $15,000 per year. The results would be spectacular, as long as you have the patience and fortitude to withstand the declines over time and have a stable reserve of funds from which to invest into stock funds during market declines.

We can calculate returns with increasing contributions too. Starting with $100 a month, and with contributions increasing by 5% each year (from $100, to $105 each month in the second year, all the way to $670 per month in the final year), our investment from January 1980 to December 2019 would have come to $1,124,249—just $10,000 more than by investing with $100 and during downturns throughout the 40 years. But the contribution amount would have been significantly higher, at just over $144,000.

How about investing through both approaches?

By investing with increasing contributions *and* adding $1,000 during each downturn, our total investment would have been about $166,000, but our return would have been a spectacular $1,526,602.

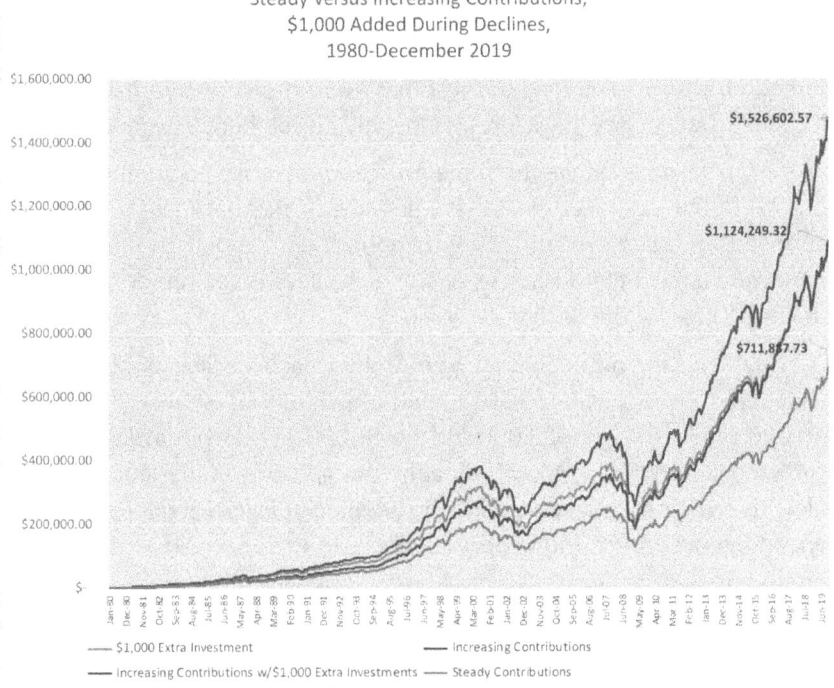

Investing with increasing contributions and adding $1,000 after each downturn of 10% yielded over $1.5 million when investing in the S&P 500 index fund from 1980 to December 2019.

The multiple components that add up to these returns will be detailed in the chapter titled *Parabolic Wealth*. But this is an illustration of what increasing contributions, coupled with investments during downturns, can add up to for buy-and-hold investors.

The trick is to apply these techniques as markets decline.

The Art of Buying into Falling Stock Funds

There are three approaches to buying into declining markets. But before discussing those, we should understand the way in which TSP participants can transfer money between funds, because it can impact our approaches to investing during downturns.

Transferring between funds is accomplished via interfund transfer. Participants can transfer money among the funds at most twice a month, as noted earlier. For our purposes, this limitation should not impact this strategy because we can hardly expect there to be a time when the markets would drop more than 20% in a calendar month. (If the markets were dropping so precipitously, I think many of us would be too busy dealing with the problems driving the sudden and steep declines to worry about our TSP accounts!)

What might impact our interfund transfers is the requirement that the transfers be in percentage amounts. The fund transfer is based on percentages of the funds, so if you have 68.273% in one fund and 31.727% in another, and you want to rebalance them, you put in 65% for the one fund and 35% for the other, or whatever percentage amounts you want to readjust to. Interfund transfers based on percentages makes the first method of buying into declining markets challenging, but not insurmountable, as you will see below.

Approach #1: Modified Thrift Van Winkle™

This first method is a modified *Thrift Van Winkle*™ approach that enables investing at least $1,000 following a decline of 10%, very similar to the examples detailed above. This approach requires participants to contribute over 5% to their TSP, preferably 10% or more.

Once your investments in one or more of the stock funds grows to $5,000, and assuming the stock funds are not experiencing any major declines (when you would want to continue investing in the stock funds, which this strategy enables you to do) change your contribution allocation to 100% to the G Fund. Continue this until you have about $500 or so—10% of your account—in the bond fund. This is why you want a significant contribution:

If you are contributing $200 a pay period to your TSP, and you get another $50 or $100 match, you can do this in two pay periods. If your contributions and match combine to $500, you could do this with one contribution allocation or continue for two until you reach $1,000. Once you have reached that amount, change your contribution allocation back to the stock funds.

Repeat this process when your stock investments reach $10,000, to bring your G Fund up to at least $1,000. Assuming the stock funds keep growing, do this again once your fund balance reaches $20,000 and for each $10,000 increment thereafter. You want to have a minimum of $1,000 available to invest during a decline, and you want a maximum of 10% of your holdings in the bond fund. Anything more and you would defeat the purpose of the *Thrift Van Winkle*™ strategy, but you want to have $2,000-$3,000 ideally available in the G Fund. (For larger accounts, you may need to focus on percentage holdings instead of dollar holdings, so that you maintain 2-3% in the bond funds to be ready for future declines.) While rare, there are times when markets have declined 20% and 30% within a few months, such as in September-October 2008 and again in January and March 2009.

Set a percentage decline to watch for in your stock funds. The standard used above was 10%, but you could set it at 8% or 12-15% or more. (Given the small amount you have to invest during times of decline, you might want to wait for a steeper decline in order to get the most out of this strategy.) Once the stock fund(s) decline that percentage amount, conduct an interfund transfer that reduces your G Fund percentage amount by the desired amount and increases your stock fund(s) by an equal amount.

Just beware! You will see a drop in your total account balance as you do this, due to the continuing decline in the stock funds. You won't like it when it's happening, but just keep reminding yourself that when the markets recover—and they'll recover eventually—you'll have that much more to gain.

Also, when you are investing in multiple stock funds, you'll find that while one fund might drop below your threshold for conducting an interfund transfer, others may not. While they are correlated (recall the correlation coefficient of .92 between the C and S Funds, and .87 between the C and I Funds), the correlation is not 100%. Thus, you may find that one fund has declined by your threshold percentage (for example, declined by 10%), while the others have declined less. Regardless, all the stock funds have probably declined by a significant degree.

This is the *art* of buying into declining markets. This approach does not lend itself to an algorithm, at least not for individual investors. You'll need to make a judgement call about when to buy into the declines. Do you take a "close enough" attitude and invest into all the funds, knowing that the funds could decline further? Or do you hold onto those reserve funds, knowing that the funds might recover completely, and that you might miss your opportunity to invest during the fleeting decline? Don't get too wrapped up in this decision process, especially in the early years of investing. You'll have plenty of opportunities to add money to declining funds, and since you are already contributing significantly to the stock funds, you're buying into them as they decline and rise anyway. This just gives you a little extra with which to work.

For the interfund transfer itself, make sure the percentages for all of the stock funds are all higher when inputting the new figures for the transfer, since the goal is to add money to funds as they decline, not sell them. Given the number of decimals in the percentages, it is easy to make a mistake in rounding. In these instances, always round up for all the stock funds, and *down* for the G and/or F Funds.

Depending on how much is in your bond fund, try to leave something after meeting the conditions for the first decline, so that you have some money left in case the market declines by another 10% or 15%. You can repeat the process when another substantial decline happens, this time drawing down your G Fund to zero and increasing your stock funds to 100%.

Once the stock markets have recovered, change your contribution allocation to the bond funds for a few pay periods, in order to increase your stable holdings to be ready for another decline in the future. However, be sure to change back to the all-stock contribution once your reserve is replenished as part of the *Thrift Van Winkle*™ approach to investing in the TSP.

Approach #2: The 80-20 Portfolio

A second way to buy into declining markets is to do so through the aggressive investor allocation of 80% stocks and 20% bonds. This has the advantage of building up a larger cushion of stable funds from the outset. Your contribution allocation is set to 80% stocks and 20% bonds, so there is no need to switch contribution allocations in the beginning.

Let's conduct the same exercise. Watch the designated stock fund(s) for percentage declines. When the chosen stock fund has declined by the designated amount, conduct an interfund transfer of a percentage point or two. Repeat upon further decreases of the given percentage amount.

This portfolio has the added flexibility of being able to put more than just a token amount to all three stock funds, if desired. A $100,000 portfolio would have about $20,000 in bonds to reinvest during major market declines, compared to the $2,000-$3,000 in approach #1. The TSP participant undertaking this approach could transfer a percentage point or more to each of the three stock funds for a total of 3% or 4% of total holdings and still have an amount left over to invest during additional significant declines like those experienced in 2008-2009. Remember that the C Fund declined by half and the S Fund by more than that over those two years! Using the 10% threshold, that would mean a TSP investor would have up to four or five opportunities to invest in a declining market using this approach. (There were five opportunities to invest from January 2008 to March 2009, for example.)

Additionally, this investor can switch from the 80-20 contribution allocation (for biweekly or monthly contributions) to 100% of contributions going to the stock funds if the downturn is significant and lasting. One approach is to reset your contribution allocations to 100% to the stock funds once they decline by 20% from their peak. You could reset it to 50-50 (or even 100% to the bond fund for a while) once the stock funds have recovered to their original prices, or even to a higher threshold like 10% above their original prices, in order to truly lock in some gains.

As an example, say a stock fund is at $50. With this approach you would transfer a few percentage points from the bond to the stock fund when it dropped to $45, and again when it dropped to $40. At this point, you also could change your contribution allocation so that 100% goes to the stock fund. Once it recovers to $50 again—or to $55, if you've set that higher threshold—you would change your contribution allocation back to its original amount, or to 100% to the bond fund, to build up your reserves to re-invest during a later decline. This has the added advantage of having slightly less volatility compared to approach #1 above (but you'll still experience some major declines in your TSP funds!). Then after some time, reset your contribution allocations to 80-20.

By now you can see that the 80-20 allocation will drift significantly over time. You may start at 80-20, and it may drift upward to 85-15. But during major market upheaval, it might go down to 70-30 or even 60-40 depending on how precipitously the stock funds decline, but as in Strategy III, you'll rebalance during those downturns, and you will additionally change your contribution allocation to 100% stocks. The key is to avoid selling or rebalancing away from the stock funds as much as possible. Let them grow for the long term, which means that your allocation will rise potentially above a 90-10 stock-to-bond fund ratio in many instances. You then can use biweekly contributions to add more to your bond funds after significant rise in the stock funds to prepare for any future downturns. In my informal calculations, most portfolios based on the 80-20 approach end up in the high-90% range in stocks by the end of the 30-year periods examined, when allowing for significant portfolio drift. Depending on your intended use and timeline for the funds, you'll want to look at how the funds are allocated based on your personal situation.

Approach #3: The 90-10 Portfolio

This is a hybrid approach. This should allow you to build up sufficient funds that can be used to reinvest in the stock funds during a downturn, but it will also allow you to enjoy more upside potential over the long-term. You won't be able to invest fully across the three stock funds during a major downturn as experienced in 2008-9, but you can invest in one or perhaps two stock funds. So a 90-10 mix works for either a concentrated portfolio (one bond fund and one or at most two stock funds) or with the understanding that you won't be able to reallocate more than a couple of times in a shorter timeframe.

The general approach is otherwise the same as the 80-20 portfolio above, just set the allocation to 90-10.

Caveats!

There are some significant caveats related to the above approaches that investors who use this approach should take into account.

First, the strategy of buying into declining markets depends on significant market volatility in order to meet the percent decline thresholds for investment. However, if markets don't decline, you won't be able to "buy" into declining funds. In short, if the stock funds remain stagnant for months or years at a time, there will be few opportunities to employ this technique.

This very situation happened in the 1990s, for example, when there was an almost seven-year gap between 10% declines. The S&P 500 index experienced a 10.2% decline that ended in January 1991, and the next decline did not fully develop until the end of October 1997, with a 10.8% decline.[49] During this time, the S&P 500 went from just over 300 in late 1990 (during Operation Desert Shield) to 951 in September 1997. And the drop in 1997 was both sharp and quick, recovering within a few weeks of the over-10% decline, giving investors barely any time to take advantage.

In general, this situation points to the challenge of "opportunity costs" in choosing one, lower-growth fund over other, generally higher-growth stock funds in anticipation of near-term declines. By putting money toward one of the bond funds and forgoing investing in a stock fund, you run the risk of that stock fund continuing to grow for years without dropping by the established percentage amount. And when the decline does happen, it might not be enough of a drop to bring it below the original amount when you could have invested earlier.

Extending the example above, with the stock market bubble during that decade the S&P 500 continued to grow to about 1500 in mid-2000 before declining to the low 800s in October 2002. While there were several 10%+ declines in the late 1990s and early 2000s from the ultimate high of around 1500, the index never dropped even close to the 300s where it stood in the early 1990s. Investors who might have waited with significant reserves to buy into a declining market would never have had the opportunity to invest those funds. That was an opportunity cost for them.

This approach also requires paying regular attention to the markets, which is the reason for the question about your interest in market activity in Strategy I. If you're just not interested in monitoring the ups and downs of markets closely, or if the financial headlines simply bore you or scare you, this strategy is not for you. Continue with either the *Thrift Van Winkle*™ strategy and completely ignore the headlines or invest in an L Fund.

The steady attention is required, though, because sometimes markets can drop quickly and rise even more quickly, so you might miss a fleeting drop below your threshold. This was the case with the flash crash in 1997, for example.

And despite the attention to the markets, sometimes the above approaches yield almost the same as just setting and forgetting an allocation. For example, in applying the 80-20 approach (#2) to the 1957-1986 timeframe, which was the median return for 30-year periods examined over the last 120 years, the result was almost exactly the same as one would have experienced by investing in the *Thrift Van Winkle*™ during that time—$934,000 versus $939,000 (the 80-20 yielded almost $886,000 on its own). That's a lot of effort to end up with essentially the same returns. Granted, there was perhaps less volatility over time. Would a 90-10 mix have performed better? Yes, but again you must ask yourself if the effort over a three-decade period is worth the potential gain. For some it is, for others, it is not.

There is one last caveat that is important for TSP investors: The individual indexes are reported separately from their dividend rates, but the TSP funds are not. This means that, while the S&P 500 index value is widely reported (in late 2019, it ended just over 3,200), this reported value does not include dividend rates. Those are reported separately; the dividend rate was just under 2% by the end of 2019, for example. For the stock funds in the TSP, the share price includes all dividends that are automatically reinvested into the funds. This is because there is no difference in tax treatment for dividends and capital gains, and because the plan funds are otherwise tax-deferred (or tax-free for Roth TSP accounts). So over time, the share prices rise a little more because of the dividends and capital gains that are automatically reinvested. This also means that a 10% fall in the index does not quite equate to a 10% drop in the share price of, say, the C Fund, because the 10% drop of the TSP fund includes both the original composition of the index fund and the additional dividends that have been added automatically to that share price. This is a minor detail for investors in general, but something to consider when setting decline thresholds.

***

All three approaches illustrate the art of investing. There is no set formula to maximize investments on either the upside or the downside. We know generally that stock funds have outperformed bond funds over the very long term, but in the short term they can decline significantly in value as well. Declines lead to buying opportunities. We just don't know when they will happen, or how deep the downturns will be. And what has worked in the past may not work in the future; plans made based on past performance may not yield the same results in the future. But based on the evidence of

120 years of investing at least, buying and holding stock funds as they decline appear to provide outsized gains over several decades of consistent investing.

Summary for Strategy IV

Strategy IV is recommended only for TSP investors who can tolerate significant declines in their TSP account balances from time to time.

- Build a minimum amount in the G and/or F Funds depending on your asset allocation strategy. For those following the *Thrift Van Winkle*™ approach, build up $1,000 for each $10,000 you have invested in your TSP using biweekly contributions, so you have a minimum of $1,000 and a maximum of 10% of your overall TSP account in one of the bond funds.

- At each 10% decline in a fund (or other preset percentage decline), transfer a percent or two of your TSP holdings from the G Fund to the declining stock fund via an interfund transfer. If other TSP stock funds in your portfolio have also declined during this time, round them up to the next highest percentage point during the transfer. Repeat this process if one or more of the declining funds falls an additional 10%.

- If stock funds have declined by more than 20%, set your biweekly contribution allocations to 100% stocks.

- Once the declining fund or funds have recovered to their original pre-loss levels or are 10% higher than their pre-loss levels (depending on the severity of the decline), rebuild your G and/or F Fund holdings by allocating all of your biweekly or monthly contributions to the bond funds, as detailed in Strategy III.

STRATEGY V
Build Further Wealth Outside Your TSP Investments

The TSP is an incredibly convenient and extremely cost-effective way for U.S. Government employees and U.S. Armed Services personnel to build wealth over time. However, it is certainly not the only method by which one can build wealth over a working career. By integrating TSP investments into a holistic personal financial strategy, you can achieve truly impressive gains in wealth and, in turn, financial security, while you devote a few years or an entire career to national service.

Strategies I-IV dealt specifically with ways to build wealth via the TSP. Strategy V will review ways to further improve one's financial situation while continuing to invest in the TSP. This strategy focuses on four additional options: (1) paying down consumer debt; (2) saving extra funds for emergencies and other purposes in appropriate savings vehicles; (3) investing in additional tax-advantaged vehicles, such as the Roth Individual Retirement Account (IRA) and the Health Savings Account (HSA) and (4) options for investing in real estate. The final section will describe further opportunities for remaining funds, such as convenient ways to contribute money to deserving charities and other efficient ways to invest extra funds.

Pay Off Consumer Debt

At first glance, paying off personal debt might seem like a strange way to build wealth outside TSP investments. After all, you can invest even while slowly paying down debt, and besides, debt is a fact of life, right? Everyone, it would seem, has debts to pay each month, such as a loan for one or more vehicles, credit card payments, student loan payments, home equity loan payments, and mortgage payments. And, as long as you can make the payments each month, what's the big deal?

Debt hinders the building of wealth in very direct ways. By having to make, for example, a $400 car payment each month, $300 each month to pay student loans, and another $500 for credit cards, you already have to set aside $1,200 each month before you can think about putting money in savings and investing plans, such as the TSP. With a paid-for car, you could invest that $400 a month and watch it grow over the years or save for a down payment on a house. The same holds for the $300 student loan payments if the loan were paid off, and for credit cards. Without these debts, you'd have $1,200 more each month to work with in your budget. In other words, when you can keep more of your take-home pay, you have more funds with which to build wealth faster, and you can breathe a little easier too.

Imagine how great it would feel to have no debt payments each month, except perhaps a mortgage payment. If you had no debt, you would only have to pay for necessities such as rent, food, gas, utility bills, and insurance—the rest of your income would be *yours to keep*. How much more could you do with that extra money in your pocket? How much more could you contribute to your TSP accounts or save up for something big, if you had fewer debt payments each month? Imagine the true wealth you could build if, instead of paying the car loan companies and credit card companies and banks, you could pay *yourself* those payments each month!

Why should banks get rich and not you?

The first edition of this book highlighted that according to the Federal Reserve, in July 2008, Americans owed $2.58 trillion in consumer debt (debt that was not secured by real estate). Over one-third of that amount—37%, or $970 billion—was owed on revolving credit, such as credit cards. This represented an increase of 26% since 2003.[50] By September 2019, consumer debt had grown to $4.149 trillion.[51]

According to the Federal Reserve Board's Survey of Consumer Finances in 2016, one-third of households had at least one vehicle loan, and the average loan was $17,200. Over 43% of family households reported having credit card debt, and those balances averaged $5,700. Almost one-fourth of U.S. households, or 22.4%, had education loans which averaged $34,200.[52]

When we talk about building wealth, we ought to refer to one's entire net worth, meaning the sum of savings and total assets, minus all debt. The U.S. Federal Reserve defines "net worth" as "the difference between families' gross assets and their liabilities."[53] If you have $50,000 in your TSP and in other savings accounts, but owe $50,000 on credit cards and a car or motorcycle (which *depreciate* or lose value over time), have you really built up any "wealth"? While you have saved up and invested a tidy sum in the TSP and in savings accounts, since you owe so much to creditors, your total net worth in this scenario is essentially zero.*

Consider also that, while you are receiving interest and dividend payments in the TSP, each of your debts is charging you interest—and in many cases considerable interest. With a balance of $6,000 on a credit card charging 15% interest, you will pay almost $500 *in addition* to the $6,000 original amount for the privilege of borrowing that money from the credit card company, assuming you pay off that amount in a year. That same $6,000 in a bank account collecting 2% interest would yield just over $120 in a year. The difference between owing $6,000 on a credit card and keeping that same $6,000 in your own bank account is $620 over one year. Once the debt is paid and you no longer have to make monthly payments of $540, you can put those debt payments to work for you by contributing more to your TSP, saving up for a house or car, or just saving for a rainy day in an interest-bearing savings account. After paying off those credit cards and other consumer debts for good, *you* control your own money.

Thus, by paying off your consumer debts, you improve your net worth, and you can then truly concentrate on building wealth by increasing the amount you invest in the TSP and other savings plans.

There are myriad approaches to paying off debt. Library bookshelves are lined with personal finance books advocating this or that approach to managing or paying down debt. While their approaches to debt management might differ in some respects, they all have a few concepts in common.

First, know how much you owe. List all of your total debts—the total amount you owe on each credit card, your car loan(s), your student loan(s),

---

* Notice too that income is not the same as wealth, as discussed in the introduction to this book. The news is filled with stories of superstar athletes and entertainers who make millions of dollars in income, but they have to declare bankruptcy because they spend too much. While those earning high incomes have the potential to build significant wealth, many fail to do so and end up broke.

boat loan(s), personal loan(s) etc.—and include your minimum monthly payment and the percentage interest rate for each debt.

Next, know how much you spend each month. Note each expense you incur for the month, starting with rent/mortgage, utilities (electricity, gas, cable, internet, and phone service), food (at home and eating/drinking out), debt payments, clothing, and entertainment and vacations. Track these expenses.

The purpose of this exercise is to determine whether your income is greater than your expenses, or vice versa. It also provides you some insight into where your hard-earned money is going. Any surprises? How much are you spending to eat out, versus eating at home? Do you have any redundant expenses, such as a cell phone bill and a home phone bill? How much are you spending on clothes, shoes, entertainment, or on "weekend getaways"?

To get serious about paying off debts for good—one goal of this Strategy—look for areas to cut back spending and devote that extra money each month to paying off one debt at a time. Cut back, for example, on eating out to only once a week, or not at all. Cut back on "drinking out," as well: Brew your coffee at home and do not drink alcohol outside the house since alcoholic beverages, wine, and beer are sold in restaurants and bars at up to three times wholesale.[54] Plan your meals for the week, and shop at the grocery store with a list for those meals (supermarkets design their stores for maximum impulse-buying opportunities). Suggest alternatives when your friends or family want to go out to eat or watch a new movie, such as a potluck dinner or renting a movie. Avoid buying new clothes or planning any vacations until you have paid off your major debts. You can also look to cut back in other areas, such as dropping to basic cable (or dropping cable altogether), shopping around for better car insurance perhaps with a higher deductible (see Strategy VI), or reducing cell and home phone service.

There are many books and sites devoted to budgeting and cutting costs out of monthly expenses. The point here is that even the small reductions can add up over time, and the extra $30 or $50 each month will help to reduce debts that much more quickly.

Which Method To Choose?

There are essentially three approaches to paying off your debts. There is the "debt snowball" approach (I prefer the term "debt melt-off"); the "debt avalanche" approach, which is sometimes called "debt stacking" or "debt rolldown;" and then there is what I would call the "minimum payments" approach.

Dave Ramsey is perhaps the staunchest advocate of paying off debts as quickly and aggressively as possible. In his Financial Peace series of books and workshops, he recommends paying off debts according to what he calls the "Debt Snowball" method. Simply order your debts from smallest to largest amount and put any extra money in your budget to the lowest debt amount first to pay it off as quickly as possible. You pay the minimum necessary to the other debts. Once that first debt is paid off, you then apply the entire amount you had been paying on the first debt toward the second debt, in addition to the minimum payment on the second debt to pay it down more quickly. Continue this method, until all of your debts are paid off.[55]

The term "debt snowball" can appear at first to be a misnomer—the debt itself is not "snowballing" or growing larger (though sometimes it feels like it!), but rather the debt payments you are throwing at various debts are gradually snowballing. I like to think of it more as a "debt melt-off," since you are trying to melt away those debts.

Separately, in her book *Pay It Down!* Jean Chatzky suggests a slightly alternative method. Instead of ranking the debt from smallest to largest, she suggests ranking the debt by interest rate and paying the highest interest-rate debt first. The repayment pattern is the same as for paying down the smallest amounts first but based on interest instead of total debt owed. Put any extra money toward the highest-interest debt to pay it off, and once that first debt is paid off, add that payment amount to the second debt in addition to the minimum payment on it, and so on. Again, the debts in this method are ordered according to interest payments, not size of debt[56]. While she does not call it by name, this is the "debt avalanche" or "debt stacking" method. (The personal finance commentator Suze Orman also advocates this approach, which she calls the "credit card roll-down" method.[57])

Below is an example list of personal debts to illustrate how these two types of payment plans would work:

Debts	Amount Owed	Interest Rate
1) Car loan	$16,000	5.90%
2) Undergraduate school student loan	$5,200	4.50%
3) Graduate school student loan	$13,600	6.20%
4) Credit card A	$2,300	0.0%
5) Credit card B	$7,700	12.00%
6) Department store card	$700	7.50%
7) Personal loan	$2,500	32%
Total owed:	**$45,500**	

If the individual holding these debts were to pay them off from smallest to largest amount owed, in the "debt snowball" or "debt meltdown" method, she would list her debts and pay them in this order:

Low-to-High Payment Plan	Amount Owed	Interest
1) Department store card	$700	7.50%
2) Credit card A	$2,300	0.0%
3) Personal loan	$2,500	32%
4) Undergraduate school student loan	$5,200	4.50%
5) Credit card B	$7,700	12.00%
6) Graduate school student loan	$13,600	6.20%
7) Car loan	$16,000	5.90%

Starting with the lowest debt first, this individual would pay off the department store card debt first, and then she would apply those same monthly payments to pay off credit card A, in addition to the minimum payments already being paid monthly to credit card A. Once that was paid off, the entire monthly payment used to pay off credit card A would then go toward the next higher amount, in addition to the minimum payments already being paid, in this case the undergraduate student loan. And so forth.

However, if this individual were to pay off the debts based on interest rates, in the "debt stacking" or "roll-down" method, she would list her debts and pay them in this order:

Interest Rate Payment Plan	Amount Owed	Interest
1) Personal loan	$2,500	32%
2) Credit card B	$7,700	12.00%
3) Department store card	$700	7.50%
4) Graduate school student loan #2	$13,600	6.20%
5) Car loan	$16,000	5.90%
6) Undergraduate school student loan	$5,200	4.50%
7) Credit card A	$2,300	0%

In the interest rate payment plan, the personal loan would be paid off first, followed by credit card A, and then the department store card. In each instance, once the previous amount was paid off, the amount going to that debt would be added to the next debt on the list, in addition to the minimum payment for that debt, and so forth until all the debts are paid off.

The "personal loan" category is illustrative of types of short-term loans such as payday or title loans. You need cash in a hurry, you put up your next paycheck or car as collateral, you agree to pay a significant fee or short-term interest rate, and you get cash with few if any questions asked. Interest rates on these loans can be quite significant. According to the Pew Charitable Trust, annual percentage rates for payday loans can reach 300% to 500% on an annualized basis, although most who take out these loans don't realize what they're paying long-term. Pew cited examples of a $1,250 loan being paid off over 10 months and requiring a "fee" of $2,450 for the loan, or a $500 loan to be paid off in 5 months in return for a "fee" of $595.[58] Title loans can be particularly pernicious, since ownership of your car is at stake.

Logically, paying off the highest-interest-rate debts first makes sense, because the higher interest rate debts cost you more money over the long term than low-rate debts. This is particularly the case with extremely high-interest rate loans or high-rate loans backed by important collateral such as your vehicle.

Under otherwise normal circumstances, though, when you don't have these kinds of loans in your life, paying off the larger amounts first might take considerable time to accomplish. If the $7,700 credit card were your first debt with the highest interest rate, this would take some time to knock off compared to the third debt, which is only $700.

It is very satisfying to pay off any debt, large or small, for good. In the low-to-high pay-off example above, the individual would have paid off two debts and started paying down a third before the individual in the second example finished paying off her first major debt, credit card B (leaving aside the usurious "personal loan"). Paying off those smaller amounts first would build confidence that these debts can all be paid off in their entirety. With the smaller debts paid off quickly, the extra payments can be applied more quickly to the larger debts. Your personal situation will of course dictate which method you use.

One popular suggestion until a few years ago was to use a home equity line of credit to pay off high-interest-rate credit cards. Those who advocated this plan pointed out that a person will pay less in interest on a home loan than on the credit card payments, and the interest on this debt is tax-deductible. With home prices having recovered, this type of debt-management approach is making a comeback.

However, this technique has multiple potential problems. For one, it is too easy to use the credit cards or other open, revolving accounts again once they are paid off to buy even more stuff. When this happens, you have to pay the extra house debt *and* the new credit card balances! Moreover, those who take out a loan against their house to pay off credit card debts can opt for a 10- or 20-year period over which to repay the loan. While they might save more on interest payments initially, the life of the loan has been greatly extended and, thus, they are less motivated to pay off the debt quickly and permanently. Finally, and most importantly, unlike credit card debts that are not secured by any of your property, the home-loan debt is now secured by your house. In other words, if you don't pay the home-loan debt, you could lose your house! Paying off debt by using more debt backed by an asset like your house carries some risk and should be avoided.

Lastly, there is the "minimum payments" approach. In this low-interest environment, this has some appeal, no doubt. You can get great 0% or very-low-interest rate deals on a one- or two-year payoff plan through a store credit card, a good deal financed through a dealership, or a debt transfer to a 0% card that lasts a year or two. With this approach, you continue to make payments without paying "interest," enjoy your new purchases, and you can continue to invest in the TSP and other investments (such as a personal residence).

That said, there are some challenges with this approach too. Almost always, the 0% interest deal is meant to spur more (impulse) buying. It is easier to rationalize a $2,000 purchase when payments are spread over 24 months (just $83 a month, and no interest!) than putting down twenty Benjamins plus a few extra for tax on the counter to finish the transaction then and there. For a lot of us, that's a good chunk of take-home pay for a few weeks! And with an open account and higher spending limit, there is the ease of adding a couple of items now and then, just out of convenience. A study as far back as 1979 found that the more credit cards a person has, the more likely he or she is to make larger purchases at department stores.[59]

It is a fact that you spend more when you buy with credit or a credit card. One 2001 study found that participants who were told they could use a credit card were willing to pay up to 100% more for sporting tickets than those who were told they would pay with cash.[60] And the tendency to spend more than anticipated appears to increase with contactless payments (with your iPhone or Android phone) too. A survey cited by a UK source suggested that three in five overspend when paying via contactless, 59% said they tended to spend more when not using physical cash, and 72% said use of contactless payments caused them to spend on impulse.[61]

Also, when you have more accounts to keep track of, there is a chance of missing a payment or of forgetting that the rate was only good for 12 or 24 months. In either case, if you misread or misremember the conditions of the 0% or low-interest account, you'll pay a pretty hefty interest rate. We're all smart enough and capable enough to keep track of the payments, use spreadsheets, and use calendar reminders, but sometimes life gets away from us. Sometimes an illness strikes, perhaps we get furloughed, things happen. Life happens. With fewer accounts open, there are fewer things to keep track of or to worry about.

These observations are not meant as value judgements. You could and probably have had long discussions with friends and family on the merits and challenges of each approach above. With that third child on the way, should you upgrade to a new or lightly used minivan or SUV that comes with five years of payments, or keep (or pay cash for) a beater? Do you take that trip to Disney when the kids are still young, even if financing on credit, or wait while you continue to buckle down to pay everything off? What about that weekend getaway with a loved one? It is an incredible feeling to have zero debt, but there is also peace-of-mind knowing your vehicle won't break down on the way to daycare in the morning. And the memories of that special trip with your loved ones or your little ones spent with Mickey and friends (when they still believe…) can last a lifetime.

All things considered, I believe you do have greater peace of mind and peace of heart when you have fewer rather than more debts. The pictures will offer great memories, certainly, but you will also remember the six months it took to pay off those cards after the trip ended (if that is what the trip required). You'll see those scratches and dents multiply on that new-ish vehicle months after driving it off the lot, and you'll remember that you still owe five figures on it. You'll think of what you could do with that money, if you didn't have to make that payment each and every month. In short, those memories and conveniences can come with both financial and psychological burdens when paid for on credit.

Incorporating Debt Payoff with TSP Investing

Here are some ways to approach paying down debt while also investing a minimum in the TSP.

First, list all of your debts, as above. List them both by total amounts, smallest to largest, then by interest, largest to smallest. Which calls out to you to tackle first? Definitely tackle those usurious accounts such as payday or title loans first, if you have any. Then close those accounts and be sure to keep the proof that you did pay them in full and closed them with a $0 balance in case any "errors" appear on your credit reports or if debt collectors start contacting you errantly (or fraudulently!) about the already-closed accounts. Promise yourself you'll never take out one of those loans again.

Second, make and stick to a budget, building in extra funds to start either a debt snowball/melt-off or debt avalanche. Budgeting is beyond the scope of this book, but a realistic budget will help you generally to stay on track in the coming months. As part of this approach, set up auto pay for the minimum amounts on all the debt payments except the one you've decided you'll tackle first, along with account reminders that they are about to be paid. But only do this if you're confident you won't overdraft your checking or savings account! You don't want to have to pay an overdraft penalty due to inconvenient timing of the autopayment in relation to getting paid. Then start to make those extra payments to the debt you've identified as the primary one to pay off.

Third, ask yourself if you should refinance any of that debt. You might get a better interest rate offer as your credit score improves or if rates drop suddenly again. If you can drop an 8% or 10% credit card account to 0%, then great! Knock out the other debts and return to that one later. But if it's just a matter of a few percentage points, maybe it's better to avoid opening more accounts if your goal truly is to get out and stay out of debt.

Fourth, one very beneficial approach is to graph progress of paying off your debts over time. This could be as simple as getting lined graphing paper, plotting the owed amount on the y-axis and dates on the x-axis, and start with "today" in the bottom-left corner. Start small—put your consumer debts on the graph, but not mortgage or student loans. This will help you maintain focus on the pressing consumer debts to pay off now. Later, once you have paid off these debts, you can revert focus to student loans or/and mortgage debt too. Hang it on the refrigerator or somewhere motivational, and you'll see the debt melt slowly over the weeks and months.

Once these are in place, revisit your budget to see how much you can still invest in the TSP while paying down debt. Give yourself wiggle-room. If you can handle a 3% contribution rate, great! You'll get most of the government match. If you can contribute 5%, you'll definitely get the match, and you'll continue to grow your investments that much faster. But if you find yourself too strapped, drop your contributions to a 1% or 2% rate as a minimum. This way, you get in the habit of investing and get half of the government contribution rate, too. Only stop your contributions in an emergency, but be sure to reinstate them at the earliest possible time.

Next, look for extra money-making opportunities. Are there opportunities for overtime? Is it possible to take a part-time job, even if just a few hours a month? Are there promotable opportunities that perhaps won't pay extra now, but will in a few months or year or two with that next promotion? Not only will this provide some extra cash to throw at your debts, but it will also provide an outlet that avoids the possibility of spending more money somewhere else. The faster you pay off your debts for good, the faster you can start significantly increasing your TSP contributions and other savings and investment plans.

As you feel more confident in paying down debt and investing in your TSP funds, you can consider graphing your increasing investments together with the debt chart. Just as it is very satisfying to pay off debts for good, it is also very satisfying to watch one's savings and investments increase gradually as well. But do this based on your investing strategy. If you are a set-and-forget investor, stick with that. Set it, and forget it. If you want to keep track on a regular basis, be ready for drops in value too. For those who lived through the 2000-2 and 2008-9 downturns, the drops were indeed painful to watch, and the values seemed to never recover. But they eventually did, and they will after the next downturn too. The graphing exercise reinforces an important positive habit of saving and investing for the long term, even as you pay off outstanding debts.

Keep in mind that by reducing your TSP contributions to pay down debt, your biweekly pay will increase as your pre-tax TSP contributions revert to after-tax income (unless you were contributing to the Roth TSP with already-taxed income—more on this to follow). But because you have switched some of those pre-tax contributions to regular pay, more of your pay is taxed. Thus, your post-tax income will not increase by the full amount of your pre-tax TSP contributions, as these formerly pre-tax contributions are now reduced by taxes as part of your income. If you reduce your $200 pre-tax contributions to $100, the extra $100 that is now paid to you as part of your regular income will be taxed, reducing it by the taxed amount for both federal and state taxes to, for example, $80.

After a few months, consider where you are with your budget. Is it realistic? Are you able to stick with it? Or is it too burdensome, too restrictive? Be realistic, and adjust expectations accordingly.

One other thing to consider is your relationship with money in general. Are you a problem spender? "Oniomania" is a compulsive shopping disorder that affects over 1 in 20 (5.8%) in the United States.[62] That rate represents those afflicted with the clinical disorder, but there are shades of "shopaholism," if one can characterize it as such (the debate continues to this day: The most recent *Diagnostic and Statistical Manual of Mental Disorders* or DSM-5 does not include shopping addiction as an official addiction, though some believe it should[63]). The financial website creditdonkey.com found surprisingly high response rates to some classic signs of shopaholism, such as how many experience a rush of excitement when they buy something (47.4%), how many buy something just because it's on sale (31.7%), and how many have items in their closet that still are in store wrappers or have tags on them (24.4%). Perhaps the most revealing positive responses were to questions about buying on credit because they don't have enough money (19.1%) and buying to improve one's mood (11% responded "frequently," which tracks more closely with the official rate of oniomania in the United States).[64] If you see yourself in these responses, look into shopping addiction therapy. This is particularly important for those with security clearances, because signs of spending issues can impact the reinvestigation process. Regardless, there is absolutely no shame in asking for help!

No doubt about it, paying off all of one's debts can take considerable time and effort, especially for recent college graduates who perhaps have credit card balances, student loans, and car payments as well. While paying down the debts might at first feel like an agonizingly slow process, it is well worth the effort as you watch the debts disappear once and for all and as you gain greater control over your personal finances.

Once you have paid off all of your consumer debts—and perhaps have just a mortgage left to pay—you can now increase your emergency fund and your contributions to the TSP and to other tax-advantaged vehicles, described below.

Save For Major Purchases Using Appropriate Savings Accounts

Now that you have paid down your debt, use the money you had been allocating to paying off debts to increase your emergency fund to at least three or four months of regular expenses. Again, make sure this savings is in an FDIC- or NCUA-insured account.* There's no need to take any risk with this money, just keep it available in an account that is quickly accessible in case you have a real emergency. This way, if your car breaks down and you

---

* As noted in Pre-Investment Strategy 2, FDIC stands for Federal Deposit Insurance Corporation (FDIC) and NCUA stands for "National Credit Union Administration." Both are insurance programs that protect savings-account holders in the unlikely event that the insured bank or credit union fails. 2010 represented the peak rate for bank failures after the 2008-9 financial crisis, when 157 banks failed, while 92 failed in 2011 and 51 in 2012. Those who had money in bank deposits insured by the FDIC were able to get their money back up to the insured amount, even after those banks failed.

need $2,000 to fix it, you can draw from the emergency fund instead of putting it all on a credit card to be paid off over the coming year (and probably with interest added to it). If you have to use your emergency fund, build it back up again for future emergencies.

Also, now that you've paid off your consumer debts, you can increase your TSP contributions from 3-5% to 7-10%, or even up to the contribution limit for the year. Since you've been budgeting carefully, you will not miss this increased TSP contribution as you start to pay yourself first instead of paying the credit card companies or banks.

Now it is time to plan for any upcoming major purchases. Do you want to buy a house? Are you shopping for a car, or preparing for a big family vacation? Prioritize your next major purchases and the time needed for each purchase. In order to focus your savings goals, save for only one major purchase at a time. If you are planning to purchase a home, do not plan to purchase a car or take a major vacation. Certainly do not do so on credit, as major purchases on credit before purchasing a home might negatively impact your credit score—the better your credit score (and the more you have saved for a down-payment), the better interest rate you will receive on your mortgage.* Only after completing the purchase of a home should you consider saving for the next major purchase, such as a new or previously owned car.

Saving for major purchases can be done through a basic interest-bearing, FDIC- or NCUA-insured savings account. Again, nothing fancy, and these savings should *not* be in stocks or stock mutual funds, as these might decline significantly in value between the time you start saving until the time you need the money to make your purchase. Remember, the more you have available for a down-payment for a large purchase—and the more debt you have paid off—the better your interest rate will be. If you pay with cash, you will not have to worry about paying any interest (and you might be able to negotiate a better deal in the process!).

---

* Also consider a 15-year fixed-rate mortgage instead of a 30-year mortgage: you'll generally get a better interest rate on a 15-year mortgage, and you'll pay off your mortgage much faster than a 30-year mortgage

"Pre-Purchase" Your Next Big Item

One way to prepare for a major purchase is to calculate in advance how much a monthly payment would be if you were to make the purchase today. But instead of actually making the purchase, put that hypothetical new monthly payment into a savings account each month. Try to do this pre-purchase exercise each month for six months or a year to see whether the payments fit your budget, even during expensive occasions of the year such as year-end holidays, summer vacations, birthdays, and anniversaries.

You can perform this exercise ahead of buying a car, for example. First, decide how much you plan to spend on a car. Then, determine what the payments would be for that car at a realistic percentage rate over three or four years. Instead of purchasing the car immediately with an actual loan, put the hypothetical monthly debt payment amount into a savings account for a year—again, to determine if these payments fit your budget throughout the year. Be sure to add an extra amount for the increased cost of insurance and property taxes, to ensure the pre-purchase exercise is realistic.

For example, you want to buy a car that costs $20,000, but you do not have the money saved up for this purchase. Monthly payments on a $20,000 loan at 3% interest over four years would come to $443. Add to this the cost of insurance, taxes, and maintenance—say, just over $100 a month for ease of calculation, although this amount will vary depending on your location—for a total of around $550 that you would be paying for this new car if you bought it now.

Instead of making the purchase immediately, save this amount each and every month over the course of a year to see if you can truly afford the payment. After a year at 2% interest, you'll have approximately $6,670 to use as a substantial down payment for this car. Incidentally, you'll find that now one-year-old $20,000 car for sale at a cheaper price. (Depending on the make and model, new cars depreciate by 20% or more within a year after leaving the new-car lot, and they depreciate another 10% or more after the second and third years of ownership). With a higher down-payment, you'd probably be eligible for a lower interest rate. In fact, you could continue this exercise for another year and you'd most likely have enough saved up to pay cash for the now two-year-old car on the spot. With a four-year payment, you'd still have 24 monthly payments of $443 still to make before owning it outright.

	Amount Saved for Car	Cumulative Debt Payments for New Car	Car Value
Year 1	$6,671	($5,316)	$16,000
Year 2*	$13,477 *Month 25: buy 2-year-old car @$14,000	($10,632)	$14,000
Year 3	$20,421 ($6,162 still in your pocket after buying a $14,000 car)	($15,948)* *with a four-year loan, still not paid off after year three!	$12,000

Assuming that a $20,000 car depreciates 20% in value the first year and 10% each of the next two years, the person who saves the same as a car payment for the first two years instead of buying the car on credit could purchase the now two-year-old car (assuming 30% depreciation) with cash at month 25 and have $50 left in savings, while the person who bought the car new on a four-year payment plan would still owe $10,300 for the same two-year-old car. By continuing to save the equivalent of a car payment in year three (minus the amount for insurance and taxes), the person who bought the two-year-old car will have over $6,100 in savings, while the person making payments will have $0 in savings and will still owe $5,227 by the end of year three for the car, which is now worth about $12,000 in both cases.

Saving up to buy a car also enables you to avoid getting into the trap of leasing a vehicle. Leasing is like a three-year rental—you make monthly payments, and then you have to give back the car once the lease expires. Yes, you can get another car (brand new!) on another lease, but then you're paying to lease again. The car is never yours, you have no equity in the car, and the payments never end because you'll need a new car once the three-year lease is over. With the above approach (and even with the four-year loan payments) you own the vehicle after that last payment. No more payments, you get to keep the car, and it still retains some value even if it has depreciated.

That said, do you need a car (or a second or third car)? Especially in a major metropolitan area, can you use public transportation and/or a car-share program instead? Perhaps your office would reimburse some or all of your public transportation expenses, and even if the car-share comes to $100 or $150 a month, you could break even when comparing total ownership costs for a vehicle (aside from the actual purchase price) when considering local and county taxes, insurance, gas, and parking. If you find that you only really need a car a couple of times a month, it could be more economical to forgo a purchase and use a car share service.

***

The same pre-purchase exercise can be done before buying a house. Let's say your rent is currently $1,000 a month, and you want to buy a house that costs around $300,000 (this was the median sales price of homes in the United States in September 2019[65]). With a 10% down payment, your mortgage would be $270,000. Financed at 4.5% interest—and including property taxes, property insurance, and mortgage insurance—your monthly payment would be about $1,800 a month. As you prepare to make your purchase, put the difference between your rent and the mortgage (just over $800) into savings each month to get a feel for how your lifestyle would change after making the purchase. Of course, you would be able to deduct the interest portion of your house debt from your taxes, but you'll also want to maintain and upgrade your property, so for the purpose of this exercise, we'll say that the interest deduction and yearly maintenance costs even out.

After a few months of "pre-purchasing" the house, you should have a pretty good feel for whether or not you can afford this payment—and, at the same time, you'll be saving for your upcoming new home, too. In this example, by the end of twelve months, you'll have saved about $9,700 from the $800 each month and 2% interest in a savings account. After another year of "pre-purchasing" the house, you'll be close to that 10% down payment for the home. You'll also have a better feel for whether you are able to afford the monthly debt payments.

Avoid Taking Out TSP Loans

The TSP allows participants in "pay" status to borrow generally up to $50,000 through two types of loans: a general-purpose loan and a residential loan. Repayment for a general-purpose loan can range from one to five years, and repayment for a residential loan can range from one to fifteen years. A TSP participant in "pay" status can hold one of each of these loans at any one time. The loan must be taken from your own contributions and earnings on those contributions and cannot be taken from matching contributions.

While taking a loan from the TSP is fairly simple to do, just because you can take out a loan does not mean you *should* take out a loan. After all, *a loan is a loan is a loan*—instead of borrowing from a bank, you are borrowing in this case from your future growth potential of your TSP account.

A commonly held view is that by using funds from your TSP account, you are simply borrowing from yourself and paying yourself interest on the amount borrowed. But there are three major reasons why borrowing from your TSP hinders the building of wealth.

First, you are taxed twice when repaying a TSP loan. In contrast to your initial tax-free TSP biweekly or monthly contributions, you pay back the loan with after-tax money, which means you lose up to a quarter of your repayment to taxes. You are repaying each $1 loan with around $0.75 or $0.80 of after-tax income. And then, when you withdraw the money in your older years, the money is taxed again. Your low-interest "loan" from yourself is taxed twice—once going in and once coming out.

Second, this loan becomes a new form of "golden handcuffs," because you are stuck in your job until you pay off your loan. "When you leave Federal service, you must repay your loan in full within 90 days after your separation is reported to the TSP," according to the TSP. If you do not pay the loan amount back in full, the outstanding loan becomes a taxable distribution and you would be charged income tax on the entire loan (assuming it was not a loan from your Roth TSP) as well as a 10% penalty. Moreover, "[y]ou will not be able to withdraw your TSP account until your loan is closed by either payment in full or taxable distribution," TSP warns.[66]

Third, you lose the benefits of potential growth. As the TSP website further warns, "[w]hen you take a TSP loan, you sacrifice the earnings that might have accrued on the borrowed money, had it remained in your TSP account," especially if you had invested in growth-oriented funds. "Although you pay the loan amount back to your TSP account with interest," the site adds, "the amount of interest paid may be less than what you might have earned if the money had remained in your TSP account."[67]

For example, let's say you borrowed $10,000 from your TSP to help finance the purchase of a house. After selling the fund shares to withdraw the money, the TSP funds from which you borrowed rise by 20%. Had you left the $10,000 in your TSP, it would have been worth $12,000—you've essentially missed out on $2,000 of growth! You'll also have to use after-tax income, so that you'd have to earn $13,000 or more depending on your federal, state, and local tax brackets (not to mention Social Security and Medicare taxes) to pay back the original $10,000 by the time you've paid off the loan. And the payments would probably be paid back into the funds you sold earlier, but since they're higher now, you're investing at a higher price.

To avoid this, it is best to plan sufficiently ahead of time by saving for or "pre-purchasing" major items separately in an interest-bearing savings account.

Investing in the 'Roth' TSP and Other Tax-Advantaged Vehicles

In 2012, the TSP inaugurated the "Roth TSP" option. Participants can now opt to make contributions with after-tax dollars, and by doing so, not only are the TSP funds tax-free, withdrawals after 59½ are too.

The Roth TSP is named after Delaware Senator William V. Roth, who sponsored the legislation in 1997 enacting a special type of Individual Retirement Account (IRA) called the "Roth IRA." The Roth IRA allowed individuals to invest taxed income that would grow over time and could be withdrawn tax-free in retirement.[68] The driving idea was that income should be taxed only once, in this case, immediately when a worker earned it. Earnings from saving and investing the already-taxed funds should be tax-free, according to this concept.

The Roth IRA and its older sibling, the traditional IRA, differ from 401(k)s and the TSP in important ways. Neither is sponsored by an employer, so investors in these vehicles do not get any sort of matching contribution. In addition to the $19,500 that can be invested in the TSP as of 2020 as either traditional or Roth contributions, those under 50 years of age are eligible to put up to $6,000 into an IRA. Those 50 and over can put an additional $5,500 in the TSP and an additional $1,000 in an IRA as "catch-up" contributions to make up for their younger years, when they were perhaps unable to contribute as much in their tax-advantaged plans.*

---

* The IRS increases these amounts from time to time, and updates can be found on the IRS website.

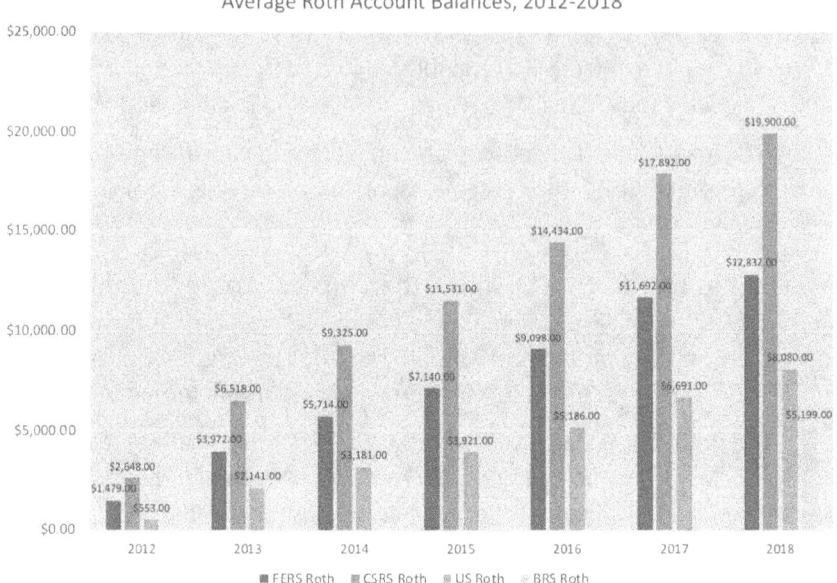

Average Roth TSP balances have grown steadily since the option was introduced in 2012.

Individual investors can deduct the amounts invested in a traditional IRA account from his or her income taxes up to a maximum modified adjusted gross income (MAGI) limit of $75,000 for single filers and $124,000 for married filers filing jointly in 2020. (These limits also gradually increase from year to year.) When this money is withdrawn after turning 59½, he or she must pay taxes on the amount withdrawn. Therefore, owners of a traditional IRA save some on taxes initially but have to pay taxes each year that money is withdrawn from the traditional IRA.

Contributions to a Roth IRA are made with after-tax money and cannot be deducted from taxes the year the investment is made. But any withdrawals taken after turning 59½ are tax free, unlike money withdrawn from the traditional TSP and traditional IRAs. There are income limits for Roth IRAs, with those who are single making less than $139,000 in MAGI and those who are married making less than $206,000 able to contribute to Roth IRAs in 2020.*

---

* Those who make more than these limits can still invest in a traditional IRA, but the amount invested is not tax-deductible, and the gains on these investments will be taxed once withdrawn after turning 59½ unless it is later converted to a Roth IRA (and taxes are paid accordingly).

Like TSP accounts, money in both the Traditional IRA and the Roth IRA can be withdrawn from the year the account owner turns 59½, without owing any penalties. The owner of a traditional IRA must begin taking minimum withdrawals for the tax year in which they turn 72 (the IRS publishes "Required Minimum Distribution" tables that dictate the minimum withdrawal amounts). In contrast, there are no mandatory withdrawal minimums for owners of Roth IRA accounts. Roth IRA owners, therefore, can continue to keep their money in the Roth IRA and let that money grow for as long as they desire.

The Roth IRA offers one other important feature. Because you've already paid taxes on the money you contribute to the Roth IRA, you can withdraw any of that contributed money at any time without any penalty. (You will have to pay taxes and a 10% penalty on any of the gains in the Roth IRA if they are withdrawn before reaching minimum withdrawal age, however.) Thus, a Roth IRA can serve as an additional emergency savings vehicle of last resort.

For example, let's say you've invested $3,000 in a Roth IRA per year for the past five years. Over the five years the Roth IRA has grown steadily, and now the $15,000 in total investments is worth $25,000. You can withdraw the original $15,000 at any time for whatever purpose without paying any penalties, although you would forfeit any potential future gains from the withdrawn amount. You cannot withdraw the remaining $10,000 growth portion of the Roth IRA, however, without paying taxes and penalties on it.

Roth IRAs became immensely popular, so much so that Roth 401(k)s started to be offered by 2006 (after Senator Roth had passed away in 2003). The TSP followed six years later. Unlike IRAs, there are no income limits restricting eligibility to contribute to the Roth TSP option. Participants can mix and match contributions, so that a portion goes to the traditional TSP and the rest goes as after-tax dollars to the Roth TSP. The combined total of your Roth and tax-deferred traditional contributions cannot exceed the elective deferral limits for that year. The government match is only made to your traditional TSP account, since there is no way to tax it as part of your income when the match is made.[69]

Because the elective deferral limit is the same for both the traditional and Roth TSP contributions, an investor could effectively contribute more by maxing out contributions ($19,500 in 2020) to a Roth account, rather than to a traditional account. Because the traditional TSP is taxed when funds are later withdrawn, the $19,500 in contributions for the year would effectively be less than the $19,500 invested with after-tax dollars in a Roth account, which are not taxed when withdrawn.

Investing in Both the TSP and a Roth IRA

As noted earlier, you can invest in the Roth IRA even when you are contributing to the TSP, assuming you are under the income limits detailed in the previous section. Of course, those who are just starting out or who are early in their government or military service careers are limited in how much they can contribute to either the TSP or a Roth IRA because of the relatively low starting salaries. And older participants who are more established in their careers, too, might be constrained by financial obligations related to raising or caring for family. While laudable, contributing the maximum $25,500 ($19,500 to the TSP and $6,000 to a Roth IRA) on a basic government or military salary would be extremely difficult, and probably unnecessary (money and investing isn't everything, after all). This is especially true for those with young children or other financial goals.

But you wouldn't need to max both out. Don't think about investing in a Roth IRA until you are able to invest a minimum of 5% of salary to the TSP, in order to get the full government match. At that point, if you can spare a few extra thousand dollars above your emergency fund, your consumer debt is paid off, and you aren't saving for any large items as outlined in the previous section, you might want to consider investing those funds in a Roth IRA. You can also set up automatic investment plans, so that funds are transferred to a Roth IRA account biweekly, monthly, or quarterly much like your TSP contributions are automatically deducted.

Here are a few reasons why you might want to contribute to both:

- You can use a personal Roth IRA as an additional emergency savings fund, since after-tax contributions can be withdrawn tax-free any time; withdrawing funds from the TSP is more complicated and usually involves taking out a loan.

- If you don't like the investment options in the TSP (either the regular or Roth option), you have many more options in a personal Roth IRA.

- You can take advantage of additional educational and other resources that many Roth IRA funds provide to learn more about saving and investing, and how other goals (such as saving for college) might be best incorporated as well.

- Your spouse can invest in a Roth IRA too, whether or not s/he is employed, as long as your combined MAGI is below the IRS limits detailed previously.

The only way for TSP participants to have access to their funds before the year they turn 59.5 is by requesting a "loan." This is true for obtaining funds from a Roth TSP too. Thus, a Roth IRA is more flexible and can serve as an extra financial cushion in times of need, in addition to providing additional investment options. You should also be less tempted to spend the funds in a Roth IRA compared to those in a checking or savings account.

You also have more flexibility on when to invest in a Roth IRA; you can put some after-tax money from bonuses into your Roth IRA, for example. And your spouse can also contribute to a Roth IRA, too. He or she is also generally eligible to put up to $6,000 into a Roth IRA in addition to your own, keeping in mind income limits.

In this way, you are diversifying your tax obligations in your later years: Your traditional TSP and government matching withdrawals will be taxable, while your Roth IRA and/or TSP contributions will be tax-free. And if you continue to work after serving with the government, you can continue to contribute to a Roth IRA in addition to any other company-sponsored plans, as long as you do not exceed the income limits.

Roth IRA investors can invest in alternative areas to further diversify their portfolios, since companies that offer Roth IRAs provide investors with many more investment options beyond those offered in the TSP. As noted in Strategy II, some portfolio strategists recommend investing in real estate, commodities, and international small-cap and international bond funds in addition to mainstream stock and bond index funds. And if you simply don't like the investment options offered in the TSP, you could just contribute enough to the G Fund to get the government match, and invest however you wish in a Roth IRA (or other investment options such as real estate, outlined below). Don't forgo the government match, though!

In all, the Roth IRA provides TSP investors with greater flexibility in diversifying both their total investment portfolio and their future tax obligations, once it is time to withdraw these funds. A Roth IRA (or non-deductible IRA for high-income workers) makes an excellent addition to any investment portfolio.

Consider an HDHP with Health Savings Account

On December 8, 2003, President George W. Bush signed legislation enabling the creation of tax-advantaged Health Savings Accounts (HSAs) in conjunction with High Deductible Health Plans (HDHPs). These new types of health accounts were included in legislation creating a Medicare prescription drug benefit. HSAs allow owners of these savings and investment vehicles to add money each year for future health-related expenditures. Unlike Flexible Spending Accounts (FSAs), contributions to HSAs do not need to be spent within the same year and can be kept and added to year after year for long-term growth. They are health-care versions of the TSP and IRA accounts.

HSAs must be used in conjunction with High-Deductible Health Plans (HDHPs), which are a type of health insurance plan that require owners to pay for initial medical expenses up to a certain high-deductible limit. For 2020, the IRS set the maximum upper limits at $6,900 for self-only coverage and $13,800 for family coverage, although individual health insurers often set lower limits. These upper limits are out-of-pocket co-pays and "deductibles," and, because they are higher than deductibles for traditional health insurance, they are called "High-Deductible" plans. Health expenses up to these maximum limits can be paid either from the HSA or out of pocket, and once the upper deductible limits are reached, the insurer covers a greater percentage of the costs associated with health care needs for that year, just like a traditional health insurer.

Because the health insurance *deductible* is higher than traditional health insurance—and individuals are required to pay more out of pocket each year for initial health care needs—the health insurance *premium* (what is paid each pay period for health insurance) is more economical than premiums for non-HDHP health insurance. (Given the special tax considerations of the HSA and the health insurance already provided to U.S. uniformed service members and retirees, HSAs are available only to civilian federal government employees who do not receive Medicare or Tricare.)

While this is a fairly new type of insurance plan, insurance providers in the Federal Employees Health Benefits Program (FEHBP) are increasingly offering HDHPs with HSAs. To sweeten the deal, up to $125 is contributed per month into participants' HSAs, although these contributions can vary from year to year depending on the size of the deductible (the higher the deductible, the more the monthly contribution offered). Those with an HDHP can contribute up to the 2020 maximum-allowed $3,550 for individual plans and $7,100 for those with family coverage to an HSA. Those 55 and over can make catch-up contributions of $1,000. Therefore, participants can add extra to their HSA, in addition to the contributions from insurance providers, as long as total contributions do not exceed the upper limits set by the IRS. Money in HSAs can be used tax-free at any time for health-related expenses, as established by the IRS. After turning 65, the owner of an HSA can use the savings for non-medical expenditures as well, but withdrawals for non-medical expenses will be taxed as regular income.

Much like the TSP, savings and investments in the HSA can enjoy potentially significant growth over time. When opened at an early age, when one usually incurs fewer medical expenses, small contributions would have many decades to grow. Contributing $2,400 a year—$200 per month, some of which might be contributed by the insurance provider—from the age of 25 at a conservative 5% growth rate, will increase to over $306,000 40 years later at age 65, assuming no withdrawals were made for medical expenses over that time. The $2,400 is less than the $3,550 and $7,100 contribution limits for individuals and families in 2020, so more could be saved and used for medical expenses each year, as necessary—and the steady increase in savings over the years provides a family with an expanding cushion for medical needs over the years. Moreover, medical expenses can be paid out-of-pocket as well, to protect the tax-advantage growth in the HSA.

By increasing this initial $2,400 contribution 4% each year (just over the average inflation rate), and if it were to enjoy 8% average gains per year for 40 years, the HSA would grow to almost *$1,140,000,* assuming that health expenses over that time were paid for out of the remaining tax-deductible contributions to the HSA. These are significant sums, compared to what one would have saved tax-free before HSAs were created—that is, nothing at all. And these savings are *in addition to* savings and investments in one's TSP and Roth IRA.

Saving for future health needs is especially important, precisely because we experience more medical needs later in life. According to the Employee Benefit Research Institute, the average couple at age 65 today could need as much as $295,000 for medical-related expenses over their lifetimes. A couple living to 95 could need as much as *$550,000* to cover medical expenses![70] While the extra savings in an HSA might not cover one's entire medical needs later in life, it could provide an additional cushion and go a long way to protecting one's remaining wealth in the TSP, IRAs, real estate, and other savings. And, like these other tax-advantaged savings vehicles, any remaining funds can be passed to family members or charities of the account owner's choice upon the passing of the HSA owner.

Coupled with the monthly contributions offered by insurance providers, contributions to an HSA should be relatively simple to incorporate into a broad investment plan. As you continue to invest in your TSP (and a Roth IRA if possible), simply choose an HDHP with the accompanying HSA, and depending on automatic additions from the insurance company, start by adding $50 or $100 a month to the account—this amount is entirely tax-deductible no matter what your income might be, so your income taxes will be reduced depending on how much you contribute during the year. Your initial goal is to have enough in the HSA to cover the full deductible for the year, which can be accomplished within a year to 18 months assuming no withdrawals for healthcare needs. It will of course take longer for those who need to make withdrawals for healthcare expenses, but at least some of this savings is deposited as an added incentive to help you manage your healthcare needs.

The biweekly premium of an HDHP with HSA is less than traditional plans too, because health insurers allow participants in these plans to manage their own healthcare needs with funds from the HSA before traditional health insurance begins, thereby helping the insurance companies reduce their expenses. However, this also means that those who need more health care over several years will have to draw more from their HSAs initially to meet these greater expenses before hitting the higher yearly deductible.

The tax-advantaged savings aspect of the HSA provides a significant incentive to shop around for better deals on medical expenses. In a personal example, after our family ophthalmologist provided a prescription for new contact lenses (the eye exam was covered by the HDHP insurance), she also offered to sell a year's worth of contacts for $316. Under a traditional plan, we would have worked through the insurance company to pay for the contacts and would therefore not have considered the price of the contacts. However, the insurance company in this case offered a flat $100 to cover the contacts, with the rest coming out of our tax-deductible HSA savings. We compared the doctor's price with those quoted by an online company and a specialty contact provider at a local warehouse store. The online company's price was less expensive than the doctor's quoted rate, at $256 for the year. However, the specialty provider at the warehouse store quoted $179—plus a $30 rebate. With the rebate and the $100 provided by the insurance company, we ended up paying $49 for a year's worth of contacts, $167 less than what we would have paid at the eye doctor's office.

But what about major family emergencies? You can't shop around for emergency services, after all…right?

This is why the deductible is so important, in conjunction with the stipend you might receive and premium savings compared to the more traditional plans. For example, in one year in the early 2010s my family had a number of health incidents. My wife had a baby, who required some additional treatment at the hospital and by specialists for most of the year. I spent some time in the hospital due to a congenital stomach issue I didn't know I had. I also injured my hip, which required some tests and several months of physical therapy (which was covered by insurance). We were all ok by the end of the year, but it was a hectic year.

We had a family HDHP, with a biweekly premium that was about $150 less than the average, non-HDHP plans (all of which also had deductibles, just not as high as our HDHP). Our plan also provided $125 per month to our HSA. Our plan's deductible was $5,000 for in-network care, and another $3,000 for out-of-network care, for a total of $8,000.

None of my family's health incidents would have been cheap on their own. Taken together, we definitely hit the maximum deductible that year, spending $8,001 and some change from our HSA. But that amount wasn't as bad as it might seem at first glance. Since we received $125 a month from the plan, that was $1,500 for the year. Also, since we saved on average $150 per biweekly paycheck, that was another $3,900. So already two-thirds of our "high deductible," or just over $5,000, was essentially covered by other savings. And because all of our contributions to the HSA was tax-deductible, we saved considerable amounts using the HSA to pay for healthcare.

And the HSA provides some extra incentive to negotiate bigger services, too. In another year, we ended up being billed for an out-of-network emergency service of over $1,700. After half-a-dozen phone calls to the company, I was able to negotiate payment in full at half the charged amount (which I put on my HSA). It wasn't easy, since there was a lot of back-and-forth between them and my health insurance provider, and it also took time to reach someone in the company with the authority to approve my request to reduce the charge. But it can (and should) be done.

In my experience at least, it all evens out in the end, but the HSA gives you more flexibility year-over-year in terms of paying for health expenses, and over the long-term for investing purposes.

Paying more initially out-of-pocket can take some adjustment in the first year or two of having an HDHP and HSA. Most people are so used to paying small deductibles and having the insurance company pay the rest that they do not stop to consider the full costs of their healthcare needs. In contrast, the HDHP/HSA account holder needs to be prepared to pay up to the deductible especially in the beginning months of the year, and this takes some planning. But the individual incentives to save and spend healthcare dollars wisely in the HDHP and HSA ultimately present a win-win-win scenario for the insurance companies, the individual worker, and for the government—which is of course financed by taxpayers. The insurance company saves money by allowing us to shop for our own basic healthcare needs. It in turn rewards us with lower insurance premiums and a monthly stipend to our tax-advantaged savings accounts. Because our insurance premiums are lower, the Federal Government—and ultimately, the taxpayer—also saves by having to pay a smaller amount for our health insurance benefits. What's not to love about the HDHP and HSA?

The HDHP with HSA is, as an aside, perhaps the greatest potential tool to help control healthcare costs in the United States, as it gives individuals the incentive to comparison shop for health care needs. This in turn increases competition and price transparency in the healthcare marketplace, which drives down (or at least helps to control) prices for healthcare expenditures. As individuals shop among hospitals, specialty providers, and health care clinics for a given procedure or service, they will demand to see, for example, the success rate and mortality rate of any given medical procedure, the training of the staff, and the itemized prices for the given procedure and for aftercare. Individual health care consumers will more carefully scrutinize prices to look for potential increased savings, and they will have a powerful financial incentive to undertake the necessary steps to stay healthier longer by eating healthfully, exercising, and not smoking.

And best of all, with the resources available in an HSA, healthcare consumers will not have to worry about any insurance company (or medical boards associated with any future single-payer system) saying "no" to a procedure or service: the HSA owner can in that case simply use money from his or her HSA to buy the health procedure or service outright, as long as the IRS considers it a qualified medical expense.

As far as investing goes, at least a few years' worth of deductibles should be saved and invested very conservatively, because money in an HSA might be needed to cover actual medical expenses and emergencies in the near term—unlike TSP or Roth IRA investments. The HSA owner should probably keep an amount equal to one-and-a-half or two times the annual deductible in the savings account itself to cover any significant health issues. Once you have saved this amount, extra money can be invested in index funds, starting with a large-cap U.S. domestic fund, for example. Unfortunately, many HSA providers currently charge significant fees and expense ratios—much higher than those found in the TSP or other index fund plans—that eat away at some of the growth potential. Hopefully, demand from HSA owners and increasing competition among HSA providers will drive down these fees and expenses and free up additional investment options in the near future.

Investing in Real Estate: Six Approaches

Although this book focuses on the TSP and investing in index funds, it would be incomplete if real estate were not included in this edition. Investing in real estate can be a significant additional builder of wealth. But it can also be a huge suck on resources including time, energy, and finances that could be better focused elsewhere. Investing in real estate is a deeply personal choice. Some love it, some hate it, some grow truly wealthy with it, others fail at it. Know what kind of person you are when considering real estate.

Investing in real estate can be conducted in conjunction with investing in the TSP, but it can't be considered "passive" investing like investing in stock or bond index funds. Only one approach detailed below involves truly passive investing. Each of the other approaches has costs involved—literally in terms of additional outlays related to the property, and figuratively in terms of the significant time, energy, and effort required to invest in real estate. Because this book is focused on passive investing, this section will lay out possible approaches for individuals to consider and areas to research further, but it will not deal with them in any significant detail.

There are six ways to invest in real estate. A TSP investor could engage in one or more of these activities at the same time as investing in the TSP or avoid them all together (spoiler alert: avoidance is the sixth choice).

1. *Purchase a residence for yourself*

Purchasing and owning your residence is empowering and, in many respects, rewarding. Home ownership offers you protection: Since you own your home, you can't be evicted as long as you pay your mortgage, taxes, homeowners association and other dues, and abide by any covenants. If you have a fixed-rate mortgage, you have some additional protection from rental inflation over the years, since you won't have to pay increased rent when your lease is up (although property taxes will certainly go up…). And at some point, you'll hopefully be in a position to pay off your mortgage, in which case you can live *rent free* (except for the taxes, maintenance, and other fees). And property appreciates in value over time, too (as do the taxes and dues…).

While all that is true, there are both pros and cons to owning your own residence. As any long-term homeowner knows, there are a lot of things that can go wrong in a house. Some new homeowners forget to adequately plan for these particular expenses. Expect for maintenance and repairs to cost anywhere from 1% to 5% of the value of the home in any given year. This can include everything from yard maintenance to a new roof or HVAC to accidental (and usually uncovered!) flooding in the basement, etc etc. You might think, *oh, I'll do all the maintenance and renovations myself…* Maybe you will, maybe you won't. Be realistic. That tall tree that looks so beautiful in the spring when everything is blooming? Maybe it collects snow and could topple at any time onto your roof. Time to take it down—or take down five just like it near your house. Tree removal can cost thousands. I don't know about you, but I'm no arborist, and I'm not going to risk my neck to save some money to take them down. There are many examples of unexpected expenses related to one's residence.

Also, the more home you have, the more it costs. This is a truism, but it's easy to forget when shopping for property. There are more rooms to fill with furniture, more walls to cover with new coats of paint and decorations, more windows to cover; it all quickly adds up.

In the end, you do need a roof over your head and a good place for your kids to grow up, but you don't want to become house-poor. You get a great house, but you might spend so much of your hard-earned salary maintaining it that you can't invest in and take advantage of other opportunities as well. Remember: To build wealth, you want to keep expenses and debt low and invest extra amounts in assets that appreciate over time.

2. Purchase rental properties

This is a traditional way of building a real estate portfolio, and it is pretty self-explanatory. You continue to live in and maintain a personal residence, and with additional funds you purchase additional property with the goal of renting it out for extra income. The rental income should pay for any monthly mortgage and dues associated with the property, allowing you to build equity over time, and it should provide some extra income to cover any maintenance, taxes, and additional funds for you to use in further building your real estate portfolio if you so choose.

Over time you can also increase rent by a few percentage points periodically, which can gradually lead to higher income. The increases in rent should over time increase dramatically compared to what should be the fixed mortgage on the property—and ultimately, the original loan should be paid off so that the rental income is all yours, even as the value of the property has increased over that time.

Another relatively new way to purchase rental properties is virtual. Companies such as roofstock.com provide online marketplaces to buy and sell rental properties or even portfolios of properties throughout the United States without having to visit them. Transactions are conducted online and include property and neighborhood data, property inspections when readying a purchase, and lending, closing, and transaction services. The companies also offer property management services, too.

Being a landlord and collecting rent from the comfort of your living room is all nice in theory. And yes, it can work out spectacularly well over time. But things can go spectacularly wrong too.

What if your tenants are unable to pay the rent for three months straight, or what if you can't get tenants for a recently vacated property for months at a time? Could you cash-flow the mortgage due on that property while waiting for rent to start coming in again? What if you suddenly need to replace a refrigerator, then a heating coil in the clothes dryer, then a leaky toilet, all within a few weeks of each other? Are you ready to be awoken in the middle of the night to hear about a burst pipe spewing water in the basement, perhaps when you are out of town on Thanksgiving or Christmas Eve even? Are you ready to pay the asking rates for the property manager to do the work for you, knowing that you can't compete the work out to potentially more cost-effective local companies?

These are not made-up stories, they've all happened; I've heard worse too. I'll refrain from providing any more anecdotes to protect the innocent... and the not-so-innocent!

3. *Purchase and PCS*™

There are two primary approaches to this strategy.

The first is to purchase a residence, depart for a PCS ("permanent change of station"), and then return to the same region and purchase another property as a new residence. Then repeat if opportunities arise.

This approach works for those who conduct hub-and-spoke PCSs, which is to say, they start their career in one location (such as the Washington, D.C. metro area), they are moved to another location, and then they return to their original location. This could happen multiple times during a career, depending on the office and opportunities.

Sometimes, though, PCSs involve regions throughout the United States, with a family never returning to a particular geographic area.

This is the second approach to the *Purchase and PCS*™ way to invest in real estate: Purchase a residence, live in it for the few years you are in a particular location, and then when you get orders to PCS again, rent the property instead of selling once you leave.

The *Purchase and PCS*™ approach in this situation still works, but with additional challenges. The first is that you will need to find different property management companies to oversee the disparate properties. At least with the hub-and-spoke approach, your real estate investments are concentrated in one area so that you could probably employ one management company to oversee all of the properties. If properties are in different geographic locations, you will have to work with different companies, and invariably some management companies will require more handholding than others.

This also might be the case with the properties themselves. Some rentals may need more attention and upkeep depending on their condition and location. State and local laws and regulations on rentals will differ. Local conditions will differ too. One property might be in an earthquake-prone region, another in a flood zone, and a third in tornado alley. The properties themselves might have specific challenges. And so on.

All of this assumes you're available to manage the properties, even if through property managers. But what if you are deployed to a war zone, or at sea for months at a time? You will have more immediate concerns, and the last thing you want to hear is, "honey, the hot water heater flooded our property in Tucson and a storm tore off the roof of our rental in Leavenworth…"

And then there is the issue of estate planning. How much of a headache do you want in planning the disposition of your estate should you—or rather, when you—pass away? This will require special planning as well, taking into consideration different state and local laws.

4. Purchase and Flip

As with the previous category, there are two approaches to this strategy as well. However, this is probably the most involved type of real estate investing individuals can undertake in the housing market.

With this approach, you purchase a residence and you plan to live in it for two or more years. You renovate and upgrade it while you live in it. After you live there long enough to have established residency for tax purposes (two or more years over a five-year period), you repeat the process and either sell the property to buy a new project with the proceeds, or you purchase a new residence and rent out the renovated property. By living in it for two years, though, you've established residency so that any profit from the sale ("capital gains") is tax-free up to $250,000 for singles or $500,000 for married couples.

For fewer than two years, you can also do what is called a "1031 exchange" and use the gains to purchase a similar property, but the window to do so is short. This approach is beyond the scope of this book.

5. Invest in Real Estate Investment Trusts (REITs)

This is by far the easiest approach to investing in real estate. Instead of purchasing and managing properties yourself, you invest in companies that are designated as real estate investment trusts, or REITs, that do that as part of their business model.

REITs are taxed differently than other public companies and are required to pay out at least 90% of their taxable income as dividends. Thus, the dividends investors receive in this category are higher than those in other categories of dividend-paying stocks. But unlike dividends from company stock, which are taxed lightly as capital gains, dividends from REITs are taxed as individual income because of how they are paid out. Holding them in a qualified account such as an IRA or Roth IRA can help to avoid taxation issues.

Investing in a REIT fund or index fund is one way to invest in real estate passively. If you invest in REITs with after-tax funds in a Roth IRA (outlined in the previous section), you could use the growth and dividends tax-free once you have reached the qualified age to withdraw funds.

While not technically "REITs," there are new crowd-funding investment platforms that allow individual investors to purchase small stakes in properties online or via mobile apps, such as the app-based apartment investment company Compound. Compound purchases condominiums, divides each property into 100,000 equity shares, and then sells the shares to investors. Roofstock also features a partial ownership investment option. These are riskier investments, however, because of the concentrated nature of the investments in single properties and because the app-based market is relatively new and untested by significant declines in property values. If it is easy for investors to invest online or via an app, it is also easy for them to try to sell, which many will probably do as declines hit the property market. Also, you can only sell if there is a buyer on the other end of the transaction, and in times of market distress investors might not be able to sell as quickly as they initially hoped or expected. Approach these investments with caution.

6. Don't invest in real estate

This sixth option is a valid choice to make, especially for those serving in the military and others who might have to PCS or move periodically. Why buy when you have to move in a couple of years? Given the costs of buying and selling real estate, it can take five years or longer to break even on a purchase of a personal residence, depending on where you live.

The financial website smartasset.com did a nationwide analysis of probable break-even points between renting and buying in 2015 and found that the average break-even point nationally was 3.8 years. There were huge differences in the data around the country, however. The Midwest, South, and Southeast had reasonable break-even points of between 2.6 (Detroit) and 4.2 years (Houston and San Antonio). Denver was 5.4 and Phoenix was 5.7 years. Purchasing a residence on one of the coasts, however, took significantly longer to break even. The California coast ranged from 8.6 (San Diego) to 14.6 years (San Francisco), while Washington D.C was 6.5, Boston was 6.3, and New York City was a whopping 18.3 years.[71] So at a minimum, you want to know that you're going to be in a residence for that long before investing in one.

Not buying was also, by the way, the smartest choice to make in 2006-2008 in many major metropolitan areas during the major bubble in housing prices. A popular saying then was, "real estate never goes down!" Another one was, "you're throwing away money by renting!" Had you bought in 2006 with a plan to sell three years later, you'd have been underwater by five or six figures.

Property ownership can also be a barrier to professional growth. Owning real estate can "anchor" you to a location. Anchoring is a concept in psychology that refers to a person being more focused on an initial situation or piece of information in making a decision than might be warranted. Having a house—or the thought of the challenges associated with having to sell it—might prevent a person from considering otherwise very good professional opportunities in other locations. You might be "anchored" to that location not just physically, but mentally as well.

It's a lot easier to break a lease to take a new position a town or a state away than it is to start the process of selling a house. And most states have laws allowing military personnel to break their lease due to new orders or deployments.

The main lesson particularly of 2007-8 is, buy only when it makes sense for your personal situation professionally, financially, familially, and time-wise.

***

One final note: There are additional ways to invest in real estate, particularly in commercial real estate. These start to become full-time endeavors, however, while the previous discussion focuses on the ability to invest even as you serve in the military or in government.

Investing in real estate can be both financially and personally rewarding. But it can also involve *huge* amounts of headaches and, if you are ill-prepared financially, significant hardship as well. Make sure you know your own personal style, you know your interests and needs, and you proceed based on the knowledge of both the risks of buying real estate and potential rewards.

Saving for College

Saving for college is challenging especially when faced with the variety of other costs involved in raising a family.

The challenge is particularly acute because college comes so fast! As a parent, you have less than two decades from the birth of a child to his or her high school graduation.

And how many of us are able to begin preparing financially for college in a child's first years? The emotional, mental, and financial adjustments take time, certainly, and they can seem overwhelming to many new parents.

When researching tax-advantaged ways to save for higher education, "529" plans are where to start. The 529 plans are legally known as "qualified tuition plans," according to the SEC, and they get their popular "529" name from the section under which they are authorized in the Internal Revenue Code. There are two types of 529 plans: prepaid tuition plans and education savings plans.[72] As of late 2019, every state except Wyoming sponsors a 529 education savings plan (Wyoming partners with Ohio in offering the "WY ABLE" 529 plan), but only a handful of states offer prepaid plans. Some private colleges and universities sponsor prepaid tuition plans, as well.

The 529 education savings plans are increasingly flexible. While contributions are not tax-deductible at the federal level, many states with income taxes offer deductions to residents for participation in the state plan. Earnings and withdrawals for qualified expenses, however, are not subject to federal tax. You can use 529 funds at most accredited post-secondary public or private schools in the United States and some abroad, including two-year or four-year technical, graduate or professional schools. Qualified expenses were expanded in the tax reform act of 2017, so that accounts can be used to pay up to $10,000 per beneficiary for K-12 tuition at public, private, or parochial schools, too. You can also change beneficiaries and reallocate unused funds to other members of the family (as long as the new beneficiary is a member of the family of the former beneficiary).

That said, there are drawbacks. Because the 529 plans are sponsored and managed primarily by the states, the 529 market is fragmented. This has the unfortunate effect of requiring account owners to pay higher fees than in some other investment vehicles. These include one-time fees associated with opening, transferring, or closing an account to ongoing account maintenance and asset management fees. The annual fees range from 0.05% (Fidelity Arizona College Savings Plan, which rises to a hefty 0.99% for actively managed funds) to 1.26% (Nebraska Educational Savings Trust Direct Plan high-end investments, which start at 0.18%). As we've seen in multiple examples in this book, and as the SEC notes, "It is important to understand the fees and expenses associated with 529 plans because they lower your returns." The SEC notes that at least some of these fees can be waived with certain account balances, automatic contributions, state residency, and electronic delivery of documents, among others.

Also note that some fund managers offer rewards credit cards that feature cash back to one's investment account. Fidelity, for example, offers a 2% College Rewards card associated with Fidelity accounts, and uPromise offers a 1.25% rewards card that offers a 15% bonus when associated with an eligible 529 college savings plan.* (Just be sure to pay off any amounts before interest is charged, otherwise the cash-back purpose of the cards is defeated!)

You are allowed to invest in any state's 529 plan. But if you live in a state that has an income tax, and if the state offers tax deductions for investing in the state's 529 plan, it probably makes sense to do so despite the fees.

Keep in mind these points when researching and deciding upon a 529 plan: (1) As discussed throughout this book, choose the low-fee option. Fees will eat away drastically at your savings and investments, and especially when saving for college, you don't have that much time to save! This usually entails: (2) Choosing index funds—I've not seen a managed fund that features

---

* Note that I have no association with and do not receive any compensation for highlighting the Fidelity or uPromise cards, or any other service noted in this book.

lower fees than index funds. But in addition to rock-bottom fees, they are also free from political interference or kick-back schemes, which can sometimes be an issue at the state level. (3) Start out slowly, if necessary, to get in the habit of saving first. Increase your savings as you get used to the new savings program and as your finances allow.

Realistically, plan for no more than 15 or 16 years of investing in growth (stock index) funds. This is because, as we have seen, drops in the market can greatly reduce one's total investment in the near- and medium-term, and it can take up to three years to recover. Therefore, be prepared to switch at least some of your investments to less-volatile options at least one year, and potentially up to three years, in advance of needing to use the funds.

Along these lines, we can test how savings approaches fared over 16-year increments much like we tested savings and investing in the TSP over 30- and 40-year periods. Let's begin with a minor investment of $50 a month, but increase that amount by 12% per year, so it becomes $56 per month the next year, $100 in year six, and $200 in year 12. This would be a total of about $25,650 over 16 years. Obviously, if you're saving for two or three children, those amounts double or triple assuming you're saving equally for all of them. One great thing about the state-sponsored plans is that almost all of them require a very low minimum investment, sometimes just $25 to get started, so a $50 starting amount should be no problem for most plans. (Just mind the account maintenance and other fees!)

Over 16-year increments, these amounts grew to an average of $52,000 in an S&P 500 index fund, versus $35,700 in an intermediate-term U.S. government bond fund. But there was significant variation, such that the lowest return for the stock index fund was $23,759; investing from 1993 to 2008 yielded a paltry $24,666.15. In total, the stock index underperformed the bond index in 18 years out of the 100 examined. As is evident in the chart below, some of those periods of underperformance recovered within a year or two, but the underperformance lasted seven consecutive years in the late 1950s and early 1960s. In most cases, waiting a year or two to start transferring funds to a cash account would have increased these amounts by thousands of dollars (albeit from a relatively low amount), but with college expenses, sometimes you don't have the luxury of waiting.

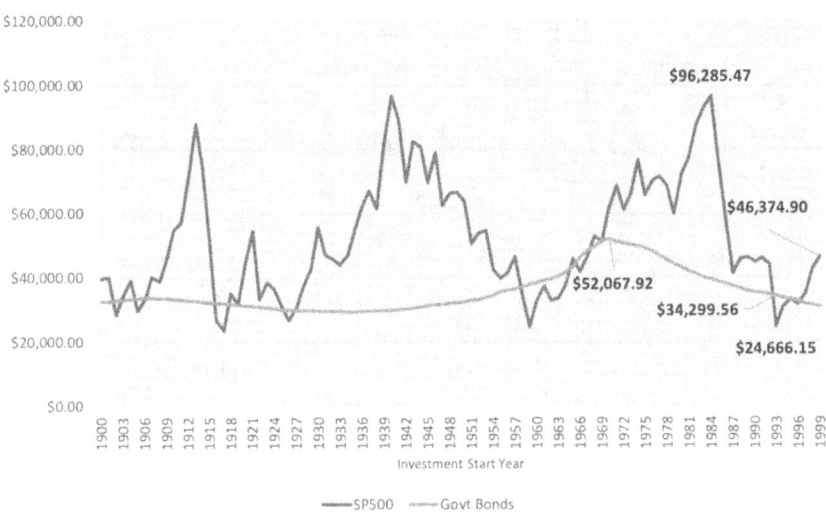

The comparative returns of investing monthly over 16-year periods in a stock index fund versus a U.S. government bond fund. Investments started at $50 a month and increased by 12% each year, for a final total of about $25,650. The stock index fund outperformed the government bond fund 82 of 100 periods examined, from 1900 to 2015.

Many 529 savings plans offer "lifecycle"-like funds that gradually reduce stock allocations and increase bond and cash allocations in line with your future withdrawal needs. Given the limited time horizon in saving for secondary education, this kind of fund based on your child's age might be a good approach when considering allocation strategies.

For some, 529 prepaid tuition plans are an option as well. In these plans, state residents lock in and prepay some or all of the state-based tuition over a much longer timeframe than the four or so years your child will attend. This can protect you from tuition inflation, and your monthly payments are spread out more evenly in advance; there are still some administrative fees involved and fees for late or non-payment, however, but the plans are tax-deductible in the states that offer it and have a state income tax (such as Virginia, Maryland, and Massachusetts), but they are obviously not tax-deductible in the states that do not have an income tax (Florida, Nevada, and Texas).

There are different drawbacks with the prepaid tuition plans, too, starting with whether your state offers it or not—most do not. Also, you won't know whether your child actually wants to attend any of the participating schools in the state until they are at least midway through their fickle teenage years. Most plans understand this, of course, but the tuition plan may pay less to the non-participating schools than to the participating ones, according to the SEC.

Whatever direction you plan to go, the mantra especially in the beginning should be: *Something is better than nothing*. If you know you won't be able to pay for a child's entire secondary education, don't beat yourself up about it! There are other options that go hand-in-hand with whatever you might be able to provide. Keep in mind that the goal in this case is not *saving* per se, but paying for college, together as a family (the kids included). This might take some pressure off of you, as the parent.

Consider some alternative approaches. You've no doubt read this in other books and columns too, but what other means are there for getting that education? Academic and/or athletic scholarships are a start, of course. Keep in mind potential scholarships at local junior colleges, for example, where a student can attend for two years and then transfer to a four-year school to finish his or her bachelor's degree. Attending a local school or junior college to get some college credits, or even attending a semester or two while still living at home, is another way to save money.

As many readers of this book no doubt know, the military is also an option: The U.S. military has tremendously generous and flexible sponsorships available for recruits (not to mention good training in its own right), whether through the G.I. Bill or through a Reserve Officer's Training Corps scholarship. This assumes your child is prepared to serve his or her country in the ways required by the military, of course.

Increasingly, there are also work-study opportunities. Starbucks, for example, offers the "College Achievement Plan" to pay for college courses for even part-time employees while working flexible hours. These courses are primarily, if not entirely, online, giving additional flexibility in how and where courses are taken. Walmart charges employees $1 a day for college courses, and the company picks up the rest of the bill. It may take a little longer to finish college through these type of work-study programs, and the self-discipline required is significant, but they're additional opportunities to explore.

There are other slightly less traditional approaches to preparing for college expenses, too. Recalculate your savings potential over the years to see if instead of contributing to a 529 regularly, you could put that extra money toward paying off your mortgage before your children attend college. If the mortgage is paid, you could devote what had been going to mortgage payments to college tuition and expenses instead—and you would be in the enviable position of having a paid-off house too! Granted, most of the money would be after-tax, so the tax savings would be less (and you would miss out on potential deductions at the state level too), but you would not need to worry about the vicissitudes of the market as your children near college age.

Separately, does your child even want or need to go to college? Other vocational-technical opportunities abound. Plumbers, machinists, HVAC technicians, electricians, and other skilled professionals make very good livings, after all, and there are many work-study programs and apprenticeships around the country where students can pick up these skills while working their trade from a remarkably young age. Even when attending a dedicated school to learn these skills, the time required to attend is much shorter compared to a four-year program, tuition is often cheaper, and the expenses are usually considered a "qualified expense" for 529 plans. They are definitely options to consider in addition to traditional four-year programs.

What About the Rest of Your Money?

You might find yourself in the enviable position of having extra funds available even after paying all your bills in full and contributing to the TSP and other tax-advantaged savings vehicles. Or maybe you suddenly come into money after winning the lottery or inheriting some money. If you are in the fortunate position where your debts are paid in full, you are maxing out your TSP and IRA contributions, you have a significant cushion in emergency savings, and you are adequately saving for any significant purchases in the medium term, you might have some income and savings left over that you don't know what to do with.

If this is the case, or if you are just comfortable with your situation and want to help others, you might consider sharing your good fortune by increasing contributions to your favorite charities directly or through very convenient payroll deductions via the Combined Federal Campaign (CFC). With additional funds—and if you are the fortunate recipient of a windfall of some sort—also consider investing in U.S. domestic and international stock index funds in addition to investing in tax-advantaged accounts.

Consider Increasing Charitable Contributions through the CFC

Many readers probably already contribute to one or more charities or non-profit organizations. A very convenient way to contribute even more to charities is through the CFC.

According to the Office of Personnel Management (OPM), the CFC is "the world's largest and most successful annual workplace charity campaign, with almost 200 CFC campaigns throughout the country and overseas raising millions of dollars each year."[73]

The CFC features literally thousands of pre-screened and deserving local, national, and international charities. Ahead of open season, which takes place in the fall of each year, OPM provides a special booklet with descriptions of the thousands of charities to which one can donate. Information also includes the total amount that goes directly for charitable works and the amount used for overhead expenses, allowing donors to see at a glance how well organizations are using donated funds.

During CFC open season, you can donate directly, and you can also sign up for a payroll deduction to start the next calendar year, much like payroll contributions to the TSP. Those who donate 1% of their salary are designated "Eagle" donors, and those who donate 2% are "Double Eagle" donors. But deductions of as little as $5 each pay period are accepted, and any little amount can add up over time to make a difference over the year. A $5 periodic contribution, for example, equals $130 in donations over the year. Every little bit helps, so consider donating to causes that are meaningful to you through the CFC in addition to direct contributions during the year.

Even if you are not yet able to make large donations currently, keep this option in mind as your wealth grows. Remember, donating even 1%* of $1,000,000 amounts to giving *$10,000*, and you'll probably be able to afford this kind of charitable giving and more as your wealth increases!

Consider Investing in Index Funds

If you still have money left over after you have all your consumer debts paid off, built up an emergency fund, maxed out your contributions to your

---

* This is half of the interest rate of the G Fund and half the dividend rate of the C Fund, for example.

TSP and other tax-advantaged savings plans, have a residence and are contributing to your favorite charities, then consider investing any extra savings in non-TSP index funds. As noted previously, index funds outperform a majority of actively managed funds and generally have expense ratios much lower than actively managed funds (see more on fees in the chapter, *Parabolic Wealth*). They are also tax-advantaged compared to regular savings and bond funds, because they are taxed at a lower capital-gains rate.

A basic allocation would match your preferred investor allocation, such as 80-20, 65-35, or 50-50 stock-savings ratios. It's as easy as that; there's no need to spend the hours required to research individual companies, no fear of underperforming the market, and capital gains taxes are easy to calculate.

And if you are still interested in playing the stock market by picking individual companies in which to invest, use these extra funds to do so.

Of course, money invested in stock funds and individual stocks should be money that you do not need for at least five to ten years, as these funds will increase and decrease in value, just as the U.S. and international stock markets go up and down over time.

Summary for Strategy V

Saving and investing do not have to be limited to the TSP, as there are many additional options available to help further enhance building and diversifying personal wealth. TSP investing should fit into a comprehensive personal financial plan that includes paying off debt and saving in other ways, such as in a Roth IRA, in an HSA, and potentially in real estate.

- Pay off consumer debts and build up an emergency fund, equal to at least three to four months' expenses.

- Plan ahead for and use appropriate savings vehicles for anticipated major future purchases.

- Avoid taking any loans from your TSP account, since this will negatively impact future account growth.

- Consider investing in additional tax-advantaged vehicles, such as a Roth IRA and an HSA in addition to the TSP.

- Consider real estate investment options that are right for you.

- Consider contributing additional funds to non-profit charitable organizations through payroll deductions via the CFC in addition to making charitable contributions directly.
- Invest remaining savings in broad, low-cost index funds.

STRATEGY VI
Protect Yourself and Your Wealth

If you build up wealth, you want to protect it. You want to protect yourself too, your family, and your legacy. Furthermore, you don't want a catastrophic event to derail your long-term plans.

How do you do all this? Get insured, have an estate plan, and protect your digital life! That's the theme of this sixth strategy.

This strategy is divided into four areas to pay particular attention to in protecting yourself and your assets. I've designated these as (1) *Personal,* (2) *Property,* (3) *Wealth,* and (4) *Digital Insurance.* The term "insurance" is used in its widest meaning, from the actual payment to a company that provides specific insurance coverage, to metaphorically "insuring" (ensuring) that you and your estate are better protected in a variety of scenarios.

Many of the topics detailed below are regulated at the state level and require insurance or legal expertise to ensure the specifics related to your situation are adequately addressed. Thus, this chapter is provided for informational purposes only as areas to consider in a holistic financial plan. Some of the details below might not be right for your situation, or the legal specifics and other details may be dated by the time you read this chapter. Ultimately, consider all of the potential challenges and catastrophic scenarios and plan for them with the help of a trusted insurance, legal, or technical professional.

This chapter does not deal with the TSP or investing, so for readers who are solely interested in investing in the TSP, skim or skip these sections. I think many readers will find the discussions useful, however, because there are some additional money-saving tips and areas of potential interest to consider as you build wealth in your TSP accounts and with other saving and investing efforts.

(1) Personal Insurance

This category of insurance protects both you and your loved ones in case anything happens to you. (Health insurance was briefly discussed in Strategy V.)

Life Insurance: FEGLI

All new civilian government employees are automatically signed up for Federal Employees' Group Life Insurance (FEGLI). This is good, basic insurance, and it requires no health exams or other applications to obtain the basic insurance. You pay two-thirds of the Basic Insurance, and the government pays the other one-third.[74] There are three other insurance options that cost extra and can be elected after you have basic coverage, discussed a little later in this section.

As you weigh the additional options, there are two things to consider: 1) Is basic FEGLI enough insurance for you and your family, and 2) Is FEGLI insurance too expensive for what you get compared to other options?

Consider that for a 35-year-old making $50,000 a year, FEGLI costs $7.80 per biweekly pay period or about $202 for the year for $102,000 in life insurance, according to OPM's FEGLI calculator.[75] That amount includes $52,000 for a "Basic Insurance Amount" and $52,000 for an "Extra Benefit". There are also Accidental Death and Dismemberment (AD&D) options, which would provide you $26,000 for losing a hand, foot, or the sight in one eye and $52,000 for the loss of two or more of those, for example. There are also some basic spousal/dependent benefit options available via FEGLI, such as $25,000 for a spouse and $12,500 for children, which start at just over a dollar per biweekly pay period.

This might suffice as basic insurance for a singleton, but for a federal worker with a spouse/significant other and possibly other family members, most experts will tell you that the amount is woefully insufficient.

However, you can add more coverage with FEGLI. Maxing out the options just discussed would cost $16.95 per biweekly pay period, and the 35-year-old's beneficiary would be eligible to receive $364,000. That is certainly better coverage, but even that amount might not be enough under some circumstances.

That said, the option that determines higher payouts after an employee's demise, option B, is based on salary. If an employee has a higher salary, s/he can get more coverage at a higher cost. If an under-35 employee made $125,000 and maxed out Option B at "5", the insurance coverage would be $879,000 with a biweekly premium of $31.55 (or a monthly cost of $68.15).

Unfortunately, but perhaps understandably, FEGLI members pay more for a decreasing amount of insurance over the years. Coverage decreases each year after the age of 35, and the cost of the coverage increases as one ages. At 40, that same individual earning $50,000 would pay $20.25 per pay period ($526 per year) for maximum insurance of $338,000. At 45, that becomes $28.95 per pay period for $312,000 in benefits. That's over $750 per year!

One option to consider, together with a basic FEGLI or potentially to replace it, is a term life insurance policy purchased on the open market. The average cost of 20-year term life insurance in late 2019 for a 35-year-old non-smoker is $29.80 per month for $500,000 of coverage, according to ValuePenguin.[76] That amount stays the same through the life of the policy—no increases!

And there are a wide variety of options on the commercial market, too. A 40-year-old male would pay about $69 per month for a 20-year, $1 million policy, or about $833 a year. This is just a few hundred dollars more than the cost of the maxed-out FEGLI life insurance, but the insured gets three times the amount of coverage.

The deals are even better for women. A 30-year-old male would pay $314 per year for a $500,000, 20-year term policy, while a female would pay $264. This compares to 30-year-old FEGLI participants paying $202 per year for $104,000 in total (basic) insurance, regardless of gender, and $338 per year for full insurance of $364,000. A $1 million term life insurance policy for a 40-year-old, non-smoking woman is $695 for the year. FEGLI offers only a third of that coverage at higher rates.

If you have a young family, definitely get insurance for both parents in the family, whether both are employed or not. The burden would be enormous if either one were to pass, and financial worries would only add to the stress. This is where term life insurance really serves a family well, when one adult caregiver has not been automatically signed up for or does not have access to FEGLI. Each head of household with a young family should be insured, whether through FEGLI, term life insurance, or both, and a spouse should have insurance too.

Term life insurance might also be financially smart for singletons as well. You might be single now, but you never know what the future holds for you. What if in two years you are suddenly married and a new parent? What if you have twins? Because term life insurance is so economical, it might be worthwhile to purchase a policy to lock in low monthly rates for 20 (or perhaps even 30) years before starting a family. This way, you increase your coverage at potentially a lower long-term rate, and you are prepared for protecting what might be an expanding family. Who knows?

There are many factors to consider before making a decision to replace FEGLI with other term insurance, however. A physical exam and other tests are often required for term life insurance. Insurance for smokers is significantly more expensive, as well. Average term life insurance for a 35-year-old male smoker is $118.36 per month, according to ValuePenguin (another incentive to quit smoking!). Some policies also might not have the full range of coverage, such as payment in the case of a lost limb or eye, but there are additional supplemental coverage options to provide for that type of coverage as well (check with your department/agency's credit union for specific deals). And ultimately, a company on the open market is not required to insure you. Note too that if you drop FEGLI, you will have to reapply, and you might be required to provide a physical as part of the application process. See the chart below for a comparison of monthly premiums and total 20-year costs between FEGLI and term life insurance ($500,000 policy) for a 30-year-old man (non-smoker or smoker) or woman.

Age	FEGLI Coverage	FEGLI Premiums (Monthly)	Term Life Insurance (Monthly)		
		$75,000 Salary	male, nonsmoker	male, smoker	female, nonsmoker
31	$529,000.00	$ 41.16	$26.00	$92.00	$22.00
32	$529,000.00	$ 41.16	$26.00	$92.00	$22.00
33	$529,000.00	$ 41.16	$26.00	$92.00	$22.00
34	$529,000.00	$ 41.16	$26.00	$92.00	$22.00
35	$529,000.00	$ 49.41	$26.00	$92.00	$22.00
36	$521,300.00	$ 49.41	$26.00	$92.00	$22.00
37	$513,600.00	$ 49.41	$26.00	$92.00	$22.00
38	$505,900.00	$ 49.41	$26.00	$92.00	$22.00
39	$498,200.00	$ 49.41	$26.00	$92.00	$22.00
40	$490,500.00	$ 57.66	$26.00	$92.00	$22.00
41	$482,800.00	$ 57.66	$26.00	$92.00	$22.00
42	$475,100.00	$ 57.66	$26.00	$92.00	$22.00
43	$467,400.00	$ 57.66	$26.00	$92.00	$22.00
44	$459,700.00	$ 57.66	$26.00	$92.00	$22.00
45	$452,000.00	$ 82.03	$26.00	$92.00	$22.00
46	$452,000.00	$ 82.03	$26.00	$92.00	$22.00
47	$452,000.00	$ 82.03	$26.00	$92.00	$22.00
48	$452,000.00	$ 82.03	$26.00	$92.00	$22.00
49	$452,000.00	$ 82.03	$26.00	$92.00	$22.00
50	$452,000.00	$114.28	$26.00	$92.00	$22.00
Total Paid Over 20 Years:		$ 14,693.00	$6,240.00	$22,080.00	$5,280.00

Difference in premiums over 20 years between FEGLI insurance and term life insurance premiums, from age 31 to 50 (sources: OPM, ValuePenguin).

Keep in mind that to be eligible for FEGLI upon retirement, you must have been insured for five years prior to the start date of your pension.[77] So by canceling FEGLI, you could also be canceling a chance to maintain FEGLI in retirement.

As for whole life insurance? Ummm, no. Perhaps for some very high-net-worth individuals there are certain tax advantages, but for the costs involved, in my opinion you get a much better deal with term life insurance and investing your savings in the TSP and in other index funds.

So look at your specific situation and the various options. Consult a financial planner if you need advice as to your specific insurance needs and how it fits into your financial plan. But before you make a final decision, make sure you have some form of insurance before dropping FEGLI, because you don't want a lapse in insurance.

Life Insurance: SGLI/FSGLI

As the name suggests, "Servicemembers' Group Life Insurance" (SGLI) is a program that provides life insurance coverage to servicemembers. It is a really good deal, especially for families.

SGLI has some additional benefits built into the program. Servicemembers can also receive TSGLI, or Traumatic Injury Protection, for an extra $1 a month. There is a long list of items that this specific insurance covers, such as loss of a limb or use of a limb, loss of one's eyesight, or other traumatic injuries. A full list of covered injuries is available on the TSGLI website, and coverage amounts generally range from $25,000 to a maximum of $100,000.[78]

FSGLI, or "Family Servicemembers Group Life Insurance," provides life insurance via SGLI for spouses and dependents of servicemembers, whether civilian or servicemembers themselves. This insurance is provided in $10,000 increments up to $100,000, and it is an easy and fast way to obtain basic insurance for one's spouse. The amount is age-based, and the price of coverage increases gradually from the age of 35.

As of 2019, basic $10,000 coverage for those under 35 started at $0.45 per pay period. A 35-year-old spouse of a servicemember can receive the maximum $100,000 coverage for about $5.30 a month, for example, while the same amount of coverage for a 40-year-old increases to $7, and on up to $29.50 per month for a 55-year-old spouse.[79]

FSGLI also provides a $10,000 life insurance policy for each child under 18 (and in certain circumstances, for dependents over that age as well). There is no additional charge for this coverage.

While FSGLI is a good starting point, term life insurance obtained on the private market might be a more comprehensive option. As noted previously, term life insurance is a particularly good value for non-smoking women. A 30-year-old woman would pay just $22 a month—$264 a year—for a $500,000, 20-year term life insurance policy. And that rate would not increase during the 20-year life of the policy, unlike FSGLI. This is a really good value for the amount of coverage a civilian spouse would receive. This kind of coverage does often require a physical and potentially other tests to get the best rates, so be sure to get the policy before canceling FSGLI. And also keep in mind that once canceled, a physical would be required to re-obtain FSGLI.

Both SGLI and FSGLI provide the ability to transition to either Veterans' Group Life Insurance (VGLI) or a commercial policy. As you look toward civilian life, definitely include planning for life insurance before separating. Those who have just separated may apply for a maximum amount of coverage that is equal to the amount of SGLI coverage at separation and can increase coverage by $25,000 on their one-year anniversary and once every for five years thereafter up to $400,000.[80]

Depending on your circumstances, however, this might not be the best option for you or your spouse, at least as your primary life insurance coverage. According to va.gov, the VGLI premium rate for a 45-year-old is $88 per month for $400,000 in life insurance, while the average rate for term life insurance is about $59 per month for $500,000 over 20 years.[81] Not only is the term life insurance potentially cheaper with greater coverage, the monthly rate for the term life insurance stays the same throughout the life of the policy, while the VGLI increases every five years. At 50, the same coverage shoots up to $144 per month, then to $268 a month at 55.

The VGLI does have an important point to consider: No proof of good health is required. Thus, those separating from the service who are otherwise uninsurable are eligible for VGLI. You must apply within 240 days of separating to avoid a health review. Otherwise, veterans must apply within one year and 120 days from date of separation.

One option is to maintain basic coverage upon separation—$10,000 in coverage is $2.20 for a 45-year-old, for example—while relying on more economical term life insurance for your primary life insurance needs. You can gradually increase or decrease over the years as necessary.

SGLI and FSGLI separately allow for a transition to commercial life insurance, but unfortunately these are only *whole life* insurance policies. In a large number of cases, term life insurance will be less expensive and provide more coverage than whole life.

In all cases, before making a decision that is right for your particular situation, read the fine print, do your research, and talk to a professional who is free of conflicts of interest (keep in mind that those advocating whole life insurance are almost always paid a commission by the insurance company to sell you their policy).

Disability insurance

The term "disability" that is used to describe an insurance product may be a bit of a misnomer, since many people consider a "disabling" event to be permanent loss of use of an extremity or eyesight. "Disability" as defined by Merriam-Webster is "a physical, mental, cognitive, or developmental condition that impairs, interferes with, or limits a person's ability to engage in certain tasks or actions or participate in typical daily activities and interactions."[82] The definition, however, does not indicate a duration but points to a certain permanency in condition. In reality, many disabling events can be temporary in nature, however, and include injuries and illnesses that "disable" only for a time. These conditions can last long enough to cause a person to miss significant amounts of work but otherwise might not be irreversibly debilitating.

Regardless of the term used to define the product, federal government employees should have a plan in place in case of a long-term absence caused by a significant injury or health issue. According to the Insurance Information Institute, 43% of all people will have a long-term disability event—defined as over 90 days—by age 65.[83] The Social Security Administration states that "just over one in four of today's 20-year-olds will become disabled before reaching age 67" (SSA does not detail the average length of disability, however).[84]

Could you survive financially if you were unable to work for over 90 days?

The truth is, a short- or longer-term disability, injury, or health event can impact any worker, young or old. For civilian federal employees, newer employees are more vulnerable to work disruption because they have less in savings and generally have fewer leave days than longer-serving workers.

Some departments and agencies provide a leave pool for those requiring extended leave to draw from in an emergency. Basically, individual members of that office's workforce can opt into the program by donating some hours of annual leave per year, and in return, they are eligible for significant additional emergency leave if they run out of annual and sick leave.

If you are not signed up for this benefit but your office offers it, *sign up now!* Yes, it probably costs some precious annual leave time that is difficult to save up in the beginning of your career, but the peace of mind and financial stability it can provide is significant in case the worst happens. Situations do occur when an employee (especially a newer one) has used up his or her entire sick leave and annual leave and has to go on unpaid leave to tend to their injury or health issue. Contact your HR department to find out if your office offers such a program.

Also, according to the Insurance Information Institute, other sources of income might be available depending on the reason for the disability. Auto insurance might cover some lost income as part of Personal Injury Protection (PIP) in the case of an auto accident. The Department of Veterans Affairs provides some replacement income for veterans, depending on the nature and reason for the disability.[85] Social Security disability benefits may also be paid for workers whose disability is severe and expected to last for 12 months or more.[86]

Some professional societies or credit unions might have special disability insurance available for members as well, so be sure to check for availability in your professional circles.

For FERS employees, there is a special category for "Disability Retirement," with some special requirements:

> *"You must have become disabled, while employed in a position subject to FERS, because of a disease or injury, for useful and efficient service in your current position. The disability must be expected to last at least one year. Your agency must certify that it is unable to accommodate your disabling med-*

ical condition in your present position and that it has considered you for any vacant position in the same agency at the same grade/pay level, within the same commuting area, for which you are qualified for reassignment." – opm.gov[87]

These are all special categories, however, and you don't want to be cast into a disability retirement where you're reliant on FERS and Social Security disability unless absolutely necessary.

For those in-between situations, when an injury or temporary disability or health issue prevents you from working for an extended period of time, disability insurance can fill that gap. If you have less than three months of sick leave and annual leave saved up and your office does not provide additional emergency leave, definitely consider disability insurance.

Long Term Care Insurance

In contrast to the previous section on disability insurance, which younger civilian workers should definitely consider, Long Term Care Insurance (LTCI) is primarily intended for older workers.

The U.S. Department of Health and Human Services' LongTermCare.gov defines long-term care as "a range of services and supports…to meet your personal care needs," which is "not medical care, but rather assistance with the basic personal tasks of everyday life, sometimes called Activities of Daily Living (ADLs)."[88] LTCI is "designed to cover long-term services" that "support…personal and custodial care in a variety of settings such as your home, a community organization, or other facility."[89]

The American Association of Retired Persons, AARP, has noted that by the time you reach 65, you have a 50% chance of needing long-term care of some sort. The average cost was $140,000 in 2018, according to AARP, and individual policies averaged $2,700 per year.[90] Policies range in price depending on the age of the insured, whether a couple is insured, and the types of coverage one signs up for.

LTCI is in a state of gradual readjustment, however. Established as a mainstream insurance product in the late 1970s and popularized in the 1980s, insurance providers came to realize in the early 2000s that they had mispriced early versions of the product. Fewer people dropped the insurance product than expected, the costs of long-term care increased more than expected, and more people were taking advantage of their policies as they aged. Thus, insurance providers are having to periodically reevaluate rates as well as benefits as changes occur in medical care and associated costs increase.

As LongTermCare.gov warns, "before you buy a policy, be aware that the insurance company may raise the premium on your policy. It is a good idea to request information on the company's premium rate history."[91] In other words, unlike term life insurance, premiums for this product can rise over time, sometimes with little notice.

The majority of claims are made later in life, according to the American Association for Long-Term Care Insurance (AALTCI), meaning the premiums and increases can add up over the decades before needing to claim any long-term care. In a study published in March 2019 of claims initiated in 2018, for example, AALTCI found that only 4.5% of claims that year were made before the age of 70, while 9.3% of claims were made in the 71-75 age group. Claims rates gradually increased and peaked at 27.2% in the 86-90 age range. The study noted that seven of the new claimants were over 100![92]

This study suggests that many individuals and couples with LTCI will pay premiums for decades before needing care, if at all. And at a minimum, an LTCI policy holder would need to be sure the amount of coverage provided by a given policy increases too, since the equivalent of $140,000 in out-of-pocket costs now would cost significantly more in three decades due to inflation and medical advances.

One strategy to consider before approaching one's 50s and 60s, when LTCI might be the most economically feasible (and given the increased lifespans and claims that are generally made much later in life), is to focus early long-term care financial planning in a Health Savings Account (HSA) associated with a High-Deductible Health Plan (HDHP). HDHPs with HSAs were discussed in Strategy V, and HSAs lend themselves especially well to this kind of planning. They are triply tax-advantaged and can grow tax-free for decades.

A monthly investment of $400—totaling just under $5,000 per year— over twenty years at 8% interest would grow to about $239,150. That amount would potentially continue to grow even when fully retired and no longer contributing to the HSA. (See the "rule of 72" in the next chapter, "Parabolic Wealth," for how this amount could double every nine years on average.) This might be a plan to consider particularly for recent empty-nesters who have fewer family-related healthcare expenses (no braces to pay for anymore!) but who still plan to work another decade or two.

Importantly, HSA funds are yours to keep and use as you see fit. You are not beholden to an insurance company to file a claim. You can include the growing investment in your estate planning as well.

Alternatively, you could do both: Invest in an HSA while working and pay for LTCI once you've reached an age where it makes financial sense. Whichever route you choose, you will need a plan in place to cover longer-term health and care expenses as you get older.

Professional Liability Insurance

Just by watching the evening news and reading the headlines, one can see that the chances of becoming directly involved in a legal procedure in Washington—whether you live there or not—are greater than zero. How many news items do we see daily of a current or recently departed official being subpoenaed, deposed, or "interviewed" related to this or that investigation?

And these are the headline-grabbing stories. How many lower-level workers are caught up in legal proceedings as well, who are called to be witnesses or are interviewed related to this or that case? Is there any chance, however remote, that you could be pulled into a legal proceeding of any sort, whether due to "politics" or your work as a supervisor or as a hiring advisor or perhaps just based on what you might have seen or heard related to a legal matter?

And what are your rights as a whistleblower? Would your employing office offer you legal protection, or simply protect its own interests?

This is where Professional Liability Insurance (PLI) comes in. You would of course want counsel that answers to you and protects *your* interests. And you don't want to have to pay the tens or potentially hundreds of thousands of dollars in legal bills out of your own pocket to obtain legal counsel. For a few hundred dollars a year, you can obtain insurance so that if needed, you will have legal counsel at your disposal who will protect your interests and rights.

The great thing about PLI is that, depending on the company, you can call one of their legal experts even if you have just preliminary questions on a matter. If you were subpoenaed, would you know where to start, or what your rights are at that moment? PLI can be the means to assist you through these challenges, and since you pay for it, the legal resources *work for you* and look after *your* interests if you need them. Depending on your profession, some offices will even reimburse you for PLI.

Consider obtaining Professional Liability Insurance.

(2) Property Insurance

This category of insurance protects you in case anything happens to what you own. Each category of property insurance noted below has many different types of coverage, some of which are regulated by state insurance commissioners and some of which are not. The below is intended for informational purposes only, as basics to consider with each type of insurance coverage. As with types of insurance discussed earlier, be sure to consult an insurance professional for coverage that fits your personal needs in accordance with state insurance regulations.

Definitely comparison-shop for insurance, since quotes can differ dramatically for similar policies. Also, ask about discounts for bundling insurance, which could include life insurance discussed above.

Renters Insurance

Renters insurance is sometimes required when signing a lease, but even when it is required it is not always enforced. Regardless of whether it is "required" or not, if you rent or otherwise live in a dwelling that is not your own, be sure to obtain renters insurance. This will protect your personal property in a variety of circumstances. It should also provide protection for personal liability and potentially for loss of use in case something unexpected were to happen to the property.

Renters insurance is quite economical for the protection it offers. The National Association of Insurance Commissioners (NAIC) says that premiums range between $15 and $30 on average per month, depending on the location and size of the dwelling and the possessions being insured.[93] ValuePenguin pegs the average cost of basic renters insurance nationally at $16 per month, with around $5 difference depending on the state the insurance is purchased in. This can provide coverage for up to $25,000 in case of theft and damage and up to $100,000 personal liability insurance. It notes that while 37% of all households rent their premises, only 40% of those renters actually have coverage.[94]

Make sure to document your personal property in advance, too. Many policies limit the amount that can be claimed in specific categories of personal property, such as jewelry or electronics—this is called "scheduled personal property," which is often the target of thieves. The documentation process lets you know if you are within those maximum amounts. If not, or if you want to insure more valuable items, work with your insurance agent or company to ensure those items are covered as well, either with higher coverage or with a personal property rider.

Check also for coverage related to specific events such as water or sewer back-up. And if the location is no longer habitable, make sure your coverage includes at least the difference between the regular cost of rent and the cost of temporary shelter, to include additional expenditures for food.

Keep documentation in a secure, fire-proof file box, and a copy in an off-site location such as in a safe deposit box at a local bank. You can also keep documentation in a secure password manager or cloud-based account, to avoid property damage ruining the actual documentation associated with the personal property (see the "digital insurance" section below). This way, if your bike is stolen from the hallway or bike rack outside the apartment complex, you have documentation that it was yours and covered; this will streamline your insurance claim for reimbursement for the loss in accordance with the insurance agreement.

Auto Insurance

This type of insurance is pretty standard for those who drive. Liability insurance (for both bodily injury and property damage) is required in almost all U.S. states, as well as personal injury protection and uninsured motorist protection depending on the state. But what about coverage for any damage done to your vehicle?

Coverage for collision and comprehensive ("other than collision") insurance depends on your vehicle and your needs. Driving a beat-up 1980s truck for work around your personal property probably calls for different insurance than that needed for driving an Audi Q7 Quattro through pothole-infested downtown D.C. and dodging jaywalking tourists and Lyft drivers. Similarly, a garaged and lightly used vehicle might not need comprehensive coverage.

The National Association of Insurance Commissioners offers a detailed overview of types of coverage and things to consider in its "Shopping Tool for Automobile Insurance."[95]

Once you've decided on whether you need comprehensive coverage, you then need to decide on your deductibles, where you might be able to save some money. Depending on your insurance company's app or website, you should be able to see how much you would save in monthly or quarterly premiums if you increase your deductible from, say, $300 to $500 in case of a claim.

This can be a bit of a gamble, though. If something *does* happen to your vehicle, then you have to pay that much more out-of-pocket for repairs. Any money you might have saved would go toward the deductible to have your vehicle repaired. It's a fine balance that will depend on your circumstances, where and how you drive, and the age and condition of your vehicle.

You can also easily increase coverage for liability insurance, which is surprisingly economical to do depending on the state insurance requirements. For those who drive a significant amount in a city or urban area, this might be something to consider.

One option is to slightly increase your deductible for damage to your vehicle, with the premium savings paying for increased liability and uninsured motorist coverage, as well as a little extra in your pocket too.

One note about a pernicious type of insurance that is offered when you are purchasing a vehicle at some dealerships. In this sales tactic, just as you're closing on the purchase after what probably amounted to considerable time coming to agreement on the sales price and other specifics, the sales manager takes you through a tiered set of insurance options to purchase in addition to any car payments. At one payment level, the dealership will cover any dents or dings to the paint. At another payment level, they'll cover some damage to the side mirrors, that sort of thing. I've seen five tiers of insurance offered at sale, for example. But there is one category that they don't include: "None of the above."

Perhaps this kind of dealer-sold insurance provides peace of mind. Particularly in a busy metro area, scratches, dings, dents and mirror damage happen all the time and aren't necessarily something that can be claimed.

But also know when going in: You can say "no" to this type of up-sold, dealer-provided insurance.

Lastly, always remember that your driving habits can impact your insurance rates. Get caught speeding beyond a certain limit or too often, and you could pay more in insurance in addition to paying hundreds for the speeding tickets and associated legal fees. Drive safely and defensively and enjoy discounted insurance. If you do have moving violations or points on your driving record, do what you can to clear them quickly and, when they do finally clear, check for better insurance rates.

Homeowners Insurance

Often, this insurance purchase is made at the same time as when a new residence is purchased—indeed, banks require it before finalizing the loan to purchase the property. In the rush to finish the deal, new homeowners might not consider the fine print as closely, nor do homeowners necessarily take the time to look for better deals in the years after closing on the property.

Standard homeowners insurance should cover damage due to fire, theft, or vandalism, as well as provide liability coverage and coverage for additional living expenses should you be unable to occupy the residence due to a covered event. But other situations might not be covered. For example, many homeowners insurance policies do not cover damage caused by standing water, seeping water, mold damage, or damage caused by earthquakes. Damage caused by fallen trees between two properties can sometimes become contentious too: which property owner (and associated insurance policy) is responsible for any property damage, when a tree on the edge of one property damages property on the other? This is particularly the case when another freestanding structure such as a shed or garage is damaged, which the insurance company might declare as uninsured.

You may want to consider riders for valuable items, which can include jewelry or expensive electronics. For maximum protection, you would want to ensure specific, high-value items are covered and document the property in terms of cost and condition, to avoid any complications with the insurance company. As noted in "renters insurance" above, this documentation can be kept in a safe deposit box at a local bank or as part of a password manager or cloud set-up, to avoid property damage ruining the original documentation (see the "digital insurance" section below for more details).

In addition to periodically shopping for better homeowners insurance, some ways to reduce premiums are to add security monitoring services, bundle insurance coverage, and increase deductibles. The latter, as noted previously, might save money on premiums, but it might also cost you money depending on future claims.

Another thing to consider, albeit in extremely limited circumstances: Homeowners insurance does not always cover catastrophic events such as terrorism or nuclear incidents, nor does it generally cover damage related to flooding or earthquakes. Double-check the fine print for these details as well.

Flood & Earthquake Insurance

For most property owners, homeowners insurance does not cover damages caused by flooding or earthquakes. Think you can get away without the cost of separate flood and earthquake insurance? Consider the risks!

For property owners, while you might not live near a major body of water, that does not mean you don't need flood insurance. Similarly, just because you live beyond an active fault line does not mean you won't be impacted by an earthquake. Yes, the chances are reduced, but they still happen.

Even a few centimeters of standing water can cause significant damage in a finished basement. The Federal Emergency Management Agency highlights that "just one inch of water in a home can cost more than $25,000 in damage…" Moreover, "more than 20% of flood claims come from properties outside high-risk flood zones." The average flood claim over the past five years, the Agency states, was $69,000 (although this figure includes damage caused by catastrophic flooding). And "homeowners/renters insurance does not typically cover flood damage," according to FEMA.[96]

With just an inch of standing water, any carpet will probably need to be pulled up, studs and drywall would probably need to be remediated, and the base of floor-level built-ins could be irreparably damaged. Hardwood floors would probably become warped. Mold could grow for months in corners and behind walls without you knowing it.

Perhaps the water comes from an open window during a torrential rainfall while you are away. Perhaps micro-cracks in the foundation (from an earthquake?) allow for unseen seepage and consequent mold growth. There are all sorts of scenarios short of a classic "flood" that could detrimentally impact your property.

Also consider: Even if you are on an upper floor of a condominium, leaks from your neighbors above you (or from one of your own rooms) could cause considerable damage to your dwelling.

Remediation for this kind of damage could cost tens of thousands of dollars and, depending on mold that might only become evident months or years later, may require additional unexpected work long after the original event occurred. For traditional homeowners insurance, water damage and associated mold claims—to include damage to personal items such as furniture—might at best fall into grey areas of coverage that could require considerable negotiation with the insurance company. In many cases, you may be stuck with the bill.

As for earthquake insurance, most homeowners insurance does not cover damage caused by earthquakes. While the possibility of an earthquake damaging your residence might be small, it is not zero in most locations. The U.S. Geologic Survey offers a great map showing the extent of earthquakes in the United States. While the well-known San Andreas fault line skirts the coast of California where earthquakes are a fact of life, earthquakes strike throughout the United States. There have been 35,683 earthquakes of 2+ or greater magnitude in the continental U.S. in the 2009-2019 decade, for example. Almost every state of the union experienced an earthquake in that timeframe.[97]

Keep in mind the costs associated with these low-probability but extremely costly events, and plan accordingly. Outside flood and earthquake zones, the cost of coverage could potentially be quite economical for the coverage it provides. Consider adding riders to your insurance coverage to plan for these events.

(3) Wealth Insurance

This category is not technically "insurance," but rather various approaches to "insure" that *you* determine how your wealth (and end-of-life health) is managed and transferred in case you are incapacitated or pass away. This is also where you can provide instructions regarding who will be the guardians of your dependents and who manages your estate in providing for them.

Consult your office of legal assistance or a qualified attorney specializing in wills and trusts for legal advice. Also consider establishing a limited power of attorney if you deploy frequently, which is beyond the scope of this book but can be established with the help of your office of legal assistance.

Make a Will

It would be unfair for your relatives or friends to be faced with figuring out your financial affairs and how you would have wanted things taken care of following your demise. If you pass away and do not have a will, you die intestate: the state becomes the executor of your estate and makes all the decisions for you. Without a will, any blood relative can make a claim on your estate.

It is also unfair to *yourself*. You have served honorably and worked hard to build your wealth. Do you want the state courts to determine what happens to your assets?

Why put off this crucial step? The process in most states is straight-forward, although there are legal specifics to be aware of, so be sure to research the process based on your state of residence. According to the Virginia State Bar, for example, in Virginia any mentally competent person who is at least eighteen years old may make a will, and the signing of a will must generally be witnessed by two competent persons, who must sign the will in front of the testator (the will's owner). The VSB adds that an exception to the witness requirement is made if the testator writes out the entire will in his or her own handwriting and signs and dates it.[98]

According to the National Notary Association, some states require notarization, while others do not; wills might be invalidated if they are notarized in still other cases, according to the association.[99] As the Virginia State Bar notes, "although the law does not require a will to be notarized, it is a highly recommended practice followed by most lawyers. If the will includes a notarized 'Self-Proving Affidavit,' the will is presumed to be properly executed and is accepted by the court without testimony from the witnesses."[100]

Thus, while the process is fairly straight-forward, you should start by visiting your legal office or a legal professional for additional resources specific to your state of residence.

Remember, no matter how small your invested assets are now, no matter how small your "estate" is, it has the potential to grow into huge amounts in later years depending on how it is managed. Perhaps you put it off now, then another year, then again a year later. Before you know it, you have $25,000, $50,000, or even six figures saved and invested in the TSP, along with insurance and other property and investments as well. The longer you put it off, the more your wealth grows; perhaps your family expands as well. You will have named beneficiaries for your TSP and life insurance, of course, but why put them through the additional challenges of going through state courts to settle all of your affairs?

Indeed, as the Virginia State Bar declares: "Every mentally competent adult should have a will." It includes important reasons such as the ability to name ("nominate") a guardian or guardians for your minor children, reducing the expenses of administering your estate, and naming the person or persons who will handle your estate and how it should be handled.

These reasons are valid for any adult resident of any state. If you do not have a will, make one now in accordance with the laws of your state of residence.

Consider a Living Revocable Trust

A living revocable trust can give you greater control in estate planning. It can also be more complicated and expensive than simply writing a will. Given the complexity and expense, most readers probably don't need to set up a trust. But consider a trust if you want more control over how your growing assets are handled after you pass.

The legal site LegalZoom details three main reasons for creating a living revocable trust: (1) It avoids probate and therefore reduces the time to settle an estate from months to weeks; (2) a living revocable trust can save money over the long-term by avoiding much of the costs associated with probate (and living trusts hold up better in court if contested); and (3) a living trust provides additional privacy because it does not go through probate, which becomes a matter of public record. A living trust can also be beneficial in case of your incapacitation, as the successor trustee can manage your affairs and avoid a court-appointed conservatorship.[101]

You, as the creator of the trust or "grantor," can designate a successor trustee to manage your assets and property according to your express wishes in the trust. The trustee can be an individual or an institution such as a bank or financial institution. The latter, called a "corporate trustee," provides some extra protection in case the original individual is no longer capable of performing the role of trustee. Because the trust is revocable, you can make changes to it as you wish.

The complexities and legal requirements for setting up a trust and transferring assets to it ("funding the trust") are not insignificant, so definitely seek the advice of an attorney specializing in trusts.

Other Legal Documents

Lastly, consider a few other legal documents particularly if you deploy often or for significant lengths of time.

A **limited power of attorney** will allow a trusted contact to manage your affairs in accordance with the powers laid out in the document, while a **special power of attorney** can be limited to specific instances (like selling a car while you are deployed). Contact your office of legal assistance for more information on these important documents.

Consider also a **healthcare proxy** and/or a **living will**. While the living revocable trust can detail how you want your financial affairs and assets handled, a healthcare proxy and/or living will detail how you want your health-related affairs handled if you are incapacitated or have passed. These documents can be drawn up by a legal professional separately or at the same time as a will and trust.

(4) Digital Insurance

These days, we do so much online. What happens if one of your devices is lost or stolen, or if one of your accounts is compromised or hijacked?

Protect your digital assets, your digital identity, and your digital life by using the below approaches.

Sign Up for Identity Theft Protection

Identify theft and fraud has evolved significantly just in the last decade. According to the Federal Trade Commission's "Consumer Sentinel Network," which tracks reports of fraud and ID theft, the number of total reported cases by year rose from 325,519 in 2001 to over one million for the first time in 2007, and reports continued to rise dramatically to over three million on average since 2015. In 2018, one in four victims of fraud reported financial losses that totaled $1.48 billion dollars, or a median loss of $375 per report—and over 18,000 victims suffered losses greater than $10,000. Military consumers, including military veterans, were victims of over 122,000 crimes in 2018.[102]

Because these are based on figures reported to the FTC usually via local law enforcement, actual figures could be larger since some victims either do not know about the theft or do not want to report their experiences to law enforcement authorities. Citing a separate report, the Insurance Information Institute highlighted that in 2018 there were 14.4 million victims of identity fraud, and 3.3 million of those victims were responsible for at least some of the liability of the fraud committed against them. The Insurance Information Institute in particular noted that criminals were increasingly targeting loyalty and rewards programs and retirement accounts.[103] (The cited report relied on survey data rather than reported data, however.)

There are numerous ways ID thieves can use stolen personal information for the purposes of financial and other fraudulent activities. Here are a few, according to the FTC and other sources:

Medical ID Theft: According to the FTC, a fraudster may use your name or health insurance information to see a doctor, get prescription drugs, file claims with your insurance provider, or obtain other care. If the fraudster's health information is mixed with yours, your treatment, payment records, and credit report could be impacted. Victims of this type of fraud will need to correct their medical records in addition to any other ID recovery efforts to ensure safe medical treatment. The FTC website has a list of steps to take to correct medical records.[104]

Child ID Theft: As the FTC details, a child's Social Security number can be used by identity thieves to apply for government benefits, open bank and credit card accounts, apply for a loan or utility service, or rent a place to live.[105] Children and dependents can usually be added to ID protection services to help mitigate this threat.

Tax-Related Identity Theft: This entails the fraudulent use of your Social Security number by an ID thief to steal your tax refund or get a job.

Familiar Fraud: The individual or group perpetrating this fraud has knowledge of the victim's personal details, and perhaps even access to the victim's personal devices. With this kind of knowledge and access, the "familiar fraudster" can potentially gain unhindered access to already-established accounts or create new accounts under the victim's name, to include new bank and credit card accounts and loans.

Non-Financial Account ID Theft: Have you noticed how your bank requires you to provide several different pieces of information (such as a pin and login that is different from your email in addition to your password) to get into your accounts? This is a good thing, as you don't want your money stolen directly from your bank account. But non-financial accounts, such as rewards programs, some mobile network providers, and many online-only accounts have basic sign-on protocols despite having a surprising amount of information about you in their systems. The theft of this information can provide fraudsters with enough information to target more sensitive accounts detailed further in the "SIM hijacking" and social engineering sections.

These sobering statistics and attack vectors are reason enough to consider signing up for identity theft protection. While no service can "protect" your identity with 100% certainty in the sense of stopping fraudsters and criminals from using your stolen identity before the crime occurs (such as with "familiar fraud" above), they can provide additional, proactive measures to monitor your credit and use of personally identifiable information (PII) online and for credit requests. This could be anything from fraudulent changes to your address and use of your identity in court or arrest records, to payday loan or other new credit account requests (which was the largest single crime in 2018, according to the FTC), to use of your PII online and in social media. When identified proactively, authorities have a much better chance of stopping the fraud before more damage can be inflicted. They also have a better chance of catching the ID thieves.

Importantly, many services also offer insurance and support for recovering your credit and reestablishing your identity in case your PII is used fraudulently. This could save you days or weeks of effort in contacting all the credit institutions involved (some of which are only open during regular business hours), waiting on hold and being transferred between customer care representatives, and figuring out how to recover from the fraudulent use of your PII.

You can also sign up for many basic ID protection services on your own for free. You can set up alerts for all of your accounts, for example, and through each of the three credit agencies. These efforts alone can go a long way to protecting yourself from fraudulent use of your identity.

The FTC maintains identitytheft.gov as a dedicated site for reporting fraud. Those who have had their personal information used to open new accounts, make purchases, or get a tax refund should report the crime on this site. The site also lists all the things you need to do to reclaim your identity, at identitytheft.gov/Steps, depending on the type of fraud you have encountered.

You also can proactively freeze your credit (which is sometimes called a "security freeze"), but this requires some additional steps. You will need to contact each of the three credit reporting agencies to freeze your credit. The freeze is in place for one year, so you will need to renew. Moreover, as the FTC states, if you plan to sign up for a monitoring service, you will need to do so *before* you freeze your accounts so that the monitoring service can access your credit files. If you want to apply for a new loan or credit card, you will need to lift the freeze first to do so, and then reinstate it afterward. Alternatively, you can place a "fraud alert" on your credit report that instructs potential creditors to contact you directly to verify your identity before opening an account. The fraud alert lasts one year and can be renewed.[106]

Some readers might be eligible for ID monitoring and insurance sponsored by the government. Were you affected by OPM's "cybersecurity incident" (as the agency now calls it) in 2015? You would be eligible for identity theft protection services through an OPM-sponsored program that is currently scheduled to last until 2026. See www.opm.gov/cybersecurity/ for details. OPM and DOD had originally awarded a $133 million contract in 2015 to pay for three years of protection for the estimated 21.5 million "victims of cybercrime" whose personal information was stolen "in one of the largest cybercrimes ever carried out against the United States Government."[107] This was subsequently extended into the 2020s. But beware! Some scammers send fake "free" offers to steal your personal information, as the FTC warns.[108] Conduct due-diligence on any company and their offerings first before signing up.

Set up an "Active Duty Alert" When Deploying

For military and civilian personnel about to deploy, you can request an "active duty alert" be placed on your credit reports to further minimize the risk of identity theft while away. According to the U.S. FTC, an active duty alert on a credit report means businesses have to take extra steps before granting credit in your name.[109]

- To request an active duty alert, contact one credit bureau; that credit bureau is then required to notify the other two credit bureaus of the alert.
- The credit bureaus also will take your name off their marketing list for prescreened credit card offers for two years, unless you ask them to add you back onto the list.
- An active duty alert is good for one year, so be sure to renew the alert if your tour of duty lasts beyond a year.

Use a Password Manager

According to the FIDO or "Fast IDentity Online" Alliance—a group dedicated to improving account security—the average individual has over 90 online accounts, and up to 51% of passwords are reused across accounts. Moreover, passwords are the root cause of over 80% of data breaches, according to the alliance.[110]

Given the centrality of passwords to securing online accounts, care should be taken in managing one's passwords across all accounts, not just financial ones.

Hackers have a variety of ways to obtain or crack a password. They can employ brute-force attacks to apply all possible combinations of letters, numbers, and special characters to discover a password. A dictionary attack is faster, since many passwords are versions of dictionary words, even with look-alike characters and numbers replacing letters. Hackers can also employ social engineering to convince a company's help desk to switch accounts away from your control or to provide them with additional personal information that the hackers can then use to seize a different account. User ID and password combinations are for sale on the dark web, as well.

And the attacks get faster as technology develops. Several online sites offer illustrations of how long it would take to crack a particular password in a given year since 1982.[111] It's eye-opening. These days, cracking six- and eight-character passwords is trivial and can take mere seconds depending on the password's strength.

Account holders' reuse of simple passwords from site to site remains a major vulnerability to this day. Not only do people reuse their passwords across accounts, passwords are usually a basic word or set of numbers, or something that is "unique" to a given user only in that they include their birthdays, names, pets, or some other combination of personal details. These latter details can be gathered from openly available social media accounts and social engineering.

In a cyber-survey of breached accounts in early 2019, the UK's National Cyber Security Centre (NCSC) found that the password "123456" was used over *23 million* times. Other top-five reused passwords included "password" and "111111". Names used as passwords included "Ashley," "Michael," and "Blink-182." (Hackers know this, and they adjust their attacks accordingly.) The NCSC also found that fewer than half of those questioned in the cyber-survey used separate, hard-to-guess passwords for different accounts.[112]

Wikipedia has a page devoted to the most-used passwords in each year since 2011, compiled from a number of sources. In addition to the most-used passwords identified in the NCSC cyber-survey, other often-used passwords include "admin" and "iloveyou".[113] Almost all of them are between six and eight characters of either lower-case letters or numbers, which take little time to crack.

Even non-English speakers reuse simple passwords. Early in 2019, security researchers noticed that the password "ji32k7au4a83" had been used in 141 occurrences of breached passwords in a dataset managed by haveibeenpwned.com. It turned out that the characters were Unicode produced by a Zhuyin (Chinese) keyboard. The characters corresponded to Chinese characters that spelled "mypassword".[114]

And as we all know, there are massive troves of data from breached or "pwned" sites available on the open internet and for sale on the dark web that include emails and passwords. The site "haveibeenpwned.com" has a section devoted to listing the breached sites in the past decade. It also maintains a closed database of over 550 million passwords for research purposes. As the site dryly notes, "exposure makes them unsuitable for ongoing use as they're at much greater risk of being used to take over other accounts."[115]

These massive data leaks have given rise to another particularly pernicious attack called *credential stuffing*. This type of attack involves the use of breached username/email and password pairs on popular sites to see if they provide access to a given account. The process can be set up programmatically, so that programs or bots input potentially millions of username/password pairs on thousands of sites, using a range of possible proxies. These programs are for sale on the internet, for example, as detailed by the developer of haveibeenpwned.com, Troy Hunt, and others.[116] Or, they could be targeted attacks if the attacker knows the username/email of a chosen victim.

There are several lessons that can be immediately drawn from the above. First, *do not reuse passwords*, especially for your financial accounts such as your TSP online account. Second, *do not use easily broken or easily guessed passwords!* Eight characters these days is too short. Twelve or even 14 characters provide much better protection currently. The UK's NCSC suggests using a string of three random but memorable words together, for example.[117]

The NCSC guidance is useful for sensitive accounts, and there are multiple approaches to generating secure passwords along these lines. The "Diceware List" approach uses five six-sided dice to choose from a list of 7,776 words for a truly random password; variations use similar approaches with different types of dice and lists. The Electronic Frontier Foundation, for example, uses a similar approach with an updated list that is easier to remember.[118]

But the average person has around 90 online or digital accounts that require passwords. None of us mere mortals could realistically remember all these accounts no matter what mnemonic devices we might employ, especially when having to change them on a regular basis.

That is why many security professionals advocate the use of a password manager. This helps you create strong passwords that are unique for each account you have. You wouldn't have to limit your passwords to 6-, 8-, or 10-character limits. You could use all cases, numbers, and special characters in 20- or even 30-character, randomly generated passwords. Passwords such as these are essentially uncrackable.

Password managers also automatically and securely detect reused passwords, both among the account holder's accounts and against passwords that have been previously breached and exposed online. They also can monitor the length of time passwords have been used on accounts. Thus, they help you manage and maintain unique and strong passwords across all your digital accounts.

In this way, if a hacker gained access to a list of passwords used for a particular site and your password was included on that list, the password manager will notify you once the breach is discovered. Some even proactively suggest new passwords for breached accounts. You simply change the password *for that site*, and you would not have to worry that the hackers can potentially get into your other accounts because you use unique passwords across all of your accounts.

Password manager security is paramount, of course. This is where you could use the three- or four-word or diceware list approaches to generate a strong password for the manager itself. Two-factor authentication would need to be enabled for the password manager at a minimum, and universal second-factor (U2F, also discussed below) would provide even better security.

If you're concerned about including your TSP account in a password manager in case the password manager itself is compromised, consider a partial approach. Keep the password in the password manager, but don't include the TSP login name (which can be masked and different from the TSP account number). You can also use a manager-recommended password and keep that version saved for regular use, but add one additional character or letter at the end of the password that only you know and that is not saved to the password manager. The pop-up to save the "new" password can become annoying in this approach, but you can feel confident that your password is safe even if your password manager somehow is breeched.

Always Use Two-Factor Authentication

In addition to using a password manager (and never reusing passwords), use what's called "two-factor authentication" or 2FA on every account for which it is available. For reasons discussed in the ID theft section above, 2FA should certainly be enabled on any banking or financial sites you may own, and on non-financial accounts as well to prevent the leaking of potentially valuable identifying digital information about you.

According to the National Institute of Standards and Technology, two-factor authentication, sometimes also called multi-factor authentication ("MFA"; 2FA is a subset of MFA), requires two of three different categories of security to access your account: (1) something you know (like a password or PIN), (2) something you have (like a personal device or smart card), or (3) something you are (like your fingerprint). They must be from different categories, so entering two different passwords would not be considered multi-factor.[119]

When enabled, 2FA requires a second authentication method in addition to a password or biometric (fingerprint, face scan, etc) to gain access to an account. Basic second factors can include a text message or call to a registered number, an email, or an app-based authenticator.

The TSP site enabled a basic two-factor capability in spring 2019, and it became mandatory to use 2FA for online account access in December 2019. The choice of factors as of early 2020 are email and text. To enable 2FA, a TSP account holder adds or updates his or her contact with this information and then verifies them with an initial code sent to those contact accounts to establish that you control them.

Once enabled, a TSP account owner signs in using the account number or username and password. Then the site asks for a special code, called a "one-time passcode" (OTP) or verification code, which is sent to one of the account holder's previously established points of contact. The account holder retrieves the code, inputs it into the site, and then gains access.

Unfortunately, TSP's mobile 2FA relies on SMS—text messages sent to your mobile phone number—as one of the two-factor protocols. While it is an important addition to your account's security since it adds to the complexity of attempting to access your account, by itself SMS is not as secure as other 2FA methods. Alarmingly, there has been a significant rise in "SMS hijacking" or SIM swapping, where criminals gain access to a user's wireless network account, change the SIM account information to a new SIM/device they control, and then use the new SIM/device to receive your text messages.

In some cases, criminals attempt to use social engineering (portraying themselves as the owner of the phone number and associated account) to convince wireless service help centers to port the number to a phone they control. In other cases, criminals pay insiders to switch the number to a different SIM card that the criminals control, sometimes for less than $100.[120] In either case, they gain access and are able to use the wireless number to receive temporary codes from any service that uses the wireless number as a backup, such as Yahoo or Google (depending on how the account's security is set up; see "U2F" below).

Criminals have used this technique increasingly since 2015 to steal cryptocurrency and high-profile social media accounts. According to the III, mobile phone account takeovers grew from 380,000 in 2017 to 680,000 in 2018.[121]

This happened to Jack Dorsey, the CEO of Twitter, as recently as August 2019. Attackers gained control of his phone number via SIM swap fraud and took control of his text-to-tweet account on Twitter-owned Cloudhopper. They then began to send offensive tweets in his name.[122] Attackers employing social engineering in 2016 targeted private accounts used by then-Homeland Security Secretary Jeh Johnson and other high-ranking government officials by conducting reverse look-ups to find their phone company information, then used social engineering techniques to trick employees into revealing additional personal information. In the case of Secretary Johnson, they were able to gain control of his Comcast account, while in another case the attackers gained control of a high-ranking official's AOL account that contained sensitive work documents.[123] While in these cases they did not take control of the officials' SIM cards, the type of attack is similar.

These attacks illustrate the vulnerability of not just mobile numbers, but email accounts too. They are another reminder that multi-factor authentication should be used on all major accounts, not just financial ones.

Moreover, these examples illustrate how authenticator apps such as Google Authenticator, Authy, Microsoft's Authenticator, or LastPass's Authenticator should be enabled as a second factor instead of texts to wireless numbers. These are called "Timed One-Time Passcode" generators, or TOTP, because the one-time codes they generate change at regular (such as 30-second) intervals. You don't need to receive any text or message in order to use them, you simply input the current code to gain access to the account. They also provide a one-time-use recovery code when first registering for the service (usually a very long string of numbers, letters, and/or special characters), but be sure to keep these in a safe place such as a safe deposit box.

Those who use app-based second factors should take into account lost or stolen devices, too, so that they do not lose access to their accounts if they lose access to their device. Authy, a cloud-based 2FA app, is particularly handy since it has a cloud back-up so you can use the same authentication setup on multiple devices. Granted, using a cloud backup for a second factor introduces the possibility of an attacker gaining access to the cloud backup, but the backups are end-to-end encrypted, and users have much greater control over how to lock down the second-factor account compared to wireless accounts. This includes the option to use security keys or tokens to further lock down the account.

Consider Enabling U2F

An even more secure solution is to enable U2F, or "Universal Second Factor," authentication where available.

U2F authentication relies on physical security keys that are plugged into the computer or otherwise use Bluetooth or nearfield communication with mobile devices to provide the second form of authentication. There are no additional passcodes to use, no text messages, no TOTP apps, therefore there are no ways to intercept the passcodes. Accessing accounts via U2F security keys also obviates man-in-the-middle attacks.

Alphabet, the parent of Google, declared in 2018 that after it instituted a U2F policy in early 2017 directing all of its 85,000+ employees to use USB-based security keys, no employee work account had been successfully phished in over a year of using the new security procedures.[124] This included phishing attempts conducted by the company's own security teams to test employees' use of the security keys.

Some U2F devices include Yubico's Yubikey line of products, Google's Titan, and the Purism Librem Key. Just make sure you have multiple keys that are kept in different locations, so that if you lose one, you can still access your accounts with another key.

U2F security can be enabled on a long and growing list of digital accounts. Most password managers can use U2F devices, for example. Some banking institutions—and many investment accounts—can be protected by U2F security keys too.

Unfortunately, while the mutual fund and investing industry has moved to adopt U2F functionality, there are no signs that the TSP will do so. It is still just limited to 2FA via text message or email.

One possible approach to increasing your TSP account security is to only associate contact information with accounts that have U2F enabled. For example, you can use a SIM-less Google Voice-based number as your 2FA contact for your TSP account, and you can further enable Google's "Advanced Protection" on the account. This will require the use of Google's Titan security key and certain other restrictions to further protect the account from being breached. But because the number is SIM-less, a potential attacker would need to gain access to your Google account in order to unlock and port it to another service. This would be virtually impossible due to the requirements to use the Titan key to log into the account.

Alternatively, in addition to using a U2F-protected email account, use a generic mobile number that is not your primary phone and that is not associated with any other accounts. This way, it is not associated with your name in public or other records; a reverse look-up would not discover this number as being associated with your name. Avoid using this number with other accounts, as data breaches could lead to discoverability of the number associated with you. This is a more expensive approach to online security, however, although companies such as Tracfone offer deals for basic talk and text for under $10 a month.

Certainly, enabling 2FA and especially U2F creates some inconveniences. It can take longer to log into your accounts, for one. You wouldn't be able to use some accounts in the office as you might have done in the past, potentially. But high-profile cases demonstrate how vulnerable your online accounts can be, and the additional steps can provide peace-of-mind as your accounts grow in value over time.

Use (Paid!) VPNs

Your browsing activity exposes a lot about you on public networks, even if the network itself is secure. How might a store or restaurant be using your data on the "free" WiFi they provide on their premises? It's no secret that some stores track you via your mobile device as you visit and move through their shopping aisles.[125] What might commercial locations do with your data when you access their WiFi networks?

Moreover, with the proliferation of spoofed WiFi hotspots that are designed to look like legitimate ones, you might mistakenly log onto a hotspot that was established to steal information from users. These are sometimes masked to resemble real WiFi hotspots, such as "my_favorite_coffee_place_ spoofed" instead of "my_favorite_coffee_place_free". They're never quite that obvious, of course.

A VPN, or virtual private network, provides an extra layer of protection from prying eyes. It creates a data tunnel from your device to an endpoint, through which your browsing and online activities are encrypted. Because it is encrypted within the data tunnel directly from your device, no one can eavesdrop on your activities.

Use of a VPN therefore should be considered particularly when traveling, and when accessing financial and other sensitive sites when away from trusted home networks.

Some suggest using a VPN domiciled in a non-"Five Eyes" country.* The theory is that because the country is outside a "Five Eyes" country, the company will not have to be responsive to U.S. government subpoenas for information on a customer's browsing history.

Personally, I don't buy that rationale. Just as I don't trust having any cloud information hosted directly in a non-Western-based server farm, I don't want my VPN browsing controlled by a company that resides outside my country of residence. A company might be outside U.S. legal jurisdiction, but that means they are potentially outside *any* jurisdiction. Who knows what other nefarious actors are targeting that VPN company, to get access to your or my VPN usage surreptitiously? That is easier to accomplish in a non-U.S., non-Five Eyes country. And should that activity be suspected or uncovered, I certainly trust U.S. or allied authorities to investigate more than I would third-country ones.

There are free VPNs available, but remember that *your* data is passing through their pipeline, and you have little control or visibility into how the company uses your information or how actively they protect it. How do they make their money to pay for the up-to-date technology and specialists to protect you? At a minimum, they have fewer resources to spend on protecting you, their "customer," and more concerning, they could be selling some of the information they gather from you as well.

---

* The "Five Eyes" countries consist of the United States, the United Kingdom, Australia, Canada, and New Zealand.

(There are also open-source approaches to building a personal VPN capability, but the technical means of setting one up are beyond the scope of this book.)

Ultimately, I prefer to use a paid, U.S.-based VPN service.

Backup Your Files

Is your computer or mobile device a "single point of failure" in your digital life? What if you lost access to the main device you use? What files, pictures, or videos would you lose as a result?

More and more these days, we must consider how we protect our devices and what is on them to ensure that, should we lose access to one, we don't lose our entire digital life.

The sections above advocated steps to protect one's digital accounts, while this section advocates steps for protecting one's digital *life*.

It's not just a loss of a device that should concern you. Ransomware became a major issue in the 2010s. Using file-encrypting software, hackers can lock unsuspecting users out of their devices. They demand payment—usually by cryptocurrency—to unlock the ransomware and restore access to the device. How you manage your digital assets can have a direct impact on how you respond to such a scenario. If you had only one digital copy of a particularly important file, or a photo collection full of memories, you might be tempted to pay. But if you have backups that were completely separate from the infected device, you could refrain from paying, however annoying a bricked device might be. (Not to mention, you would avoid the feeling of your privacy being both violated and held hostage.)[126]

Moreover, how secure are your files and documents should a tornado rip through your neighborhood while you were away? Would your main device *and* local hard-drive backups be destroyed as a result of the natural catastrophe?

These scenarios are not fun to consider, but it's important to think through in order to protect your digital assets.

You should consider keeping at least three backups: (1) backups on multiple devices, (2) backups on a digital storage device that is separate from the internet and the other devices, and (3) a virtual backup.

A cloud service is probably the easiest way to manage backups across devices as well as in a virtual environment. It is also probably the most durable solution in case of a natural disaster destroying your other devices and backups. There are multiple, reputable and secure services available from Apple, Google, and Microsoft, to Dropbox and Box, to name some of the big ones. There are plenty of other smaller companies as well.

Depending on your views, a cloud service may or may not best serve as a virtual backup for your digital files. You might consider a cloud service insecure because of celebrity hacks in the early 2010s, or perhaps you just don't trust public clouds with all of your data.

Cloud services have come a long way since the well-publicized hacking incidents early in the decade. Most cloud service providers either enable 2FA by default, or they make 2FA and even U2F widely available and user-friendly. Cloud-enabled sharing also provides much greater control over file and photo sharing. You can determine who is able to see a given file or photo, how they see it, and for how long. You can revoke the shared links and folders as well. For the security conscious who avoid public social media accounts, a cloud-based private network can serve many of the same functions offered by mainstream social media platforms.

With some technical savvy, you also can set up and host a private cloud on your own network. OwnCloud, Nextcloud, and Seafile are a few of the open source cloud solutions that you can install and maintain on your own. Since you control everything from the downloading and installation to the configuration and access controls you should have no concern about commercial clouds "tracking" you or otherwise having access to your personal files (if you are indeed concerned about that). They also provide solutions for updating and syncing files, photos, contacts, calendars, and other data across your devices. And they employ and are compatible with many 2FA authenticators and security keys.

The one drawback to a private cloud solution is that it is usually locally hosted and thus still vulnerable to local conditions, everything from power outages to natural disasters. There are cloud hosting services based on these open-sourced options, but they can cost about the same as the more mainstream (and more user-friendly) cloud services. Federated private clouds are an exciting possibility in this regard. You can mitigate locality risk by setting up and connecting multiple and privately-run cloud servers with friends and/

or family that are hosted in different locations (that is, where your friends and family live). While this would require more maintenance and upkeep, it does help to mitigate against natural disasters wiping out your digital life. You can still maintain granular control over who can access what files, too.

New, hybrid solutions are coming to market as well. Some companies are introducing cloud servers that can be self-hosted and also include periodic and automatic cloud back-ups for a yearly fee. They also include the ability to set up your own domain and associated private and secure email. Helm, for example, markets a server that is purchased and hosted locally, but backs up encrypted files and email to a cloud service for a yearly fee.[127]

Whichever solution you choose, definitely enable 2FA or U2F for personal and cloud accounts, as noted above.

***

Insure What You Need to Insure, and Update!

For each of the aforementioned sections, there will be nuances specific to your situation that might not have been addressed, or the details may become outdated by the time you have read this chapter. Definitely do additional research, read the fine print, and consult *independent* financial, insurance, and/or legal experts—ones who are not compensated for selling you a specific investment or insurance product—before making a decision.

One last exercise you must undertake on a regular basis: Review your beneficiary information regularly and update your documents with every life event!

Parabolic Wealth

Throughout this book, we have examined the growth of investments by making periodic and gradually increasing contributions over a career. A career—your career—could be entirely with the military and/or federal government, or with a number of different employers in the private as well as public sectors. Or maybe you start your own company, or you go on to teach. Wherever you go, you can take your TSP investment with you, and you can continue to add to it in an IRA or other employer-sponsored plan (being mindful of any fees these may charge).

Now it is time to examine how dividends, interest, and growth rates, coupled with a number of other factors outlined below and compounded over time, can positively impact investments in profound ways, particularly in later years.

Linear Growth, Exponential Growth, and Parabolic Growth

Growth can take many shapes. A basic growth rate is linear growth.

Linear growth is what it sounds like, a line going up steadily over time. You probably remember from high school math the function for a line, $y = mx + b$, where b is the intercept on the y-axis, and m represents the slope. The slope is the growth rate for a line, assuming it is positive (if it's negative, that of course means you're losing money).

To illustrate, take $10 growing by $1 at each time period. At period one it adds $1 to make it $11, then another $1 to make it $12, and so on. At this rate, it would take 10 intervals or time periods to double to $20. But the growth rate is the same, at $1. To double again to $40, it now takes 20 intervals or time periods (20 times adding of $1 each time). And then to double again to $80, it now takes 40 intervals.

You see the challenge with this situation. The growth rate is no more and no less. It simply takes longer and longer to build wealth! As investors looking to build personal wealth over the long term, we want to avoid linear growth rates.

A really exciting growth rate is called *exponential growth*. Instead of steadily increasing by the same amount at each interval, exponential growth rates double at each interval, so one doubles to two, and two doubles to four, and then to eight, and so on. The function here is $f(x) = ab^x$. This results in rapid growth rate—*exponential growth rate*. The line growing exponentially slopes ever more rapidly higher, as you can see in the chart below comparing hypothetical linear and exponential growth rates.

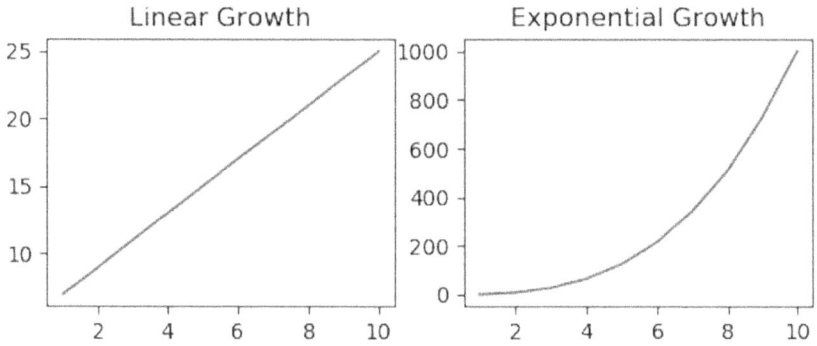

These two charts compare linear versus exponential growth rates. Despite the same timespan on the x-axis (0-10), the hypothetical linear growth rate rises to 25, while the hypothetical exponential growth rate rises to 1000, while its slope continues to bend upward.

A great illustration of this in action is the penny riddle. Would you rather have an amount that starts with $0.01 that doubles each day for 30 days, or would you rather have $10,000 right now?

Think carefully! $10,000 is *a lot* of money, after all, and it could be yours right now (in this hypothetical exercise) without waiting a whole month to get whatever you might receive starting from that measly penny. It takes a whole week to even reach $0.64, after all.

But keep going with that calculation, and you'll be astounded. Follow along if you can: Open up your favorite spreadsheet, and in the first cell type in ".01". Then in the next cell, put in a formula that doubles the previous cell. Continue for 30 cells. The amount takes a while to grow, certainly. It takes 18 days to reach the $1,000 mark, and 21 days—three full weeks—to reach $10,000. It reaches the $100,000 mark four days later, however, and then it crosses the $1,000,000 mark after day 28. At the end of 30 days, the grand total is a whopping $5,368,709.12. This, all from starting with a penny!

That is *exponential* growth.

Alas, this doesn't happen in the real world of investment returns. For investors, high linear or pure exponential growth rates are impossible. Scam artists and Ponzi schemes will promise this type of steady but dynamic growth. They'll claim: "Invest with me, and you will enjoy 12% to 15% growth rates annually, with no downturns!" Sometimes the claimed growth will be greater, sometimes it will be less. But the hallmarks of these scams are: (1) claims of higher growth rates than normally available elsewhere, and (2) claims that your money is "safe" in the given investment.

As you've seen in example after example in this book, based on real data, the only "safe" investment in terms of never declining has been the G Fund. All the others experience declines, often multiple significant declines, over any 30-year period. But the G Fund's near-linear growth rate has averaged around 2% in the second half of the 2010s. Any promises for regular and significant growth above this rate, with no declines in value, are at best over-confident and at worst criminal.

Rather, growth comes in fits and spurts that trends upward over time, in what can become parabolic in nature. And with those spurts come negative parabolic events as well, which will be illustrated below. Growth forms a larger parabola slopping upward, but at times the parabola inverts, so that our sloping curve turns negative and trends downward for a time. These are important events, and they help reset markets. They are also important buying opportunities, as we've examined previously.

The below graph shows the typical rise and fall of a given market, which slopes upward. But the movements can be fitted to parabolic movements, in either upward or downward directions.

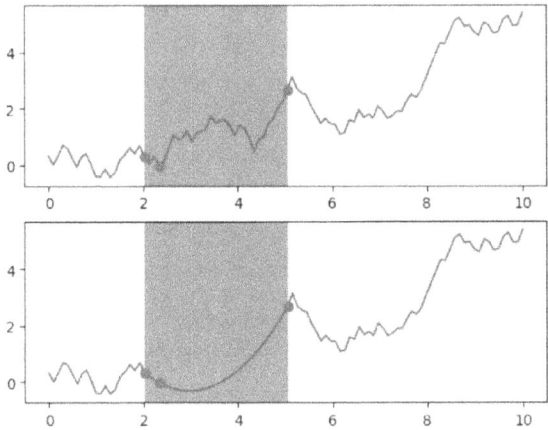

These hypothetical line graphs show how market trends can switch between convex and concave parabolic forms, even as the movement trends upward over time.

These negative parabolic events, when the slope turns negative, always (eventually) invert and go positive again, which is when parabolic wealth is truly experienced. By continuing the exercise of dollar-cost-averaging during the negative parabolic events, our greater parabola grows more significantly over time. Before examining parabolic wealth further, let's first examine the 'rule of 72' and compound growth.

Compound Growth and the 'Rule of 72'

Compound growth is a significant driver of wealth-building over time.

To illustrate with an example that is more realistic than the penny-doubling example above, we'll use the $100,000 figure from previous chapters again. Let's say that $100,000 grows in value through dividends, interest, and asset growth by 10% over a year, without any contributions added to it. So that $100,000 becomes $110,000 after a year.

Now let's say it grows again the following year by the same 10%. So that would be $120,000 after the second year, matching the $10,000 return of the first year, right? Wrong. That $110,000 grows to $121,000—it increased by *$11,000* this time, not by $10,000.

The $10,000 original growth amount also increased by 10%, or $1,000, in the second year. And in the *third* year, that $121,000 would grow to $133,100 assuming a 10% return, or an additional $12,100 that year. The $21,000 earned in the first two years grows by 10% ($2,100) in addition to the 10% of the original $100,000 ($10,000).

This is an example of compound growth: the growth of the original amount in value, plus reinvested dividends or interest, is compounded so that there are increasing returns both in the original amount and in the reinvested amount. A 10% return each year, in the example above, does not mean a $10,000 return each year, but rather growing returns of $10,000 in year 1, $11,000 in year 2, $12,100 in year 3, $13,310 in year 4 and so forth.

In fact, with a 10% return compounded over time, that original $100,000 would double in value in just over seven years.

This is the essence of the rule of 72. To calculate the amount of time it would take an original investment to double over time, you divide 72 by the real number of the interest rate. In this case, 72 divided by 10—the 10% annual return in the example above—is 7.2 years. It therefore takes any given investment about 7.2 years to double, with a 10% annual rate of return.

Thus, a 5% annual return would double in about 14.4 years, an 8% return would double in 9 years, and a 12% annual return would double in 6 years. As you can see, lower growth rates take longer to double. At 2% interest, it would take just about 36 years for an investment to double. (And because the 2% is just above the rate of inflation, there is actually little growth with this rate of return.)

With the 'rule of 72' formula, we can now calculate the doubling of any number with any interest rate. An original amount of $25,000 would become $50,000 in 7.2 years at 10%, but it would take 24 years at 3% compound growth rates to double. Similarly, $1,000,000 would become $2,000,000 in 7.2 years at 10%, but it would take 24 years to double at 3% compound growth rates.

The real power of the 'rule of 72' and compound growth is seen with multiple doublings. This is like the penny example above, although it takes much longer in the real world.

In the original $100,000 example, we saw that it would become $200,000 in 7.2 years at 10% compound growth. Continuing that example, that $200,000 would double again in another 7.2 years to $400,000, and that figure would double again to $800,000 in 7.2 years. In just under 29 years in total, that $100,000 would turn into $1,600,000 with 10% returns—or a doubling of four times, according to the rule of 72.

And that is *without* any additional investments over those 29 years.

Again, this formula can be applied with any given amounts. A $50,000 investment enjoying 8% returns would take 45 years to double five times to reach $1,600,000, while a $200,000 investment enjoying a 12% compound annual growth rate would take just 18 years to double three times to reach $1,600,000.

Markets do not enjoy steady returns each and every year. The higher returning funds have an extreme rate of variability (volatility), as we have seen already. The challenge is staying invested through thick and thin, through the ups and downs and market gyrations, to enjoy the 'rule of 72' multiple-doubling growth rates.

Are You 'Crazy' Enough to Get Rich?

Emotion can be a powerful driver of investor behavior. Even the descriptions of market behavior, in a sense, reflect our emotional reactions to them. Think of the terms "severe downturn" or even "crash" when markets drop compared to "market swings" and reaching "market highs" when they rise. If we are focused too closely on the market's gyrations and how they are described in popular media, we can become elated when markets rise and deflated when they fall. The popular media especially uses lots of emotive words to describe market behavior even after a relatively minor movement of a percent or two. The constant use of these terms can impact us emotionally and in turn nudge us to make investing decisions that might be contrary to our long-term interests.

An important phenomenon in behavioral economics is "loss aversion," which was briefly discussed in an earlier chapter. We are naturally inclined to avoid losses, and this is surely ingrained in us as a survival mechanism. Some sources suggest that the fear of losing money is up to twice as strong as the pleasure of gaining.[128] Knowing that investments can go down often, and sometimes go down significantly for long periods of time, some potential investors avoid putting money in funds even though they have shown over very long periods to have very good overall rates of return. This perhaps explains why the G Fund has made up close to 40% of total TSP holdings in the 2010s.[129]

"Myopic loss aversion," in turn, is the tendency to be overly focused on and make decisions in response to short-term volatility of one's investments, even when the decisions are counter to long-term interests. During times of extreme market volatility, these investors are prone to sell their investments due to the potentially mistaken belief that this will protect what they have in the current moment from further declines, rather than holding and buying into the market declines. (The popular media's use of overly emotive terms only exacerbates this emotional response.) The decision to sell can in turn lead to "status-quo bias" and "sunk cost" thinking in "waiting out" the market declines until they have risen again. This effectively "sells" one's investments "low" and "buys" them back again "high," which is the antithesis of prudent investing.

But one type of investor is essentially fearless, and they have shown to be better investors than the rest of us because of their unique mental condition.

In one 2005 study, researchers examined how three groups of people would perform in a 20-round investing scenario. The researchers divided participants into "target patients," "control patients," and "normal participants." The target patient group all had lesions in areas of their brains that were critical for processing emotions, but otherwise had normal IQs. Essentially, this group's sense of fear as traditionally defined was impaired. The control group also had lesions, but not in areas associated with control of emotions. And the normal group was otherwise unaffected by any lesions.

The researchers compared how the target group would do by investing over 20 rounds compared to the control group taking part in the same study. According to the odds of the scenario, a participant would do better by investing than not investing in the entire 20-round period 87% of the time, whether the investor "won" a round or "lost."

Over multiple rounds of investing, those with inhibited senses of emotion did substantially better than both the control patient group and the group of normal participants. The target group continued to invest almost equally whether they won (84%) or lost (85.2%) a round, while reinvesting fell considerably for both the control (37.1%) and normal (40.5%) groups after a "loss" round.

The researchers likened this to a driver who hits an icy patch on the road. The untrained and emotional drivers are prone to panic and brake, causing their vehicles to skid out of control, but the trained (or "fearless") driver eases the car through any tailspin without panicking or braking out of fear.[130]

In another example, the famed bond investor Bill Gross announced that he had Asperger's syndrome, often described as a mild form of autism. Gross said in a February 2019 interview with Bloomberg News that the condition helped him to compartmentalize and "focus on the long-term things" and not get caught up "in the details."[131]

This is exactly the type of mental outlook we need to have when investing what is essentially our life savings into market indexes that can experience significant volatility over relatively long timeframes. While these individuals certainly aren't 'crazy,' their special mental outlook points to how successful investors should undertake long-term investing. Essentially, investors have to be metaphorically 'crazy' not only to stay invested during major market declines, but to continue to invest during these declines. It is tough to stay focused on the big picture during times of market crisis, but the history of returns shows that investors are always well-rewarded in the long run when they do.

Little Things Make the Big Things Happen

There are many seemingly little things that can ultimately have a major impact on building wealth over time. We've examined them earlier in the book, but we'll detail them all here together to see how much they impact your final investing results. They are: (1) low fees; (2) dividend reinvestments; (3) contributions; and (4) time.

The Impact of Fees on Investments

We saw earlier how small fees can impact a large investment on a yearly basis. The fees can take a variety of guises: direct fees charged for services, fees for transactions, account maintenance fees, and "expense ratios" and other fund-related fees to keep a fund operational.

Some of these fees are understandable and necessary. The expense ratio is a necessary fee. Without it, none of the TSP funds could operate. It costs money to buy and sell the stocks and bonds of individual companies and to account for the transactions. And if you feel more comfortable getting advice from a human being, who takes his or her fiduciary responsibility seriously and puts your interests first, that fee gets you a lot in return. You'll get sound advice during difficult times and advice to keep you from buying into the latest fad and keep you focused on the big picture. If the fee is percentage-based, the better your investments do, the better your investment manager does. He or she wants you to do well because then he or she does well too. That is a good incentive for both of you to work toward long-term growth of your funds. This kind of fee, when reasonable, is well worth what you pay.

But multiple fees can be buried in the fine print, with different fees charged at different times. And they can add up quickly. A percentage fee for managing your funds is in addition to the expense ratio charged by your investment funds, on top of account maintenance and other fees. Also some funds, especially actively managed ones, give kickbacks to investment managers for recommending their funds over other, potentially better ones, so your investment manager could potentially get the fees you pay him or her directly, while also a little extra for steering your money to that investment. That is a conflict of interest, which is why you should ask about your investment manager's sources of direct and indirect compensation.

Let's say your investment manager charges 0.46% yearly fees, in addition to the 0.04% expense ratio for the index fund(s) you're invested in. Let's be charitable and say these are the only fees you pay because you only invest in index funds. (Usually they'll steer you to other, active funds too; there is a case for low-fee active funds, although I've never been convinced by those arguments, for reasons detailed in chapter 1).

In this example, you're paying 0.5% fees of your portfolio in total, yearly. No big deal, right? Even with $500,000 invested, that's just $2,500 per year, which grows as the investments grow. Well, here's the total reduction in your investment for 0.5% fees per year versus 0.04%, for each 30-year period of investments in the S&P 500 index since 1900.* The results are astounding.

---

* The results are based on monthly investments that start at $250 a month in the first year and rise by 5% per year, to $1,029 in the 30th year. The amounts are invested into the S&P 500 index, with dividends adjusted and reinvested monthly. The investor's contributions amount comes to $199,316 in total over the 30-year period. In order to provide an apples-to-apples comparison of hypothetical investments over 30-year timeframes during real-world investing situations since 1900, the figures are not adjusted for inflation.

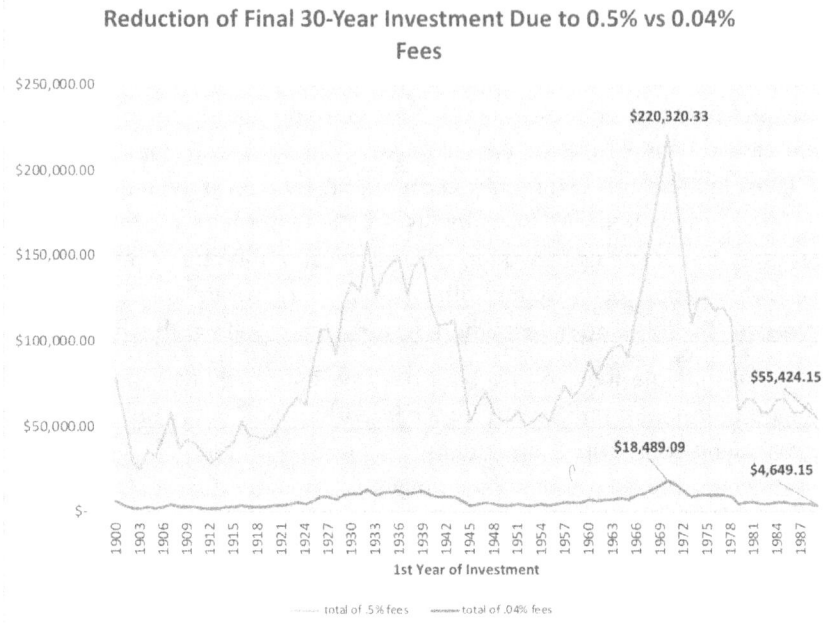

Annual fees of 0.5% can dramatically reduce an investor's final amount by tens or even hundreds of thousands of dollars compared to the approximately 0.04% fees for basic index funds or TSP funds.

The chart illustrates the total reduction of your investment compared to the index final return after a 30-year period with a 0.5% each year, and the line at the bottom represents the total reduction of your investment with 0.04% in yearly fees. For the last 30-year period available as part of this study, 1989-2018, the 0.5% fees over that time reduced your final amount by $55,424, while the 0.04% fee structure reduced your final investment by only $4,649. The 0.5% fee-structured investment ended 2018 with $619,099, versus $669,874 for the 0.04% fee structure. That's a difference of over $50,000, all because of less than half a percent difference in fees.

For the 30-year period beginning in 1970 and ending in 1999, as another example, the investor would have received $220,320 less with a 0.5% fee structure, versus a mere $18,489 reduction with the 0.04% paid in fees. (The amount peaked here because the timeframe ended in December 1999 and included the bubble years of the late 1990s.) What an investor paying 0.04% over that time would have made, which was $2,376,283, was reduced to $2,174,451 dollars. That is a decrease for the investor of almost *a quarter of a million dollars!* The index itself, without fees, returned $2.394 million during that time.

The 0.5% fee structure is relatively miniscule compared to the fee structures of some funds, as noted earlier. If you combine the average fee structure for some funds, which according to the Brightscope study cited in chapter 1 was 0.58%, with management and account fees, the total fees come to over 1%. Again, the total of 1-1.5% in annual fees (some of which is hidden by charging different fees at different times) might seem low at first glance, but it means that the total fees paid over 30 years is double or even triple what is represented in the chart above. They are so high, in fact, that I could not represent them on a single chart. That $55,424 in fees for 1989-2018 grows to as much as $166,272 reduction due to total fees, and the $220,000 reduction for 1970-1999 grows to a $660,000 reduction due to fees. This would've reduced your $2.376 million to $1.716 million. Those seemingly small fees directly reduce your personal wealth, potentially in some cases by over a half-million dollars.

And this is just for average 30-year periods. Below you'll see how amounts can really grow after 35- and 40-year periods. The potential losses in growth just to fees is mind-boggling in these cases.

When illustrating the impact of fees on returns, the type of investment itself does not matter. If government bonds returned this much over time and had the same 0.5% in fees per year, you'd get the same reduction as a result. If you invested in pork bellies and platinum over 30 years and had the same returns and same fee structure, the reduction in your personal wealth would've been the same. It's a function of the fee structure itself over time that lowers returns rather than the investment.

Reinvestment of Dividends

There is another investment that TSP participants often forget about but that is integral to significant returns over time, and that is reinvestment of dividends. We discussed the important role dividends play in investing in previous chapters, but here we'll see how they impact investing returns in total.

You can see a stark difference between 30-year returns from 1900 to 2018 with and without reinvesting dividends. The difference in returns is particularly evident when compared to returns of government bonds. As noted previously, every 30-year period of investing in a U.S. stock index fund (S&P 500) did better than government bonds, when reinvesting dividends on a regular basis. In contrast, just investing in the U.S. stock index fund, without reinvesting dividends, meant the index investing at times *underperformed* government bonds.

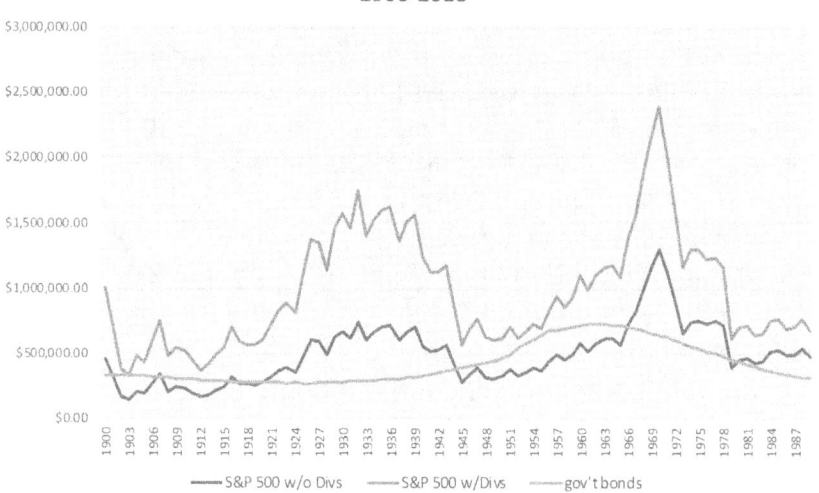

As you can see in the chart, simple index fund investing (without reinvesting dividends) underperformed government bonds when beginning the 30-year investment at the outset of the 1900s, specifically in the two decades after World War II and at the end of the 1970s. Index investing when reinvesting dividends, in contrast, outperformed during all of these periods.

Take investing from the early 1980s as an example. Returns in the 30-year periods that started in the 1980s (from 1981 to 2010, for example) when starting with $250 monthly contributions and increasing those monthly contributions by 5% each year, averaged $483,647 in the U.S. stock index fund without reinvesting dividends, and a whopping $706,382 when reinvesting dividends. These returns were driven by compounding: Dividends were reinvested and bought more fund shares, which in turn provided more dividend payouts to be reinvested in still more fund shares. Government bonds returned an average of $367,339 during this time. Thus, the index fund with dividends reinvested on average outperformed the non-dividend-reinvestment strategy by about $223,000, and government bonds by almost $340,000. Not reinvesting dividends produces almost as poor returns as government bonds, on average—and sometimes it produces worse returns.

As noted previously, TSP investors do not have to worry about reinvesting dividends and interest with their TSP holdings, since all interest and dividends are automatically reinvested. But this is something to understand when investing in funds outside the TSP, and in general when considering compound growth.

Increasing Contributions

In line with keeping fees low and reinvesting dividends, one should regularly increase one's contributions each year when possible. It doesn't have to be increased by much, and often pay raises will provide some of those increases naturally over time. But the difference between steady contributions and increasing contributions by even 5% per year is amazing. We saw an example in the previous chapter, illustrating the difference between $1,000 invested each year and increasing contributions each year, from 1980 to 2019.

Many of the calculations in this book started with $250 monthly investments. This is because many who are reading this book and who are just starting to invest early in their careers can only afford to contribute a small amount in the beginning. (I remember how difficult it can be—I could barely afford to contribute $50 per pay period in my first year of full-time civilian employment.) The 5% annual increases in contributions represent a low-end projection of a full career, without considering inflation.

Adding to these amounts over time, both with a higher contribution rate starting early in one's career and higher percentage rate increases with additional promotions, will propel wealth-building potential significantly.

Let's say you're a lieutenant/O1 or a GS-7 just out of college. Instead of starting with $250 a month, you add a percent or two to your personal contributions, and together with the slightly larger government match, you start by adding $350 a month to your TSP account in your first year of investing. Further, let's say you work hard and are pretty good at what you do, and you're regularly promoted for your work and abilities. Your TSP contributions and matches rise accordingly. Over the 30-year period, you're able to increase your TSP contributions by the equivalent of 6% a year, which brings your total monthly addition to your TSP in the 30th year to the equivalent of almost $1,900 a month, or just under $23,000 a year (taking advantage of "catch-up" contributions).

Using returns for the 30-year period from 1957 to 1986 (the median of the returns for periods examined since 1900), by starting with $350 a month and increasing contributions by 6% per year, an investor's final total balance after using the *Thrift Van Winkle*™ strategy at the end of December 1986 would be $1.48 million, compared with $937,000 by starting with $250 and increasing contributions by 5%. The total contributions and government match at $350/6% increases would have totaled $332,000—if split evenly between the individual and government, that would have been a $166,000 on the part of the TSP participant. (This will be further illustrated in the next section.)

Time

Time is another factor that influences returns. There are three factors related to time in this analysis.

The first is the amount of time your money stays invested in general. The more time you have to keep your money invested, the more time the 'rule of 72' and compound interest have to work. Not only are your original contributions growing, but the reinvested dividends and interest are growing too, and they in turn are generating more dividends and interest that are reinvested.

Let's look at the most extreme case during the 1900s: the Great Depression and ensuing war years in the 1930s and 1940s. Now it again must be recognized that this was an extremely challenging time for the country and for the world. The Great Depression was marked by very high unemployment and economic deprivation experienced by tens of millions of Americans. And with the onset of World War II, millions more Americans served and sacrificed—and hundreds of thousands made the ultimate sacrifice—for freedom in the 1940s. Any approach to examining potential investing behavior must include the context of the times. You can't invest if you don't have a job. Furthermore, at that time the very fate of freedom and democracy that underpin free markets, investing, and the ability to build wealth were in jeopardy on multiple fronts. (Which is why fighting for and preserving freedom and democracy are so important.)

Here is a chart that illustrates the returns over the 30-year period from 1906 to 1935. Similar to previous examples, this chart compares investing in either the stock index fund or government bond index fund, starting the monthly $250 contributions that increase by 5% each year.

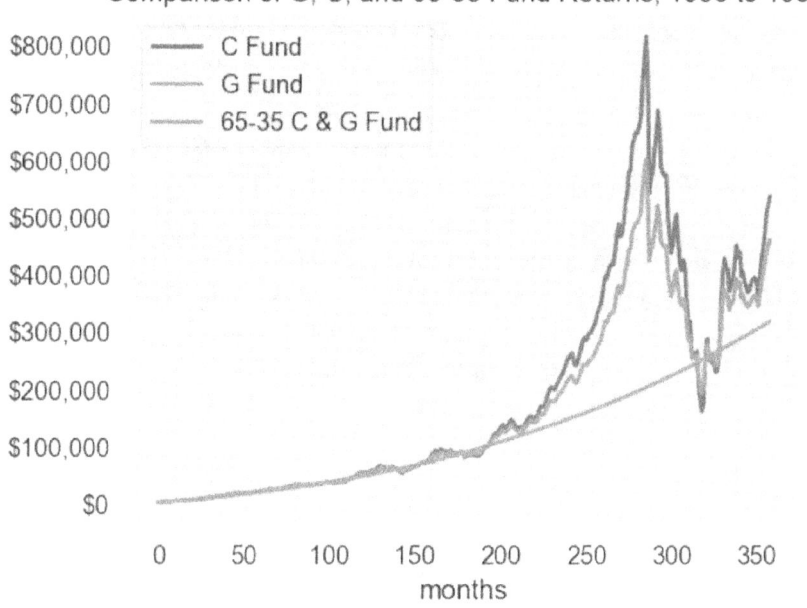

A chart comparing returns of investing in an all-stock index fund versus an all-U.S. government bond fund from January 1906 to December 1935, starting with $250 per month and increasing contributions by 5% per year.

This was by any measure a very difficult period to invest in because of the times. As you can see, a hypothetical investor in a stock index fund (the C Fund) would have enjoyed tremendous growth for 24 years of his or her investing lifetime. But then there was an almost immediate and severe drop in the stock market, in this case from over $800,000 to about $550,000—this was due to the famous Black Tuesday and Great Market Crash that took place from 24 to 29 October 1929. The declines continued for several years due to poor domestic economic policy and severe protectionist policies represented by the Smoot-Hawley Tariff Act of 1930 and other legislation.* The prolonged decline meant that the all-stock investor's portfolio dropped almost 80% to below $200,000 in two-plus years (even as the individual continued to contribute monthly). That kind of decline for anyone would've been devastating. The returns drop well below those of an investor who has invested solely in government bonds.

But even then, within two years the amount rises above returns on government bonds. While it does not end anywhere near the $800,000 high in year 24, the investor here ends the 30-year period with almost $550,000.

This again illustrates why investors, particularly aggressive or all-stock investors, must be mentally and emotionally prepared for severe, extreme drops. Even if the data shows that for every 30-year period (except for 1903-1932, when final returns were essentially even) the stock investor enjoys better final returns than the bond investor when continuing to contribute throughout that time, the experience can be excruciating. This is also why it takes a 'crazy' person to stick to a majority-stock investment plan! (There are less crazy and balanced approaches discussed in Strategy II that work really well too.)

---

* Thus, it's important to understand that the October 1929 market crash did not on its own cause the depression. There are many downturns and crashes in markets that, contrary to the experience of the early 1930s, recover relatively quickly in time or are marked merely by recessions (two or more consecutive quarters of decline in gross domestic product). They can be painful in the short-term, certainly, but recessions are nowhere near depressions in terms of economic pain. In fact, in the charts presented in this section, you can see the recovery begin shortly after the nadir of the market crash, but then the markets decline again because of the impact of continuing poor management of the economy. Free-market policies matter, for businesses, workers, and investors alike.

But what if this same investor continued to invest for 35 and 40 years? Those returns are illustrated in the next chart.

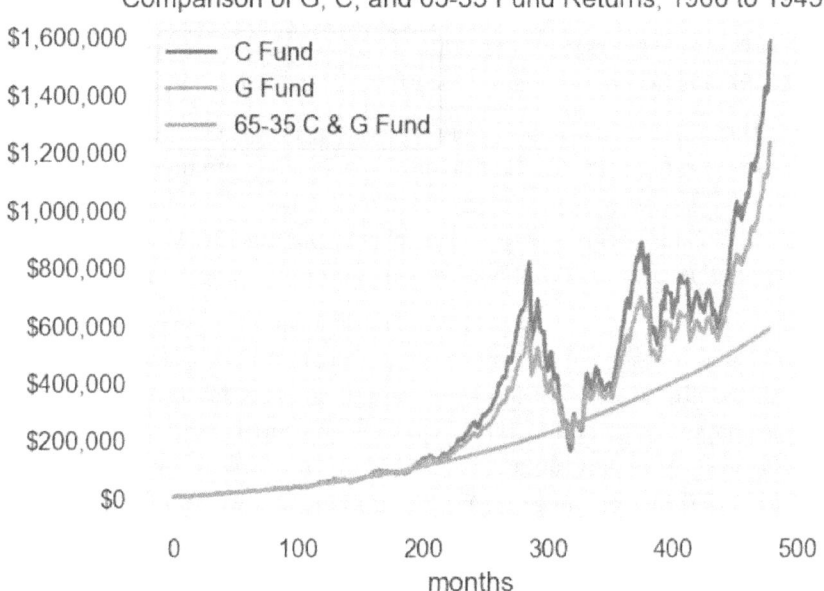

A chart comparing returns of investing in an all-stock index fund versus an all-U.S. government bond fund from January 1906 to December 1945. The investor starts by contributing $250 per month in the first year and increases contributions by 5% per year to $1,676 per monthly contribution in year 40, with contributions totaling just over $362,000.

By extending one's investment horizon another ten years through these extremely difficult circumstances to December 1945, this individual substantially increases his or her returns from just over $500,000 to almost $1.6 million. Extending the amount of time investing and staying invested, the investor can enjoy greater returns.

The second important factor related to time is the time it takes to recover from a downturn. Reviewing the market returns over the past 120 years, the data indicates that it takes about three years to recover from the nadir of most significant downturns, if one continues to invest via the TSP. That assumes that the investor does not sell and continues to invest in the stock funds during the downturn.

To enjoy good long-term results, you don't want to start withdrawing your funds during a major downturn. Recall that among the top-10 best eras for 30-year periods, the absolute best began in 1970 and ended in December 1999. That was almost at the very top of the market bubble in the late 1990s. Fast-forward ten years, and the era from 1979 to 2008 ended substantially lower, coming as it did in the middle of the 'Great Recession'.

The 30-year investment periods starting in the late 1970s coincided with the bubble-era 1990s, the downturns in 2000-2, and then the deep sell-off in 2008. The prior 30-year period, which began in 1978, ended 2007 right before the major declines with $1.161 million. But the 30-year period starting in 1979 and ending in 2008 finished with a mere $618,000. Ouch!

If, instead of using those funds immediately, the investor continued to work and invest for a few more years, the amount dropped even further several months to a low of $541,000, at the absolute bottom of the market rout in the spring of 2009. But five months after that, it increased again to over $700,000. Twenty-six months—just over two years—after the 30-year period ended in December 2008, the amount was worth over $1 million. The amount rose and fell in the next couple of years, but after five years the investment was worth $1.527 million. This is more than 2.5 times the value at the end of December 2008, and almost three times the amount at the absolute bottom of the market.

In other cases, one's investments can recover and go higher within a year or two. This was the case in the early 1960s, when investors in 1962 suffered a drop of more than 20%, but a year later the large cap S&P 500/C Fund had zoomed past its original amount and continued higher by the mid-1960s. Within a few years, that significant drop seemed like just a minor dip during the time.

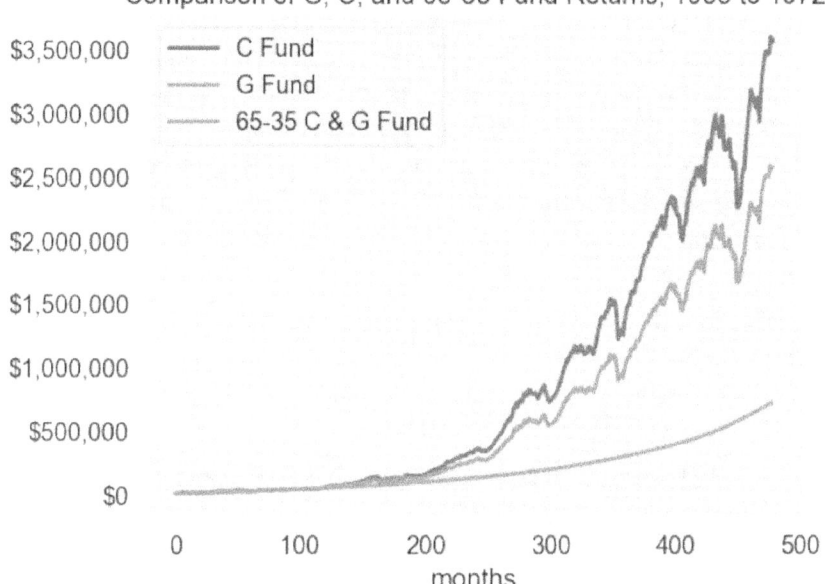

A chart comparing returns of investing in the C Fund, the G Fund, and a 65-35 mix of C and G fund (not rebalanced), over 40 years from 1933 to 1972. Investors experienced a major dip in 1962 (at about month 360), but markets recovered quickly and investments continued to grow through the 1960s.

Here is another finding of the 120-year study: Every 35-year period that ended in the post-war years had a final total amount of at least $1 million, after starting with $250 monthly contributions that rose by 5%, totaling $270,957 (the final year of contributions had grown to $1,313 per month, or just under $16,000 for that year). The lowest total amount was $1.13 million for the 35-year period starting in 1940. There were a number of 35-year periods in the $2 million range, and some in the $3 million range too.

However, a few 35-year periods that began in the early 1900s, such as those that started in 1906 and 1907, suffered heavily during that time. These investments, ending as they did in the early war years, finished with $688,512 and $581,188 respectively. These amounts compared to government bonds returning around $430,000 in those same periods, so they still outperformed bonds and outperformed total amount invested. (That said, I doubt many of us would be "retiring" during national emergencies such as in the middle of a major world war.)

And the 40-year periods performed spectacularly well. Every 40-year period in the post-war era returned at least $2 million, and many returned in the $3- and $4-million range. The 40-year period ending in the 1990s bubble era returned over $6 million. Even the 40-year periods of investing during the late Great Depression and world war years ended with more than $1 million, except for those that began in 1902 and 1903 (which ended during the early war years).

These should all be adjusted for one's personal investment approach, of course. A 65-35 portfolio, with some rebalancing over time, will feature a smoother performance, but will not perform in absolute terms as well as the above portfolios. But they'll do well, nonetheless.

The last point about time is timing, or rather, *not* timing.

'Timing' the market refers to the attempt to buy into a market at its low point, and sell at high points. Obviously, if you could buy low and sell high consistently, you would have *spectacular* returns. Unless you're clairvoyant, you can't do this. A person might get lucky once or twice, but that would be it.

Keeping a balanced portfolio based on set percentages or rebalancing during specific times of year (such as the beginning of the year or on your work anniversary) is not timing. Similarly, keeping a little extra available to invest during market dips or downturns based on specific percentages is a separate approach detailed in Strategy IV. But in general, selling with the idea of buying in the near-term based on a hunch or other "data" or "signals" that the market will drop further can be detrimental to your long-term investment returns.

The data shows again and again how the markets fall fast, but then they can recover swiftly as well. Don't miss out by trying to "time" the market.

Parabolic Wealth

Here, then, is the formula for parabolic wealth.

Understand your investment style, knowing that markets will fall from time to time. Choose at least some growth; the more oriented your portfolio is toward growth (in the stock funds), the higher returns you will receive on average over the very long term. But growth-oriented investments will fall significantly in value from time to time, so understand how much risk you are willing to take, as defined by how much of a decline you can withstand in your total investments (remember, as long as you don't sell during the declines, you haven't *lost* anything, because the value of the shares goes back up when markets recover).

Contribute at least enough to get the government match, but try to contribute more if your budget allows. By having low-to-no debt, you will be able to afford to contribute more than if you have significant debt. Try to pay off consumer debt as soon as possible. Avoid high-payment items like a new car or large house payment if possible. When you are able to, consider increasing your contributions by a percent or two if you receive a promotion, or at the beginning of the year when pay scales might be readjusted.

Always be aware of fees and of costs related to investing. While TSP participants do not have to worry about fees related to their TSP accounts, be mindful of what your other investments might be costing you. If you invest in an HSA, chose the low-cost stock index fund over other more expensive managed funds, for example. And if you are presented with a choice, reinvest your dividends as you are investing (you can live off your dividends later in life, though).

Time is your friend. Invest early and continue to invest regularly even if you decide not to make the military or government service a career. Starting at 18 or 22 means you can continue to invest for 40 years or longer, with potentially spectacular results.

Here is one example of a 40-year period, starting with $350 a month in contributions and increasing those contributions by 6% each year.

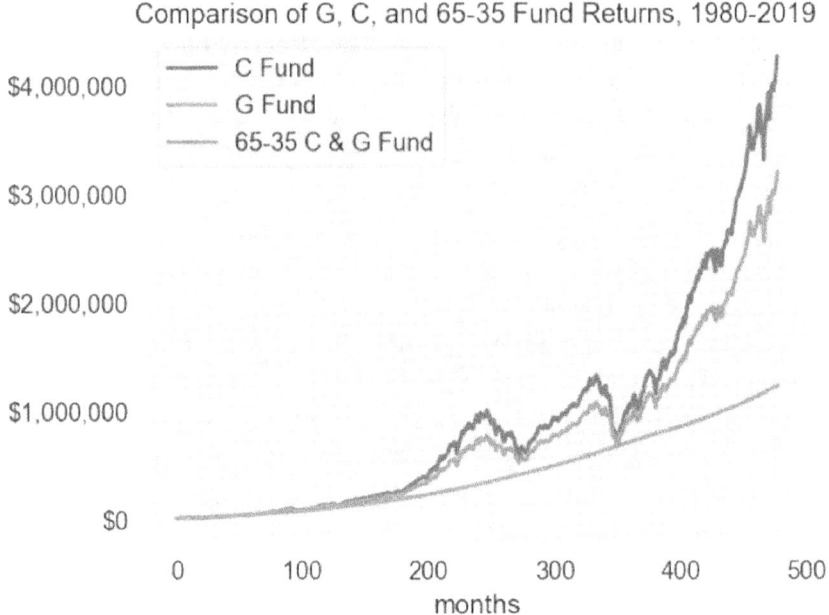

Comparison of 40 years of returns from 1980 to December 2019, investing $350 a month and increasing contributions by 6% each year. The monthly return figures are for the actual C and G Funds from 1988, while the 1980-1987 figures are from the S&P 500 index/dividend ratio and the 10-year government bond returns.

The 40-year period from 1980 to December 2019 included a major bubble period (the late 1990s), some short-term downturns (such as in October 1987) and two major downturns. The second one, in 2008-9, was the worst period for stocks since the Great Depression. In this case, the *"Thrift Van Winkle"*™ and 65-35 moderate portfolios had dropped to within a few hundred dollars of the G Fund total, with the C Fund falling from a high of $1.28 million in month 328 to $666,633 in month 349, compared to the G Fund's $666,339 that month. The C Fund quickly rebounded, though, and it rose to above $1 million by month 358, less than a year later (almost at the 30-year mark). Already by year 35, the C Fund was well above $2 million, and the 65-35 moderate portfolio was on its way there. The G Fund was hitting $1 million by that point. By year 40, the C Fund/Thrift Van Winkle portfolio was hitting the $4 million mark, and the 65-35/moderate portfolio rose above the $3 million mark.

This is just one 40-year period, but it uses real figures for the C and G Funds for the monthly returns from 1988 to 2019. Other 40-year periods did much better with these larger contribution rates. Investments starting in the late 1920s and ending in the late 1960s ended in the mid-$6 million range, and investments that began in the late 1950s and in 1960 ended at the top of the bubble market in the late 1990s in the $9 million range.

Here is a chart that shows 40-year investment periods for every five years starting with the year after World War II.

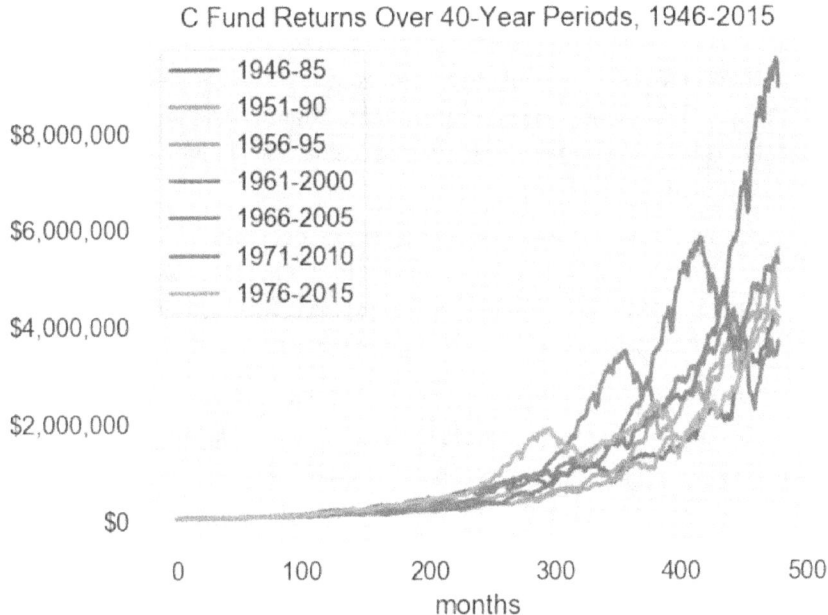

Comparison of rolling 40 year returns of the S&P 500/C Fund, when starting with $350 monthly contributions and increasing those contributions by 6% each year. The returns are for 40-year periods at five-year increments, starting from 1946.

This isn't adjusted for inflation, but even if the figures above are cut in half as a result of inflation, these are still significant amounts. And as noted previously, you own these accounts, this is your money to do with as you please. And these funds are in addition to any other savings and investing plans, such as an HSA, IRAs, a personal residence or other real estate, and other accounts.

So, stay invested through thick and thin. Have an affordable, low-debt lifestyle. Always get a match and watch those fees. In down markets, remember that it can take anywhere from one to three years of additional investing to recover losses. Above all, have faith in the U.S. economy and other free market economies—which are absolutely the best wealth-creators and wealth-builders in the world.

***

The word *parabolic* has a second meaning. It relates to parables or stories that illustrate or symbolize a particular moral attitude.

There have been a lot of charts and graphs presented in this book, a lot of math-y stuff, but when it comes down to it, wealth, or rather the generation of wealth, is itself a parable. What inherent value does money have, in and of itself? At the end of the day, so what?

As the economist John Maynard Keynes declared in 1923: "The long run is a misleading guide to current affairs. In the long run we are all dead." Leave it to an economist to state it so bluntly! But why sacrifice, scrimp, and save when ultimately, we all meet the same ending?

The answer, your answer, is your personal parable.

I like the topic of saving and investing because I like the math and the charts. I like the rule of 72, I like seeing numbers grow and double and double again. I also like the sense of independence one can draw from learning to create and build wealth, and the good that can be derived from it.

Perhaps you're the same. Perhaps you believe, like I do, that the pleasure is in the process, and this relates to both the service (work) and the math (compounding). Perhaps you want to leave a personal legacy to your kids, to your alma mater, to your favorite charities. Perhaps you want to live the good life in your later years, however you might define it, whether drinking Mai Tais on the beach, fishing in the Ozarks, or sponsoring orphanages in India. Wealth is a vehicle, a means to get somewhere special, do special things, help those with special needs, to help develop and build great organizations and great things.

The journey requires sacrifices, especially in the beginning, but every journey worth taking does. What drives you through those sacrifices? What is your story, your parable—what drives you to build wealth? Wealth creation and wealth building are byproducts of your focused efforts, of service to others, certainly in the public sector but also in the private sector too. If you don't like how you are focusing your energies, or who or what you are serving, not only will the building of wealth lose meaning, you will suffer spiritually and emotionally.

So define your story. Find and understand the parable driving your quest, your story, what motivates you and why. In doing so, you'll find true wealth.

NOTES

CONCLUSION
Bringing it All Together

With the TSP and other tax-advantaged savings vehicles, Federal Government workers and their military counterparts are no longer bound by "golden handcuffs" of lifetime government service merely for retirement benefits. By maximizing savings and investing opportunities through the TSP and by using other personal finance techniques, federal workers and uniformed military personnel can choose to serve just a few years, 10 or 20 years, or an entire lifetime and still enjoy opportunities to build wealth during their government or military service and beyond.

This book explored ways to save and invest in the TSP while also using other personal finance techniques to build personal wealth over the long term.

Pre-Investment Strategy 1 at the beginning of this book suggested building and maintaining savings for emergencies amounting to at least six weeks' worth of expenses starting out, and Pre-Investment Strategy 2 recommended starting out contributing 5% of pay to the TSP if possible.

Strategy I helped the TSP investor establish his or her interest in and risk tolerance for investing. Strategy II, in turn, advocated allocating savings and investments among the TSP funds based on one's interest and risk tolerance, so that the TSP investor is not tempted to sell during significant declines in the market. Laying out research of market investing over rolling 30-year periods since 1900, Strategy II detailed the *Thrift Van Winkle*™ approach to investing solely or primarily in the C Fund, albeit with significant volatility inherent in the approach. For risk-conscious investors, Strategy II proposed a 50-50 allocation between TSP stock and bond funds for conservative investors, a 65-35 stock-bond fund allocation for moderate investors, and an 80-20 stock-bond fund allocation for aggressive investors, who are comfortable with potentially significant swings in their TSP total account value. For those who are simply not interested in following their TSP funds or the markets on a regular basis but who still want some potential growth in their investments over the long term, the strategy proposed investing in one of the TSP's L Funds as an alternative.

Strategy III discussed approaches to re-balancing periodically by allocating one's biweekly or monthly contributions to the under-weighted TSP funds, to allow greater growth potential of TSP funds over the long term. It suggested re-balancing via interfund transfers when TSP funds drifted more than 5% from target allocations, for example.

For aggressive investors, Strategy IV proposed a method to make additional investments over time by buying into stock funds that drop by 10% or more. While market declines—and corresponding declines of TSP fund totals—are sometimes severe, past experience suggests that investing during these market drops can provide greater returns over the very long term.

As one continues to invest in the TSP, Strategy V suggested paying off outstanding debts for good, especially consumer debts such as credit cards and car loans. With no debt, the TSP investor has more income available with which to both invest and save for future large purchases, such as a car or house. Strategy V advocated "pre-purchasing" or saving for future purchases based on how much debt payments would be for that item for at least a year. After a year or two, money used to "pre-purchase" an item can be used as a down payment or for the outright purchase of the item. Once consumer debts are paid off, the TSP investor can increase TSP contributions and consider other savings vehicles such as a Roth IRA. Investors can also consider a High Deductible Health Plan with a Health Savings Account for even more wealth-building potential.

And as you build wealth, consider donating some of it to charities of your choice through the CFC and directly, as desired. Additional funds can also be invested in tax-efficient index mutual funds for long-term growth.

Strategy VI focused on insuring yourself and your family against catastrophic events with your health, your personal property, your professional life, and your digital life. It also discussed TSP password and account security.

Lastly, the chapter on Parabolic Wealth brought together all of the concepts to demonstrate how real wealth can be built over a lifetime of consistent, focused, buy-and-hold investing in growth-oriented stock funds, starting from nothing.

The building of wealth is a gradual process that takes time, effort, and patience. It requires making conscious decisions to save and invest. But over several decades you, as diligent savers and investors, can have a sizable amount of wealth available in your later years—you will have built personal legacies for yourselves, your families, and your favorite charities.

I wish you, my federal and military colleagues, success in your personal journeys of saving, investing, and building wealth during your time in service and in your post-government and post-military careers. All the best!

Endnote References

[1] "Retire," Merriam-Webster, https://www.merriam-webster.com/dictionary/retire, last accessed on November 7, 2019.

[2] Bargh, J. A., Chen, M., Burrows, L. J. Pers. Soc. Psych. 71, 230–244 (1996), https://psycnet.apa.org/record/1996-06400-003, last accessed on November 21, 2019; see also: "Does Thinking of Grandpa Make You Slow?" psychologytoday.com, March 2003, https://www.psychologytoday.com/us/blog/social-brain-social-mind/201203/does thinking-grandpa-make-you-slow.

[3] Ed Yong, "A Failed Replication Draws a Scathing Personal Attack From a Psychology Professor," Discover Magazine, March 10, 2012, https://www.discovermagazine.com/mind/a-failed-replication-draws-a-scathing-personalattack-from-a-psychology-professor, last accessed on November 21, 2019.

[4] Military Leadership Diversity Commission, "Reenlistment Rates Across the Services by Gender and Race/Ethnicity," April 2010, https://diversity.defense.gov/Portals/51/Documents/Resources/Commission/docs/Issue%20Papers/Paper%2031%20-%20Reenlistment%20Rates%20Across%20the%20Services.pdf, last accessed on November 11, 2019.

[5] Michael Wald, "Turnover Up as More Workers Quit the Federal Government," Fedsmith March 22, 2018, https://www.fedsmith.com/2018/03/22/turnover-workersquit-federal-government/, last accessed on November 11, 2019.

[6] See, for example, "Thrift Savings Fund Statistics," Federal Retirement Thrift Investment Board, July 2019, https://www.frtib.gov/pdf/minutes/2019/Aug/MM-2019May-Att1.pdf; updated stats are available at tspstrategies.com.

[7] This short history of the federal government pensions draws from a 1995 overview written by the Government Accountability Office at the request of Congress: see GAO's "Overview of Federal Retirement Programs," http://www.gao.gov/assets/110/106032.pdf, last accessed on November 8, 2019, and other U.S. government documents.

[8] "United States Life Tables, 1929-1931," U.S. Department of Commerce, Bureau of the Census, pp 4-10, https://www.cdc.gov/nchs/data/lifetables/life30.pdf, last accessed on November 7, 2019.

[9] "Life Expectancy for Social Security," Social Security Administration, http://www.ssa.gov/history/lifeexpect.html, last accessed on November 7, 2019.

[10] Havemann, Judith. "Federal Workers Are Facing Fundamental Pension Choice; New Plan May Loosen 'Golden Handcuffs,'" in Washington Post, 20 July 1987: A01.

[11] Causey, Mike. "The Federal Diary," in Washington Post, 2 November 1988: D02.

[12] "Investing in the TSP: The Individual Funds," Thrift Savings Plan, https://www.tsp.gov/PlanParticipation/BeneficiaryParticipants/investing/individualFunds.html, last accessed on November 8, 2019.

[13] Gallup, "2017 Participant Satisfaction Survey," November 2017, https://www.frtib.gov/ReadingRoom/SurveysPart/TSP-Survey-Results-2017.pdf, last accessed on November 7, 2019.

[14] "The BrightScope/ICI Defined Contribution Plan Profile: A Close Look at 401(k) Plans," Brightscope, December 2014, pp 41-42, https://www.ici.org/pdf/ppr_14_dcplan_profile_401k.pdf, last accessed on November 8,2019.

[15] Weller, Christian E. and Shana Jenkins. "The 401(k) Fee Effect: The Costs of 401(k) Accounts Are Eating Into Americans' Retirement Returns. What Should Be Done?" in Financial Planning, 1 May 2007: 1.

[16] Adam McCullough, "2018 Morningstar Fee Study Finds That Fund Prices Continue to Decline," Morningstar, April 30, 2019, https://www.morningstar.com/articles/925303/2018-morningstar-fee-study-finds-thatfund-prices-continue-to-decline, last accessed on November 7, 2019.

[17] Berkshire Hathaway Inc., 2004 Shareholder Letter: p 4, www.berkshirehathaway.

com/2004ar/2004ar.pdf, last accessed on March 8, 2019. The material is copyrighted and used with permission of the author.

[18] Berkshire Hathaway Inc., 2006 Shareholder Letter: p 21, www.berkshirehathaway.com/letters/2006ltr.pdf, last accessed on March 8, 2019. The material is copyrighted and used with permission of the author.

[19] Loomis, Carol. "Buffett's Big Bet." 9 June 2008, money.cnn.com/2008/06/04/news/newsmakers/buffett_bet.fortune/, last accessed on March 8, 2019.

[20] David Carrig, "Warren Buffett wins $1M bet against hedge funds and gives it to girls' charity," USA Today, January 2, 2018, https://www.usatoday.com/story/money/markets/2018/01/02/warren-buffett-bet-againsthedge- funds-girls-charity/996993001/, last accessed on November 7, 2019.

[21] Allison Ingersoll, "Long Slide in Hedge-Fund Fees Leaves the '2 and 20' Model on the Ropes," Bloomberg, July 16, 2019, https://www.bloomberg.com/news/articles/2019-07-16/hedge-fund-fees-long-slide-leaves-2-and-20-model-on-the-ropes, last accessed on November 7, 2019.

[22] A full list of stock exchanges in the United States can be found at http://www.worldstockexchanges.net/usa.html, last accessed on November 7, 2019.

[23] For more discussion on the history and background of ticker symbols, see "Stock Symbol (Ticker)," Investopia, June 13, 2019, https://www.investopedia.com/terms/s/stocksymbol.asp, last accessed on November 7, 2019.

[24] Malkiel, Burton. A Random Walk Down Wall Street. (New York: Norton, 2003), p 357.

[25] French, Kenneth R. "The Cost of Active Investing," in Journal of Finance, Vol 63 Iss 4, August 2008, ssrn.com/abstract=1105775, last accessed on March 8, 2019.

[26] For detailed information about the BRS, see "Uniformed Services Blended Retirement System," https://militarypay.defense.gov/blendedretirement/, and the linked informational brochure, "A Guide to the Uniformed Services Blended Retirement System," last accessed on November 8, 2019.

[27] Siegel, Jeremy. Stocks for the Long Run. 4th ed. (New York: McGraw-Hill, 2008), p 13.

[28] J. B. Maverick, "What is the average annual return for the S&P 500?" Investopia, May 21, 2019, https://www.investopedia.com/ask/answers/042415/what-average-annualreturn-sp-500.asp, last accessed on November 7, 2019.

[29] Siegel, Jeremy. Stocks for the Long Run. 4th ed. (New York: McGraw-Hill, 2008), p 13.

[30] "Remarks by Chairman Alan Greenspan At the Annual Dinner and Francis Boyer Lecture of The American Enterprise Institute for Public Policy Research, Washington, D.C." 5 December 1996, www.federalreserve.gov/boarddocs/speeches/1996/19961205.htm, last accessed on October 8, 2008.

[31] Berkshire Hathaway Inc., 1999 Shareholder Letter: p 3, www.berkshirehathaway.com/letters/1999htm.html, last accessed on March 8, 2019. The material is copyrighted and used with permission of the author.

[32] Buffett, Warren and Carol Loomis. "Mr. Buffett on the Stock Market," in Fortune Magazine, 22 November 1999. Accessed 8 March 2011, in money.cnn.com/magazines/fortune/fortune_archive/1999/11/22/269071/index.htm. The material is copyrighted and used with permission of the author.

[33] Buffett, Warren. "Buy American. I Am," in New York Times, www.nytimes.com/2008/10/17/opinion/17buffett.html?dbk, last accessed on March 8, 2008. The material is copyrighted and used with permission of the author.

[34] "Changes in U.S. Family Finances, 2013 to 2016," Federal Reserve Bulletin, September 2017, p 17, https://www.federalreserve.gov/publications/files/scf17.pdf, last accessed on November 8, 2019.

[35] Figures taken from "Estimates inflation-adjusted to 2016 dollars," available at "Survey of

Consumer Finances," https://www.federalreserve.gov/econres/files/scf2016_tables_public_real_historical.xlsx, last accessed on November 8, 2019.

[36] "Changes in U.S. Family Finances, 2013 to 2016," Federal Reserve Bulletin, September 2017, p 17, https://www.federalreserve.gov/publications/files/scf17.pdf, last accessed on November 8, 2019.

[37] Figures taken from "Estimates inflation-adjusted to 2016 dollars," available at "Survey of Consumer Finances," https://www.federalreserve.gov/econres/files/scf2016_tables_public_nominal_historical.xlsx, last accessed on November 8, 2019.

[38] "Changes in U.S. Family Finances, 2013 to 2016," Federal Reserve Bulletin, September 2017, pp 20-23, https://www.federalreserve.gov/publications/files/scf17.pdf, last accessed on November 8, 2019.

[39] "Thrift Savings Fund Statistics," FRTIB, July 2019, https://www.frtib.gov/pdf/minutes/MM-2019Aug-Att1.pdf, last accessed on November 8,2019.

[40] "Changes in U.S. Family Finances, 2013 to 2016," Federal Reserve Bulletin, September 2017, p 24, https://www.federalreserve.gov/publications/files/scf17.pdf, last accessed on November 8, 2019; "Thrift Savings Fund Statistics," FRTIB, December 2013, https://www.frtib.gov/pdf/minutes/MM-2014Jan-Att1.pdf, last accessed on November 8, 2019; "Thrift Savings Fund Statistics," FRTIB, December 2016, https://www.frtib.gov/pdf/minutes/MM-2017Jan-Att1.pdf, last accessed on November 8, 2019; "Thrift Savings Fund Statistics," FRTIB, July 2019, https://www.frtib.gov/pdf/minutes/MM-2019Aug-Att1.pdf, last accessed on November 8, 2019.

[41] For more discussion about volatility, see Justin Kuepper, "Volatility Definition," Investopedia.com, October 16, 2019, https://www.investopedia.com/terms/v/volatility.asp, last accessed on November 11, 2019.

[42] Stanley, Thomas J. and William D. Danko. The Millionaire Next Door: The Surprising Secrets of America's Wealthy. (New York: RosettaBooks, LLC, 2010), p 100.

[43] "Share Price Calculation," tsp.gov, https://www.tsp.gov/InvestmentFunds/FundsOverview/sharePriceCalculation.html, last accessed on November 11, 2019.

[44] Ibbotson Associates, "Stocks, Bonds, Bills, and Inflation 2006 Yearbook," p 41.

[45] To determine returns over rolling 20-, 30-, and 40-year periods from 1900 to 2019, I relied on two data sets that were similar to the TSP's G Fund and C Fund throughout the 1900s. To represent the G Fund, I relied on the U.S. 10-year Treasury Bond interest rate, reported monthly, because the G Fund is almost perfectly correlated with the 10-year bond. For the C Fund, I used S&P data for the S&P 500 and legacy indexes since 1926 and Case-Shiller's "U.S. Stock Markets 1871-Present and CAPE Ratio," available at http://www.econ.yale.edu/~shiller/data.htm, to normalize monthly S&P index month-end closing values and dividend ratios from 1900 to 2019. Scripts used to calculate rolling returns are available on Github at bit.ly/TSP2ndEd. Dividends were reinvested on a monthly basis, although the scripts can be adjusted to calculate reinvestment on a quarterly or annual basis instead. Dividends were calculated monthly because the C Fund automatically reinvests dividends as individual companies pay them and not as a single payout on a quarterly basis. I chose the two funds for this study for several reasons. The two asset classes are consistently uncorrelated or slightly negatively correlated, as discussed in a separate section of this book. They had the most consistent month-over-month data for the entire 120-year timeframe. Also, the G Fund/U.S. 10-year Treasury Bond had never experienced a decline in value, thus the asset class was a good proxy for an ultra-safe asset during times of extreme financial stress. Additionally, they have consistently been the two most popular funds in the TSP since their inception in 1987-1988, based on holdings and average participant allocations (updated statistics are available at bit.ly/TSPallocations). Moreover, the calculations for the data sets over the final 20- and 30-year timeframes of the study match very closely with calculations using

actual monthly returns of the C Fund and G Fund (from 1988 to 2019). The S&P 500 index returns matched within about 98.6% accuracy of actual monthly returns of the C Fund, and the 10-year government bond returns matched with greater than 99% accuracy of the G Fund returns. (Expense ratios were not included in the calculations unless otherwise noted.)

[46] "Income of Families and Persons in the United States: 1950," U.S. Census Bureau, Report Number P60-09, March 25, 1952, https://census.gov/library/publications/1952/demo/p60-009.html, last accessed on November 14, 2019.

[47] Craig L. Israelsen, "Investment Portfolio Torture Chamber," Financial Planning, https://www.financial-planning.com/news/sequence-of-returns-can-affect-a-retirementportfolio, last accessed on November 20, 2019.

[48] Lynch, Peter. Beating the Street. (New York: Simon & Schuster, 1994), p 33.

[49] "Past Correction: Drops of 10 Percent or More in the S&P 500," Fox Business, February 8, 2018, https://www.foxbusiness.com/markets/past-corrections-drops-of-10- percent-or-more-in-the-sp-500, last accessed on December 5, 2019.

[50] Federal Reserve Statistical Release. "Consumer Credit." 8 September 2008, www.federalreserve.gov/releases/G19/Current/, last accessed on October 8, 2008.

[51] "Consumer Credit Outstanding," Board of Governors Federal Reserve System, September 2019, https://www.federalreserve.gov/releases/g19/current/, last accessed on November 24, 2019.

[52] Federal Reserve Bulletin, "Changes in U.S. Family Finances from 2013 to 2016: Evidence from the Survey of Consumer Finances," Board of Governors of the Federal Reserve System, Vol 103, No 3, September 2017, p 22, https://www.federalreserve.gov/publications/files/scf17.pdf, last accessed on November 24, 2019.

[53] "Changes in U.S. Family Finances from 2007 to 2010," Federal Reserve Bulletin, Vol 98, No 2, p 16, https://www.federalreserve.gov/pubs/bulletin/2012/pdf/scf12.pdf, last accessed on November 8, 2019.

[54] "Restaurant Wine Markups," The Reluctant Gourmet, October 31, 2019, https://www.reluctantgourmet.com/restaurant-w-wine-markups/, last accessed on November 25, 2019; one article's title says it all: "Why You Pay $52 for a $15 Wine in a Restaurant," The Globe and Mail, May 14, 2013, https://www.theglobeandmail.com/life/food-and-wine/wine/why-you-pay-52-for-a-15-wine-in-a-restaurant/article11919459/, last accessed on November 25, 2019.

[55] Ramsey, Dave. Financial Peace Revisited. (New York: Viking, 2003), pp 89-92.

[56] Chatzky, Jean. Pay It Down! From Debt To Wealth on $10 a Day. (New York: Portfolio, 2004), pp 159-170.

[57] Suze Orman, "Roll Down You Credit Card Debt!" https://suzeorman.com/dt/DebtRolldown.html, last accessed on December 12, 2019.

[58] "Payday Loan Customers Want More Protections," Pew Charitable Trusts, April 19, 2017, last accessed on November 25, 2019.

[59] Elizabeth Hirschman, "Differences in Consumer Purchase Behavior by Credit Card Payment System," Journal of Consumer Research, Volume 6, Issue 1, June 1979, pp 58–66, https://doi.org/10.1086/208748.

[60] Drazen Prelec, Duncan Simester, "Always Leave Home Without It: A Further Investigation of the Credit-Card Effect on Willingness to Pay," Marketing Letters (2001) 12: 5. https://doi.org/10.1023/A:1008196717017, last accessed on November 24, 2019.

[61] Hannah Jones, "Contactless Payments: Do They Make Us Spend More?" February 3, 2019, https://www.youngmoneymatters.co.uk/contactless-payments-do-they-make-usspend-more/, last accessed on November 25, 2019.

[62] Donald Black, "A review of compulsive buying disorder," World Psychiatry. 2007 Feb; 6(1): 14–18, https://www.ncbi.nlm.nih.gov/pmc/articles/PMC1805733/, last accessed on November 27, 2019.

⁶³ Isabela A. Melca et al, "DSM-5 and the Decision Not to Include Sex, Shopping or Stealing as Addictions," Current Addiction Reports, https://www.researchgate.net/publication/264051559_DSM-5_and_the_Decision_Not_to_Include_Sex_Shopping_or_Stealing_as_Addictions, last accessed on November 27, 2019.
⁶⁴ Charles Tran, "Survey: Shopping Addiction Statistics," surveymonkey.com, November 13, 2013, https://www.creditdonkey.com/shopping-addiction.html, last accessed on November 27, 2019.
⁶⁵ "Median and Average Sales Prices of New Homes Sold in United States," U.S. Census Bureau, September 2019, https://www.census.gov/construction/nrs/pdf/uspricemon.pdf, last accessed on November 27, 2019.
⁶⁶ See TSP website, "TSP Loans: Nonpay Status," https://www.tsp.gov/PlanParticipation/LoansAndWithdrawals/loans/nonPayStatus.html, last accessed on November 27, 2019.
⁶⁷ See TSP website, "TSP Loans: Loan Basics," https://www.tsp.gov/PlanParticipation/LoansAndWithdrawals/loans/index.html, last accessed on November 27, 2019.
⁶⁸ "The Congressional Papers of William V. Roth, Jr.: Biography," Delaware Historical Society, http://dehistory.org/research-collections/senator-william-v-roth-collection/rothbiography, last accessed on November 28, 2019.
⁶⁹ See https://tspstrategies.com/roth-tsp/roth-tsp/ for more information.
⁷⁰ Fronstin, Paul. "Savings Needed to Fund Health Insurance and Health Care Expenses in Retirement," Employee Benefit Research Institute, Issue Brief No. 295, July 2006, www.ebri.org/pdf/briefspdf/EBRI_IB_07-20061.pdf, last accessed on March 8, 2011.
⁷¹ "How Long You Have to Live in America's Biggest Cities for Buying to Make Sense," Smartasset.com, May 1, 2015, https://smartasset.com/mortgage/rent-vs-buy#us/5, last accessed on November 24, 2019.
⁷² "An Introduction to 529 Plans," U.S. Securities and Exchange Commission, https://www.sec.gov/reportspubs/investor-publications/investorpubsintro529htm.html, last accessed on December 12, 2019.
⁷³ Office of Personnel Management website, www.opm.gov/cfc/index.asp.
⁷⁴ Office of Personnel Management. "Life Insurance," https://www.opm.gov/healthcareinsurance/life-insurance/, last accessed October 25, 2019.
⁷⁵ Available at https://www.opm.gov/retirement-services/calculators/fegli-calculator/ as of late-October 2019.
⁷⁶ "Average Cost of Life Insurance (2019): Rates by Age, Term and Policy Size", https://www.valuepenguin.com/average-cost-life-insurance, last accessed October 25, 2019.
⁷⁷ For expanded discussion of the FEGLI program and requirements, see the Office of Personnel Management's Federal Employees' Group Life Insurance (FEGLI), June 2019, available at https://www.opm.gov/healthcare-insurance/life-insurance/referencematerials/publications-forms/feglihandbook.pdf.
⁷⁸ "Servicemembers' Group Life Insurance Traumatic Injury Protection (TSGLI), https://www.benefits.va.gov/insurance/tsgli_schedule_Schedule.asp, last accessed on October 29, 2019.
⁷⁹ "Family Servicemembers' Group Life Insurance (FSGLI)", https://www.benefits.va.gov/insurance/fsgli.asp, last accessed on October 29, 2019.
⁸⁰ "Veterans Group Life Insurance," https://www.benefits.va.gov/insurance/vgli.asp, last accessed on October 29, 2019.
⁸¹ "VGLI Premium Rates," https://www.benefits.va.gov/INSURANCE/vgli_rates_new.asp, last accessed on October 29, 2019.
⁸² "Disability," Merriam-Webster, https://www.merriamwebster.com/dictionary/disability, last accessed on November 4, 2019.
⁸³ "How can I insure against loss of income?" https://www.iii.org/article/how-can-iinsure-against-loss-income, last accessed on October 25, 2019.

[84] "Benefits Planner: Disability," Social Security Administration, https://www.ssa.gov/planners/disability/, last accessed on November 4, 2019.
[85] "How can I insure against loss of income?" https://www.iii.org/article/how-can-iinsure-against-loss-income, last accessed on October 25, 2019.
[86] "Disability Benefits", Social Security Administration, https://www.ssa.gov/benefits/disability/, last accessed on November 4, 2019.
[87] "FERS Information: Disability Retirement," Office of Personnel Management, https://www.opm.gov/retirement-services/fers-information/eligibility/, last accessed on November 4, 2019.
[88] "What is Long-Term Care?" US Department of Health and Human Services, https://longtermcare.acl.gov/the-basics/what-is-long-term-care.html, last accessed on November 4, 2019.
[89] "What is Long-term Care Insurance?" https://longtermcare.acl.gov/costs-how-topay/what-is-long-term-care-insurance/, last accessed on November 4, 2019.
[90] Ellen Stark, "5 Things You Should Know About Long-Term Care Insurance: A new breed of policy is taking off, but it can be pricey," AARP Bulletin, March 1, 2018, https://www.aarp.org/caregiving/financial-legal/info-2018/long-term-care-insurancefd.html, last accessed on November 4, 2019.
[91] "What is Long-term Care Insurance?" https://longtermcare.acl.gov/costs-how-topay/what-is-long-term-care-insurance/, last accessed on November 4, 2019.
[92] "Ages When Long-Term Care Insurance Claims Begin: 2018 Study," American Association for Long-Term Care Insurance, March 1, 2019, http://www.aaltci.org/news/long-term-care-insurance-association-news/ages-when-longterm-care-insurance-claims-begin-2018-study, last accessed on November 4, 2019.
[93] "For Rent: Protecting Your Belongings With Renters Insurance," https://www.naic.org/documents/protecting_your_belongings_with_renters_insurance.htm, last accessed on October 30, 2019.
[94] "Average Cost of Renters Insurance (2019)," ValuePenguin, https://www.valuepenguin.com/average-cost-renters-insurance, last accessed on November 6, 2019.
[95] "A Shopping Tool for Automobile Insurance," National Association of Insurance Commissioners, 2014, https://www.naic.org/documents/committees_c_trans_read_wg_related_shopping_tool_auto_singles.pdf, last accessed on November 6, 2019.
[96] "The Cost of Flooding," Federal Emergency Management Agency, https://www.floodsmart.gov/why/why-buy-flood-insurance, last accessed on November 6, 2019.
[97] "Search Earthquake Catalog," United State Geological Survey, https://earthquake.usgs.gov/earthquakes/search/, last accessed on November 6, 2019.
[98] "Wills in Virginia," Virginia State Bar, https://www.vsb.org/site/publications/wills-invirginia, last accessed on November 6, 2019.
[99] "Notarize a Will," https://www.nationalnotary.org/knowledge-center/tipstutorials/notarize-wills, last accessed on October 30, 2019.
[100] "Wills in Virginia," Virginia State Bar, https://www.vsb.org/site/publications/wills-invirgnia, last accessed on November 6, 2019.
[101] Michelle Kaminsky, "Top Five Benefits of a Living Trust," LegalZoom, August 2019, https://www.legalzoom.com/articles/top-5-benefits-of-a-living-trust, last accessed on November 6, 2019.
[102] "Consumer Sentinel Network Data Book 2018," Federal Trade Commission, February 2019, https://www.ftc.gov/system/files/documents/reports/consumer-sentinel-network-data-book-2018/consumer_sentinel_network_data_book_2018_0.pdf, last accessed on November 6, 2019.
[103] "Facts + Statistics: Identity theft and cybercrime," Insurance Information Institute, https://www.iii.org/fact-statistic/facts-statistics-identity-theft-and-cybercrime, last accessed on

November 6, 2019.
[104] "Medical Identity Theft," Federal Trade Commission, https://www.consumer.ftc.gov/articles/0171-medical-identity-theft, last accessed on November 6, 2019.
[105] "Child Identity Theft," Federal Trade Commission, https://www.consumer.ftc.gov/articles/0040-child-identity-theft, last accessed on November 6, 2019.
[106] "Identity Theft Protection Services," Federal Trade Commission, https://www.consumer.ftc.gov/articles/0235-identity-theft-protection-services, last accessed on November 6, 2019.
[107] OPM, "OPM, DoD Announce Identity Theft Protection and Credit Monitoring Contract: Victims of Cybercrime to Receive Three Years of Services," September 1, 2015, available at https://www.opm.gov/news/releases/2015/09/opm-dod-announceidentity- theft-protection-and-credit-monitoring-contract/, last access on November 8, 2019.
[108] "Identity Theft Protection Services," Federal Trade Commission, https://www.consumer-ftc.gov/articles/0235-identity-theft-protection-services, last accessed on November 6, 2019.
[109] See "Active Duty Alerts," Federal Trade Commission, https://www.consumer.ftc.gov/articles/0273-active-duty-alerts, last accessed on November 6, 2019.
[110] FIDO Alliance, https://fidoalliance.org/what-is-fido/, last accessed on November 5, 2019.
[111] "Estimating Password-Cracking Times," https://www.betterbuys.com/estimatingpassword-cracking-times/, last accessed on November 1, 2019. See also, "How Secure Is My Password," https://random-ize.com/how-long-to-hack-pass/.
[112] "Millions using 123456 as password, security study finds," BBC News, April 21, 2019, https://www.bbc.com/news/technology-47974583, last accessed on November 5, 2019.
[113] "List of the most common passwords," Wikipedia, https://en.m.wikipedia.org/wiki/List_of_the_most_common_passwords, last accessed November 4, 2019.
[114] Jones, Rhett, "Why 'ji32k7au4a83' Is a Remarkably Common Password," March 4, 2019, https://gizmodo.com/why-ji32k7au4a83-is-a-remarkably-common-password-1833045282, last accessed on November 1, 2019.
[115] "Pwned Passwords," https://haveibeenpwned.com/Passwords, last accessed on November 1, 2019.
[116] "Password reuse, credential stuffing and another billion records in Have I been pwned," May 5, 2017, https://www.troyhunt.com/password-reuse-credential-stuffingand-another-1-billion-records-in-have-i-been-pwned/, last accessed on November 1, 2019.
[117] "Millions using 123456 as password, security study finds," BBC News, April 21, 2019, https://www.bbc.com/news/technology-47974583, last accessed on November 5, 2019.
[118] Joseph Bonneau, "Deep Dive: EFF's New Wordlists for Random Passphrases," Electronic Frontier Foundation, July 19, 2016, https://www.eff.org/deeplinks/2016/07/new-word-lists-random-passphrases, last accessed on November 5, 2019.
[119] "Back to basics: Multi-factor authentication (MFA)," NIST, https://www.nist.gov/itl/tig/back-basics-multi-factor-authentication, last accessed on November 5, 2019.
[120] Nathaniel Popper, "Hackers Hit Twitter C.E.O. Jack Dorsey in a 'SIM Swap.' You're at Risk, Too." New York Times, September 5, 2019, https://www.nytimes.com/2019/09/05/technology/sim-swap-jack-dorsey-hack.html, last accessed on November 5, 2019.
[121] "Facts + Statistics: Identity theft and cybercrime," Insurance Information Institute, https://www.iii.org/fact-statistic/facts-statistics-identity-theft-and-cybercrime, last accessed on November 6, 2019.
[122] Russell Brandom, "The frighteningly simple technique that hijacked Jack Dorsey's Twitter account," The Verge, August 31, 2019, https://www.theverge.com/2019/8/31/20841448/jack-dorsey-twitter-hacked-account-simswapping, last accessed on November 5, 2019.
[123] Kim Zetter, "Teen Who Hacked CIA Director's Email Tells How He Did It," Wired, October 19, 2015, https://www.wired.com/2015/10/hacker-who-broke-into-cia-directorjohn-brennan-email-tells-how-he-did-it/, last accessed on November 5, 2019.

[124] Brian Krebs, "Google: Security Keys Neutralized Employee Phishing," KrebsonSecurity.com, July 23, 2018, https://krebsonsecurity.com/2018/07/googlesecurity-keys-neutralized-employee-phishing/, last accessed on November 5, 2019.

[125] Brian Fung, "How stores use your phone's WiFi to track your shopping habits," Washington Post, October 19, 2013, https://www.washingtonpost.com/news/theswitch/wp/2013/10/19/how-stores-use-your-phones-wifi-to-track-your-shopping-habits/, last accessed on November 5, 2019.

[126] Another important story to read on this topic is Mat Honan's "How Apple and Amazon Security Flaws Led to My Epic Hacking," Wired, August 6, 2012, https://www.wired.com/2012/08/apple-amazon-mat-honan-hacking/, last accessed on November 5, 2019.

[127] See https://thehelm.com for more details.

[128] "Loss Aversion," Behavioraleconomics.com, https://www.behavioraleconomics.com/resources/mini-encyclopedia-of-be/loss-aversion/, last accessed on December 11, 2019.

[129] See https://tspstrategies.com/tspstats/ for the latest statistics.

[130] Shiv, B., Loewenstein, G., Bechara, A., Damásio, H., & Damasio, A. R. (2005). Investment behavior and the negative side of emotion. Psychological Science, 16, 435-439.

[131] Erik Schatzker, "The Bill Gross You Didn't Know: Taxes, Deficits and Asperger's," Bloomberg, March 1, 2019, https://www.bloomberg.com/news/articles/2019-03-01/taxesdeficits- and-asperger-s-the-bill-gross-you-didn-t-know, last accessed on December 12, 2019.

www.ingramcontent.com/pod-product-compliance
Lightning Source LLC
Chambersburg PA
CBHW052346220526

45465CB00003BA/981